GARVEY AND GARVEYISM

GARVEY
AND
GARVEYISM

Amy Jacques Garvey

<small>INTRODUCTION BY JOHN HENRIK CLARKE</small>

Collier Books
Collier-Macmillan Ltd., London

We are all merely human beings;
what we do to others
affects not only them but ourselves—
our dispositions, our actions,
which all leave their impress;
these history records.

A.J.G.

INTRODUCTION

The publication of this popular edition of *Garvey and Garveyism* proves, if proof is needed, that we are now in the midst of a Marcus Garvey Renaissance. In nearly all matters relating to the resurgence of black people, in this country and abroad, there is a reconsideration of this man and his program for the redemption of people of African descent throughout the world. His dream, which seemed impossible in his lifetime, is now the stimulation for a new Black Nationalism, which in his terms is really Black Nationhood. His prophecy has been fulfilled in the independence explosion that brought more than thirty African nations into being. The concept of Black Power that he advocated, using other terms, is now a reality in large areas of the world where the people of African origin are predominant.

Due to the persistence and years of sacrifice of Mrs. Amy Jacques Garvey, widow of Marcus Garvey, a large body of work by and about this great nationalist leader has been preserved and can be made available to a new generation of black people who will have the power to turn his dreams into realities. Like all great dreamers and planners, Marcus Garvey dreamed and planned ahead of his time and his peoples' ability to understand the significance of his life's work. A set of circumstances, mostly created by the world colonial powers, crushed this dreamer, but not his dreams. This book and the new interest in his life and teachings is indicative of the rebirth of "Garvey and Garveyism." There is no way to understand this book without some knowledge of the genesis of Marcus Garvey the man and his ideas.

When he was born in 1887, in Jamaica, West Indies, the

so-called "scramble for Africa" was over. All over Africa the warrior nationalists who had opposed European colonialism throughout the nineteenth century were either being killed or sent into exile. The Europeans with territorial aspirations in Africa had sat, at the Berlin Conference of 1884 and 1885, and decided how to split up the continent among them. In the United States, the Black Americans were still suffering from the betrayal of the Reconstruction in 1876. The trouble within the world black community that Marcus Garvey would later grapple with had already been started when he was born. In the years when he was growing to early manhood, his people entered the twentieth century and a new phase of their struggle for freedom and national identity.

In 1907, Marcus Garvey was involved in the Printers' Union strike in Jamaica. After this unsuccessful strike ended in defeat for the printers, he went to work for the Government Printing Office and soon after, edited his first publication, *The Watchman*.

In 1909, Garvey made his first trip outside of Jamaica, to Costa Rica. In this poor and exploited country he observed the condition of black workers and started an effort to improve their lot. His protest to the British Consul brought only bureaucratic indifference. He was learning his first lessons about the arrogant stubbornness of a European colonial power.

In 1912 he was in London, working, learning, growing, and seeing new dimensions of the black man's struggle. The ideas that would go into the making of his life's work were being formulated. His close association with Duse Mohammed Ali, an Egyptian scholar and nationalist, helped to sharpen his ideas about African redemption. He worked for a while on the monthly magazine edited by Duse Mohammed Ali, *The African Times and Orient Review*. Here in London he read a copy of the book *Up From Slavery* by Booker T. Washington. This book and its ideas had a strong influence on his concept of leadership and its responsibility.

The seeds of what would later become Garveyism had been planted during his first years in London.

In the pamphlet "Marcus Garvey," Adolph Edwards gives the following capsule history of the early days of the Universal Negro Improvement Association:

> Garvey landed in Jamaica on 15th July, 1914. The Caribbean isle had not changed. Kingston remained hot, depressing, inactive; above all, the social atmosphere was just as stultifying as before. Garvey's brain was afire and his existence was a world of thoughts. Within five days of his arrival he organized and founded the movement whose name was destined to be on the lips of millions—The Universal Negro Improvement Association. Briefly, the purpose of the Association was to unite "all the Negro peoples of the world into one great body to establish a country and government absolutely their own." The Association's motto was short and stirring: "One God! One aim! One destiny!" Garvey was designated President and Travelling Commissioner.
>
> The UNIA did not only have plans for the universal improvement of the Negro, but it also had plans for the immediate upliftment of the Negro in Jamaica. The most important of these was the proposed establishment of educational and industrial colleges for Jamaican Negroes on the pattern of the Tuskegee Institute in Alabama, which had been founded by Booker T. Washington. This plan received the support of a few prominent citizens, including the Mayor of Kingston and the Roman Catholic bishop, but on the whole, it came in for sharp criticism within the more articulate circles. Garvey tells who were his persecutors and the decision he made: "Men and women as black as I and even more so, had believed themselves white under the West Indian order of society. I was simply an impossible man to use openly the term 'negro'; yet every one beneath his breath was calling the black man a 'nigger.' I had to decide whether to please my friends and be one of the 'black-whites' of Jamaica, and be reasonably prosperous, or come out openly, and help improve and protect the integrity of the black millions, and suffer. I decided to do the latter."

In *Philosophy and Opinions* Marcus Garvey would later ask himself: "Where is the black man's government? Where is his king and his kingdom? Where is his president, his country and his ambassador, his army, his navy, his men of big affairs?" He could not answer the question affirmatively, so he decided to make the black man's government, king and kingdom, president and men of big affairs. This decision is the basis of *Garvey and Garveyism*. He taught his people to dream big again; he reminded them that they had once been kings and rulers of great nations and would be again. The cry "Up you mighty race, you can accomplish what you will" was a call to the black man to reclaim his best self and reenter the mainstream of world history. When Marcus Garvey came to the United States in 1916, World War I had already started. The migration of black workers from the South to the new war industries in the North and eastern parts of the United States was in full swing. Dissatisfaction, discontent and frustration among millions of black Americans were accelerating this migration. The atmosphere and the condition was well prepared for the message and the program of Marcus Garvey.

He came to the United States in 1916, one year after the death of Booker T. Washington. He had exchanged correspondence with Booker T. Washington with the hope of securing some means to build, in Jamaica, a school similar to Tuskegee in Alabama. Unfortunately, Booker T. Washington had died the previous year.

In the book *New World A-Coming*, Roi Ottley has observed that Marcus Garvey leaped into the ocean of black unhappiness in the United States at a most timely moment for a savior. He further observes that

> he had witnessed the Negro's disillusionment mount with the progress of the World War. Negro soldiers had suffered all forms of Jim Crow, humiliation, discrimination, slander, and even violence at the hands of the white civilian population. After the war, there was a resurgence of Ku Klux Klan influence; another decade of racial hatred and open lawlessness

had set in, and Negroes again were prominent among the victims. Meantime, administration leaders were quite pointed in trying to persuade Negroes that in spite of their full participation in the war effort they could expect no change in their traditional status in America. Newton D. Baker was particularly vocal on this issue. The liberal white citizens were disturbed by events, but took little action beyond viewing with alarm.

Negroes were more than ready for a Moses—and only a black man could express the depth of their feelings. Intellectuals of the race tried to rationalize the situation, but not so the broad masses; their acknowledged leader, Du Bois, had gone overboard with the war effort and now found himself estranged from his people. Negroes were faced with a choice between racialism and radicalism. Marcus Garvey settled the question for thousands by forming the Universal Negro Improvement Association, called U.N.I.A. for brevity, and preaching with great zeal for a pilgrimage of black men "Back to Africa." He rallied men to the slogan, "Africa for Africans!"—for talk was then current about self-determination for subject peoples.

Marcus Garvey's plans for the self-determination of his people are outlined in the following excerpts from "Aims and Objects of Movement for Solution of Negro Problem" issued by Marcus Garvey as President-General of Universal Negro Improvement Association, 1924.

The Universal Negro Improvement Association is an organization among Negroes that is seeking to improve the condition of the race, with the view of establishing a Nation in Africa where Negroes will be given the opportunity to develop by themselves, without creating the hatred and animosity that now exist in countries of the white race through Negroes rivaling them for the highest and best positions in government, politics, society and industry. This organization believes in the rights of all men, yellow, white and black. To us, the white race has a right to the peaceful possession and occupation of countries of its own and in like manner the yellow and black races have their rights. . . . Only by an honest and liberal consideration of such rights can the world be blessed with the peace that is sought by Christian teachers and leaders.

The Spiritual Brotherhood of Man. The following preamble to the Constitution of the organization speaks for itself: The Universal Negro Improvement Association and African Communities' League is a social, friendly, humanitarian, charitable, educational, institutional, constructive, and expansive society and is founded by persons, desiring to the utmost, to work for the general uplift of the Negro peoples of the world. And the members pledge themselves to do all in their power to conserve the rights of their noble race and to respect the rights of all mankind, believing always in the Brotherhood of Man and the Fatherhood of God. The motto of the organization is: One God! One Aim! One Destiny! Therefore, let justice be done to all mankind, realizing that if the strong oppresses the weak, confusion and discontent will ever mark the path of man, but with love, faith and charity toward all, the reign of peace and plenty will be heralded into the world and the generations of men shall be called Blessed.

The declared Objects of the Association are: To establish a Universal Confraternity among the race; to promote the spirit of pride and love; to reclaim the fallen; to administer to and assist the needy; to assist in civilizing the backward tribes of Africa; to assist in the development of Independent Negro Nations and Communities; to establish a central nation for the race; to establish Commissionaries or Agencies in the principal countries and cities of the world for the representation of all Negroes.

The early twenties were times of change and accomplishment in the Harlem community. It was the period when Harlem was literally put on the map. Two events made this possible: a literary movement known as the Harlem Renaissance and the emergence in Harlem of the magnetic and compelling personality of Marcus Garvey. He was the most seriously considered and the most colorful of the numerous black Manassehs who presented themselves and their grandiose programs to the people of Harlem.

Marcus Garvey's reaction to color prejudice and his search for a way to rise above it and lead his people back to Africa, spiritually if not physically, was the all-consuming passion of his existence. His glorious and romantic movement exhorted the black people of the world and fixed their eyes on the bright star of a future in which they could reclaim and rebuild their African homeland and heritage.

Garvey succeeded in building a mass movement among American blacks while other leaders were attempting it and doubting that it could be done. He advocated the return of Africa to the Africans and people of African descent.

He organized, very boldly, the Black Star Line, a steamship company for transporting cargoes of African produce to the United States. A little-known, though very important aspect of the founding of this black steamship company was the urgent pleas of West African farmers and producers to Marcus Garvey for a shipping service that would relieve them of being victimized by white shipping agencies and produce dealers who offered them very low prices for their produce, delivered at the wharf. African passengers paid for first-class service and were given second-class treatment.

Marcus Garvey and his movement had a spectacular early development in the United States, and because of this spread rapidly throughout the Caribbean area and Central and South America, among West Indian migrant laborers. And due to the effectiveness of the American mass media of communication, it penetrated into the continent of Africa.

One year after he entered the United States, in 1917, he made a speaking tour of the principal cities, building up a national following. By 1919 he had branches well established all over the world preparing to send delegates and representatives of fraternal organizations to "the first International Convention of the Negro Peoples of the World," which was held in August 1920 in New York City.

The first public mass meeting was held at Madison

Square Garden—the largest auditorium in the state, and white reporters conceded that about 25,000 assembled inside the auditorium, and there was an overflow standing in the streets.

The significance of this thirty-day convention was that for the first time representatives of African people from all over the world met in sessions to report on conditions under which they lived—socially, economically and politically—and to discuss remedial measures.

Garvey and his movement had a short and spectacular life span in the United States. His movement took really effective form in about 1919, and by 1926 he was in a Federal prison, charged with misusing the mails. From prison he was deported home to Jamaica. This is, briefly, the essence of the Garvey saga in America.

Marcus Garvey, who was duly elected Provisional President of Africa by his followers, was never allowed to set foot on African soil. He spoke no African language. But Garvey managed to convey to African people everywhere (and to the rest of the world) his passionate belief that Africa was the home of a civilization which had once been great and would be great again. When one takes into consideration the slenderness of Garvey's resources and the vast material forces, social conceptions and imperial interests which automatically sought to destroy him, his achievement remains one of the great propaganda miracles of this century.

Garvey's voice reverberated inside Africa itself. The King of Swaziland later told Mrs. Marcus Garvey that he knew the names of only two black men in the Western world: Jack Johnson, the boxer who defeated the white man Jim Jeffries, and Marcus Garvey. From his narrow vantage point in Harlem, Marcus Garvey became a world figure.

After years of neglect, new interest in the life and ideas of this remarkable man has created a Marcus Garvey Renaissance. In his homeland, Jamaica, he has been proclaimed a national hero. All over the black world he is being reconsidered with respect and reverence. His greatness lies in the fact that he was daring enough to dream of a better future for black people, wherever they live on this earth.

JOHN HENRIK CLARKE

CHAPTER ONE

From early history to the present we learn of men and women who have emerged from their environment and so far out-distanced their contemporaries in thought and action, that in their day they were apt to be called "mad, dangerous or fools." Long after their death, when the truths they espoused or the experiments they conducted are validated, or the dangers which they pointed out come to pass, then they who have been convinced by experience are prone to admit that the visionary was right, and must have been inspired to have been so persevering.

Heredity and environment seem to influence these extraordinary persons, and to be used by them to carry out a spiritual urge in a given line—an experiment, a mission or task. They seem to have a supreme purpose in life, and once started, even against personal interests, will not give up. They are, as it were, impelled to go on, even to death.

In this category we may well place Marcus Mosiah Garvey, born on the 17th day of August 1887, to Marcus and Sarah Garvey in Jamaica, an island in the Caribbean, discovered by Columbus on his second voyage to the New World, and called Xaymaca—Isle of Springs. The Spaniards decimated the Arawaks—the aborigines—and controlled the island for 161 years, during which time they brought Africans to work on the plantations. When the English captured the island in 1657, most of the Africans fled to the hills and led a free life, so they were called Maroons from "Cimarron"—the wild ones. Although many military expeditions were sent against them, they defeated the trained soldiers. The English, exhausted by these guerrillas from the caves and hills, signed a peace treaty of friendship with them, allowing them to live on their lands without paying taxes, and to be directly governed by their own chiefs. Many more shipments of Africans were brought to the island by the English to work as slaves, but the Maroons always regarded themselves as superior.

Garvey's father, who was always an enigma to his neighbors in St. Ann's Bay, St. Ann ("the Garden Parish"), is said to have been a descendant of the Maroons. An eighty-nine-year-old Jewish lady who knew both Mr. and Mrs. Garvey well, being a resident of that parish herself, described them as follows:

> Mr. Garvey was a master mason, he did both stone and brick work beautifully, but he always acted as if he did not belong among the villagers; he was well read, and gave advice as a local lawyer. He was silent, stern, seemed to have the strength of an ox, his complexion was not very black, but his features were broad, and nose flat. He was "Mr. Garvey" to everyone, even to Sarah, his wife, and his children.
>
> She was just the opposite to him in every way. She was one of the most beautiful black women I have ever seen. She had European features; her skin was black and soft as velvet; her eyes jet black, large, liquid and sad. Her voice was gentle and caressing, her figure well shaped and erect. She was a regular Church-goer at the Wesleyan Methodist Church. Mr. Garvey only attended funerals, which were not often. Mrs. Garvey used to make delicious pastries from coconuts, guavas etc., and sell them, as Mr. Garvey took jobs when he felt like it, and would rather lock himself in his room and read.

This strange union brought forth eleven children, but all except Indiana and Marcus died in childhood. He was the youngest, and although all the other boys had biblical names given them by their mother, yet Mose, as he was called, had been named Marcus by his father, who believed in planetary influences, and said, "Any boy born under the planet Leo—the lion—when the Sun is in the ascendancy, is bound to be a leader in his line." Mrs. Garvey wanted him named Moses, so he compromised and added Mosiah to

Marcus, and she said, "I hope he will be like Moses and lead his people."

In the domestic arrangements Mr. Garvey dwelt apart—he built a large room, several feet away from the home. In this room he housed his books and newspapers; he lived there when he wanted to be alone, and that was almost always; he stored imported canned foods, fruits, cheese and biscuits, so that he could read and munch to his heart's content without interference.

Mose grew up very close to his mother; he was her baby, her comfort, her handy one. She was co-owner with a single brother of a property at Chalky Hill; when pimento and citrus came to reaping time, she sent Mose to help in the reaping, selling and bringing back her portion of the proceeds. Crop-time was a big time for him, as his Ma would be sure to give him something new from her allotment. Such trifles as Mose's wants did not worry Mr. Garvey; he was too engrossed in himself and his brooding.

Mose was puzzled over his father's moodiness and abstraction; he used to sit by the sea and wonder why his old man was so cross, why his mother was so patient with him. Would he ever have money to go on one of the big ships which took logwood and pimento to Germany, sugar and citrus to England, and bananas to America? He longed to see the people and places he read about in his father's books. Everything seemed to move so slowly in the town; the big plantation owners sent their children to England to high schools and colleges, the small planters sent their children to Kingston (the capital) for higher education. He had hopes that he too would go there.

But his father's peculiar disposition, his unreasonable stubbornness was causing him to lose his properties. For twenty years he had been getting newspapers from Mr. Gaul, the owner-publisher, and understood it was a gift—for what Mr. Garvey read, others in the village would be sure to read. So it went until the owner died; and when in winding up his estate his executors sent Mr. Garvey a bill for thirty pounds ($150), he refused to pay it. He was sued, contested the case, lost, and still refused to pay claim and costs; so by court order one of his properties was attached and sold for much less than its value.

He became more irritable, as he felt that he was unjustly dealt with. He quarreled with a neighbor about a boundary line of a few feet, with another about cutting down a cedar tree which he claimed, and so he was in and out of court, losing each time as costs piled up against him, until he lost all of his lands, except just a house spot.

So at fourteen Mose had to leave elementary school (public school) and was apprenticed to his godfather, Mr. Burrowes, to learn printing. At a small country printshop one learns everything in connection with the trade; besides, Mr. Burrowes had many books, and the "wise heads" of the Town would drop in, especially on market days, to swap news and discuss happenings. After two years Mose was full of knowledge, but his pockets were thin. He was always reminded when he asked for a raise that he was learning "a good trade."

A hurricane swept the countryside in 1903, destroying valuable trees; flood rains ruined the ground food, such as yams, cocos and cassava. Ma Garvey was in desperate straits, as all her crops were lost. Mose confided only to her his plans to go to Kingston to his maternal uncle, and get a job as a printer, so that later on he could send for her.

He kept his word, but she did not like city life and fretted over her losses in the country. To her, real life was plenty of fruit trees, basking under their cool shade, getting water from the river, without having to pay for it, tending her garden, and having chickens and ducks in her yard. Without this domestic freedom and natural living, she felt cooped-up in a room, looking out on paved streets, thinking of what might have been. She soon died.

To Mose, city life lacked the natural beauty, calm and neighborliness of village life, but it brought a quickening of other activities, contacts with people who had traveled on ships to all parts of the world, civic consciousness and exposure to vocal expression. Barbershop forums and parkbench discussion groups after work contributed to his mental expansion. At first he was a silent listener, hesitant to enter discussions; for his first attempt he was rudely rebuked and told, "Country boy, shut your mouth." This retort galled him; he determined after this to learn how to be a good speaker. He knew he had views which were different from those of his comrades, but they would chaff at his youth and disregard his points of argument; so he must learn to press them with logic and persuasion.

At this period there were in Jamaica no elocution classes and no concert or stage groups, so every Sunday he visited different churches to get pointers in platform deportment and oratory from the preachers. In his room he read aloud passages from school readers and poems, and tried out gestures he thought apt, while pacing the floor.

In January 1907 occurred a great earthquake and fire which destroyed Kingston, killing over 800 persons, and destroying buildings and property to the value of two million pounds. Money was loaned by the English government to help rebuild the city. Wages were very low, money lost more of its purchasing power, chiefly because of scarcity of commodities, and workers felt the pinch. The first union to be formed in the island was a printers' union, and Garvey was foremost in it. They made demands for an increase in wages, and better working conditions, which were not met. They struck; and although Garvey was a foreman at Benjamin's Printery and he personally was promised an increase in pay, he struck with them. The union received financial help from American printers, but the union treasurer left the island with the money, and broke the morale of the men.

After this Garvey went to work at the Government Printing Office. Saturday nights he and others used to have discussion groups at Victoria Pier; fanned by the sea breezes, and lighted sometimes by the moon, they would hold forth on all sorts of subjects; but what was uppermost in Mose's mind was how to improve the lot of the poor working people. Thus he helped to form the first political club in Jamaica—the National Club—which issued a publication fortnightly called *Our Own*.

By this time he could speak fluently and endeavored to help others. In 1910 he used to train young men and women in elocution and arrange concerts and elocution contests. Prominent persons donated the prizes. The first black man to inspire leadership in him was Dr. Love, who was born in Nassau, Bahamas, educated in England and on the Continent. He spent his best years in Jamaica, fighting for the uplift of the black masses. He published a paper called *The Advocate*. Courageous and outspoken, he spent all his time and means in this work, and in the practice of medicine, especially among the poor.

Garvey now realized that his cultural and political activities were full-time work. He gave up his job at the printshop, and published a little paper called *The Watchman*. But he had nothing to sustain him, and could not get help. He decided to go to Costa Rica to one of his maternal uncles, to earn enough money to return and continue his work. Off he went, where a fruit company was clearing and planting bananas. His uncle got him a job as a timekeeper, but what his black people had to brave in order to earn a living sickened him: Daily they had to encounter snakes, swamps and wild tigercats; at weekends when they got their pay and went to the nearby towns to buy the week's supplies, the Costa Rican bandits would waylay them on their return trip, chop them up like logs with their Spanish machetes, and take away money and goods. Mutilated black bodies in the rivers and bush were common sights. Garvey could stand it no longer, and returned to Port Limón, the capital. There he discovered that those who had put their money in the banks suffered great risks, as the banks were not under government control, but were run more like private money-exchange agencies. Garvey then asked the British Consul what could be done to protect the lives and moneys of these black British subjects. Quite nonchalantly he was told that nothing could be done by him as Consul; he could not change conditions in Costa Rica. Garvey then realized that white men did not regard the lives of black men as equal to those of white men, and had no intention of trying to protect blacks or giving them a square deal.

With what money he had earned, he started a paper called *La Nacionale*, but he could not carry it on for long, as his people were not organized and enlightened enough to help him fight their own battles. His uncle helped him to go to Bocas-del-Toro, Republic of Panama, where he saw much of the same abuse of the labor and theft of the money of his people. He worked there for some months, then went to Colón and started another paper called *La Prensa*. The Panama Canal was dug with West Indian labor under American contract, but previously thousands had lost their lives from malaria and other diseases because of the unsanitary conditions. Frenchmen started the canal, American dollars finished it, but black men's sweat and blood were spilled copiously to make this dream come true. Yet they were called "Silver Employees," underpaid and jim-crowed in separate quarters, not as good as "Gold Employees," meaning white men.

He left Panama and went to Ecuador, South America, where West Indian labor was being used on tobacco fields and in mining. Again he saw the awful conditions under which they labored—no protection from the British Consul, and no efforts made for their welfare. The same conditions obtained in Nicaragua, Spanish Honduras, Colombia and Venezuela. Sickened with fever, and sick at heart over appeals from his people for help on their behalf, he decided to return to Jamaica in 1911, and contend with the government there, as well as to awaken Jamaicans at home to the true conditions on the Spanish mainland.

From the government he was faced with the same inertia and disinterestedness towards the suffering by which black

peoples earned a living and helped their poor relatives back
home. The Governor said he was not inclined to get in bad
graces with the Spanish republics, and if conditions there
were intolerable, Jamaicans should return. But, argued Garvey, "return to do what?" To this the government was
mum.

The people urged Garvey to form an association for the
betterment of black West Indians at home and abroad.
Again money handicapped him, and the government frowned
on his efforts. He called the organization the Universal Negro
Improvement Association. The word "Negro" created opposition and prevented help from "better-off colored people," who
felt that Negro was synonymous with low, good-for-nothing.
To the few whites it suggested an organized black majority,
which they felt would be dangerous to their economic overlordship. These oppositions were subtle and undermining, so
he decided to go to England, and try to enlist the sympathy of
black seamen and students from Africa.

He had heard of conditions in Africa and Europe from
the lips of Jamaicans and Barbadians who had been soldiers
in the West India Regiments used in Africa to suppress
Africans and take their territories. The last such event was
the Ashanti war. The West Indians were urged to fight
Africans, so that they could be "subdued, Christianized,
and taught the modern way of living." It is said that when
the Africans saw black men coming toward them, many
threw down their primitive weapons and surrendered, regarding them as long-lost relatives. But both were disillu-
sioned soon afterwards, as white traders and soldiers took
possession of Africans' lands and began exploiting their
labors. Many Barbadian ex-soldiers settled in Jamaica.

All this Garvey digested, and determined that amends
should be made for the deception practiced on Africans and
their relatives abroad. The year 1912–13 found him in England and on the European Continent, contacting African
seamen and students, who opened to him new vistas of
Africa and Asia. He worked on the *African Times and*

Orient Review, published in London by Duse Mohammed Ali, an Egyptian scholar and traveler. From him he learned much of Africa's ancient history, topography, mineral potential and the labor conditions of semislavery and serfdom: all this suffering in order to mine and produce wealth to enrich Europeans, and turn their wheels of industry, thereby providing gainful employment for their peoples, with the attendant educational and cultural facilities. The ingrates! thought he. Who are making them rich and puffed-up? Africa, India and Malaya. How long is this deception to last? Only so long as they continue to keep all subject peoples ignorant of each other's conditions of exploitation and abuse, half-starved and uneducated. He now knew that the colored races outnumbered the whites, as three quarters of the earth's population were colored. What if these vast numbers discovered their potentialities and the possibilities for them to act as free men and women guiding their own destiny?

Garvey spent much time in the libraries reading, among others things, of the rise and fall of empires, economics, etc.; he also attended Trinity College, but found it hard to study and earn enough to keep himself in warm clothing and good food; he decided to return to Jamaica, full of added information to continue the work of the Organization.

In one of his articles in the *African Times and Orient Review*, dated mid-October 1913, under the title, "The British West Indies in the mirror of civilization—history," he described the appalling economic conditions of the masses, and made this prophecy in closing:

> As one who knows the people well, I make no apology for prophesying that there will soon be a turning point in the history of the West Indies, and that the people who inhabit that portion of the Western Hemisphere will be the instruments of uniting a scattered Race, who before the close of many centuries will found an Empire on which the sun shall

shine as ceaseless as it shines on the Empire of the North today.

This may be regarded as a dream, but I would point my critical friends to history and its lessons. Would Caesar have believed that the country he was invading in 55 B.C. would be the seat of the greatest Empire of the world? Laugh then as you may at what I have been bold enough to prophesy, but as surely as there is evolution in the natural growth of man and nations, so surely will there be a change in the history of these subjected Regions.

CHAPTER TWO

On board ship one night as he lay thinking of all he had seen and heard in England and Europe, the whole African program came to him as a revelation. Silently he questioned himself and prayed for the answers and directives. Thought he, the conditions in Africa certainly are a reflection on Westernized black people; once black people were made aware of the situation, and whatever the handicaps, to continue this estrangement would be inexcusable. Yes, he must tell them, he must show them their true relationship toward each other, that the condition of one reflects on the others. After all, exploitation of blacks and discrimination were everywhere, in a greater or lesser degree. Where was the black man's government strong enough to protect him? A black man seemed to have only one true passport, and that was his black face; no matter what other passport he presented as a subject or citizen of any country in which he was born, his black face finally decided the way he should be treated, and that was usually as less than a white man.

Where were the black man's ships to carry his minerals and produce to make him economically secure? White companies took black men's cargoes, and carried them as passengers only when it suited their convenience. Their attitude was, "If you don't like it, then swim the oceans or get your

own ships." Where were black men's factories to provide
employment for their people? Why should black men always walk hat in hand begging white men for jobs? It is
because the black man is not economically self-reliant that
he is kicked around, and gets the refuse; this is why he is
treated with contempt, sometimes with pity, but never with
respect as a race.

Up from his bunk Garvey rose, got his notebook, and
added a co-title to his organization—"African Communities'
League."

Aims and Objects:

To establish a Universal Confraternity among the race; to
promote the spirit of pride and love; to reclaim the fallen; to
administer to and assist the needy; to assist in civilizing the
backward tribes of Africa; to assist in the development of
Independent Negro nations and communities; to establish a
central nation for the race, where they will be given the
opportunity to develop themselves; to establish Commissaries
and Agencies in the principal countries and cities of the world
for the representation of all Negroes; to promote a conscien-
tious Spiritual worship among the native tribes of Africa; to
establish Universities, Colleges, Academies and Schools for
racial education and culture of the people; to improve the
general conditions of Negroes everywhere.

Thus his embryonic ideas took on more expansive
growth, and the words of the old hymn became a prayer on
his lips, "For service, Lord, O let me live, My love, my All
to others give."

The preamble to the constitution which he wrote before
he left for England reads:

The Universal Negro Improvement Association and African
Communities' League is a social, friendly, humanitarian,
charitable, educational, institutional, constructive, and expansive Society, and is founded by persons desiring to the utmost,
to work for the general uplift of the Negro peoples of the
world. And the members pledge themselves to do all in their

power to conserve the rights of their noble race, and to respect the rights of all mankind, believing always in the Brotherhood of Man and the Fatherhood of God. The motto of the Organization is: One God! One Aim! One Destiny! Therefore, let justice be done to all mankind, realizing that if the strong oppresses the weak, confusion and discontent will ever mark the path of man, but with love, faith and charity towards all, the reign of peace and plenty will be heralded into the world and the generations of men shall be called Blessed.

In 1914 he returned to Jamaica, and for nearly two years he struggled to unite Jamaicans to a consciousness of race —a gigantic task, as educated, well-off blacks ignored the cause of the black masses. They were purposely accepted into the society of the whites, and told they were "different." This was done to weaken the black majority economically and intellectually. The ambition of blacks when they got money and education was to "lift up the color" of their children by marrying white or near-whites. They argued that these children would be accepted in society and get better business opportunities and jobs; this was a social and particularly an economic expedient, but it created a color-of-skin bias. Garvey tried to show them the falsity and trickery of it, and that outside the shores of the islands they were classified and treated as belonging to a poor, rejected race. But prejudice based on "class" was an English institution, and to ape the English and be snobbish made blacks feel "high and mighty." This is one of the phases of "divide-and-rule" policy of imperialism in colonial territories, to reduce the people of a particular country—the real owners of the land—to impotence in thinking as a group, and acting in their own interest.

Garvey spent many months of hardship and disappointment unable to get the masses to unite and cooperate for their own good, but still he plodded on. He was up against the plantocracy—the land barons, the white shipping and fruit companies (who made millions yearly out of the islands and Africa) and newspapers, whose policy was to make the island safe for big business at any cost, as they were the stockholders. Added to this combine were the people he was trying to reeducate, who for over a century had been steeped in the almost divine might of imperialist European nations. "It can't be done," was the innermost thought of even those who were helping him; yet they knew that he was but expressing their hopes and ambitions.

The subtle economic thralldom under the colonial powers in the Caribbean fools many West Indians who say, "All I want is money to do business, or good-paying, steady work. . . . I can buy a good house anywhere I want to live, I can send my children to good schools as long as I can pay for them. . . . I can live like a real man and be respected. . . . All I want is money." True. But to get it for the masses was the almost impossible task. To make this possible at once would necessitate revolutionary measures, which would be impractical and horrifying. But this foolish thinking, this mirage, taunted the masses and made Garvey's work harder.

Seamen traveling on banana ships told him of opportunities in America; he also heard of the help Booker T. Washington got for his work in the Southern states, so he wrote him, and Washington encouraged him to come up. Garvey felt that if he could get funds, he would return and open a trade school like Tuskegee. This would give practical help to the masses, who then had no such opportunity for training; at the same time he could inculcate in them race love, and strengthen his African program in the entire island. The trade school would in time furnish competent men and women as technical missionaries to be sent to the mother country—Africa.

He planned to set up branches of the Universal Negro Improvement Association and African Communities' League under colored American leadership, and return to Jamaica to establish his trade school and black cultural center, where he could keep in touch with the American and African branches, and go periodically to America, which could be used as a meeting-ground for conventions, because there was freedom of speech and press, greater latitude of movement, and the largest black population in the Western World.

When he arrived in the United States of America in March 1916, Washington had died. By traveling through most of the states he got an overall picture of the true conditions of his race. Opportunities? Yes, but out-weighed by disenfranchisement, lynchings, jim-crowism and discrimination. He got busy organizing groups, but the people lacked faith in their local leaders, who regarded their following as so many votes to be bartered for personal gain, or a few jobs for their henchmen. Thus their voting power was split among Republicans, Democrats, Socialists and Communists. Garvey realized that it would take some time to inspire in them the altruism of real race leadership, and to stress the dire need of uniting Africans, West Indians and themselves for a common cause.

To him, they lacked long-ranged vision, they were not overseas travelers as some of the whites, they knew practically nothing of the countries beyond their shores, and nothing of the history of their African ancestors; they regarded Africans as "naked savages," and West Indians as "monkey-chasers" (although they only saw monkeys in the zoo). Many earned good wages in the big industrial cities, but as earnestly as they worked for it, they set out to spend it recklessly.

On the other hand colored Americans could not understand why that "foolish foreigner" would go hungry and stand up talking about Africa until he brought tears to the eyes of some of his sidewalk hearers, when he could use that "silver tongue" to live well and wear good clothes. Twice Garvey got dizzy and fell off soapboxes because he was hungry (unkind remarks were that it was a stunt to get the sympathy of the crowd). He caught many colds because his shoe soles had holes in them. But Garvey had seen black men back home with bare feet or board sandals emerge from their wattle-and-daub rooms, look out on their two or three acres of cultivation and small stock, and smile—the smile of contentment—and walk with the air of a lord or baron, knowing in their minds and repeating to themselves, "These are mine. I am master of them." Garvey grew up in these surroundings, which had taught him that fine clothes and liquor did not make a man a real man. One had to possess the good earth unmolested, to have the means of economic stability, to be able to plan and administer one's own destiny—that was freedom, and that was being "somebody" with "something" in this material world.

He was not the product of sidewalks, although he used them to speak to crowds. He was a child of nature, who used to hear the thunder roll, the lightning flash during tropical storms, to see the havoc wreaked by them, and to replant again with zeal and hope; he watched the turbulent blue sea that bore on its bosom ships with people and goods; he dreamed his dreams by her shores, and they were as far-reaching as her waters; he knew that as he lived those dreams they would have stormy sailings as well as balmy days. As a boy he delighted to look in awe at the "Roaring River Falls," as the spray kissed his cheeks, and its churning waters gurgled over the rocks into the "Roaring River" beneath, which could be heard for miles around; he wondered if ever he would be able to roar loud enough to voice his turbulent thoughts, which made him restless and eager—for what? He knew not. Even the science of nature taught him: storms and calms, violence and gentleness; it gave him courage, yet a simplicity and love for lowly things and humble poor people.

Africa to him was like his birthplace; he loved the profusion of tropical growth; he loved the people who lived near to nature. Africa! nearly twelve million square miles of it! What a wonderful gift from God! If only he could get his people to appreciate it the way he did, and use it as God predestined. He must! He will fulfill God's purpose.

CHAPTER THREE

Garvey's "Appeal to the Soul of White America," written for the *Negro World*, October 1923, and reproduced in Volume 11 of the *Philosophy and Opinions of Marcus Garvey*, sets out the doctrine of Garveyism as it applies to the U.S.A., and his arguments in support of these principles. It was written because all over the nation the cry was: "This is a white man's country, and by God we intend to keep it white." Garvey wrote:

"Surely the soul of liberal, philanthropic, liberty-loving, white America is not dead. It is true that the glamour of materialism to a great degree destroyed the innocence and purity of the national conscience, but still, beyond our soulless industrialism, beyond our politics, there is a deep feeling of human sympathy that touches the soul of white America, upon which the unfortunate and sorrowful can always depend for sympathy, help and action. It is to that feeling that I appeal for four hundred million Negroes of the world, and fifteen millions of America in particular.

"There is no real white man in America who does not desire a solution of the Negro problem. Each thoughtful citizen has probably his own idea of how the vexed question of races should be settled. To some the Negro could be gotten rid of by wholesale butchery, by lynching, by economic starvation, by a return to slavery and legalized oppression; while others would have the problem solved by seeing the race all herded together and kept somewhere among themselves; while a few—those in whom they have an interest—should be allowed to live around as wards of a mistaken philanthropy; yet none so generous as to desire to see the Negro elevated to a standard of real progress and prosperity, welded into a homogeneous whole, creating of themselves a mighty nation, with proper systems of government, civilization and culture, to mark them admissible to the fraternities of nations and races without disadvantages.

"I do not desire to offend the finer feelings and sensibilities of those white friends of the race who really believe that they are kind and considerate to us as a people; but I feel it my duty to make a real appeal to conscience and not to belief. Conscience is solid, convicting and permanently demonstrative; belief is only a matter of opinion, changeable by superior reasoning. Once the belief was that it was fit and proper to hold the Negro as a slave, and in this the bishop, priest and layman agreed. Later on, they changed their belief or opinion, but at all times, the conscience of certain people dictated to them that it was wrong and inhuman to hold human beings as slaves. It is to such a conscience in white America that I am addressing myself.

"Negroes are human beings—the peculiar and strange opinions of writers, ethnologists, philosophers, scientists and anthropologists notwithstanding. They have feelings, souls, passions, ambitions, desires, just as other men; hence, they must be considered.

"Has white America really considered the Negro in the light of permanent human progress? The answer is NO. Men and women of the white race, do you know what is going to happen if you do not think and act now? One of two things. You are either going to deceive and keep the Negro in your midst until you have perfectly completed your wonderful American civilization with its progress in art, science, industry and politics, and then, jealous of your own success and achievements in those directions, and with the greater jealousy of seeing your race pure and unmixed, cast him off to die in the whirlpool of economic starvation, thus getting rid of another race that was not intelligent enough to live; or you simply mean by the largeness of your hearts to assimilate fifteen million Negroes into the social fraternity of an American race that will neither be white nor black. Don't be alarmed. We must prevent both consequences. No real race-loving white man wants to destroy the purity of his race, and no real Negro conscious of himself wants to die; hence there is room for an understanding, and an adjustment; and that is just what we seek.

"Let white and black stop deceiving themselves. Let the white race stop thinking that all black men are dogs and not to be considered as human beings. Let foolish Negro agitators and so-called reformers,—encouraged by deceptive or unthinking white associates,—stop preaching and advocating the doctrine of "social equality," meaning thereby the social intermingling of both races, intermarriage and general social co-relationship. The two extremes will get us nowhere, other than breeding hate, and encouraging discord, which will eventually end disastrously to the weaker race.

"Some Negroes, in the quest for position and honour, have been admitted to the full enjoyment of their constitutional rights. Thus we have some of our men filling high and responsible government positions; others, on their own account, have established themselves in the professions, commerce and industry. This, the casual onlooker, and even the men themselves, will say carries a guarantee and hope of social equality, and permanent racial progress. But this is a mistake. There is no progress of the Negro in America that is permanent, so long as we have with us the monster evil—prejudice.

"Prejudice we shall always have between black and white, so long as the latter believes that the former is intruding upon their rights. So long as white labourers believe that black labourers are taking and holding their jobs; so long as white artisans believe that black artisans are performing the work that they should do; so long as white men and women believe that black men and women are filling the positions they covet; so long as white political leaders and statesmen believe that black politicians and statesmen are seeking the same positions in the nation's government; so long as white men believe that black men want to associate with, and marry white women, then we will ever have prejudice, and not only prejudice, but riots, lynchings, burnings and God to tell what next will follow.

"It is this danger that drives me mad. It must be prevented. We cannot allow white and black to drift along unthinkingly toward this great gulf and danger that is nationally ahead of us. It is because of this that I speak, and call upon the soul of great white America to help. It is no use putting off. The work must be done, and it must be started now.

"Some people have misunderstood me. Some don't want to understand me. But I must explain myself for the good of the world and humanity. Those of the Negro race who preach social equality, and who are working for an American race that will, in complexion, be neither white nor black, have tried to misinterpret me to the white public, and create prejudice against my work. The white public not stopping to analyze and question the motive behind criticism and attacks aimed against new leaders and their movements, condemn without even giving a chance to the criticized to be heard. Those of my own race who oppose me because I refuse to endorse their programme of social arrogance and social equality, gloat over the fact that by their misrepresentation and underhand methods, they were able to discredit me, so as to destroy the movement that I represent, in opposition to their programme of a new American race; but we will not now consider the opposition to a programme or a movement; but state the facts as they are, and let deep souled white America pass its own judgment.

"In another one hundred years white America will have doubled the population; in another two hundred years it will have trebled itself. The keen student must realize that the centuries ahead will bring us an over-crowded country; as the population grows larger, opportunities will be fewer; the competition for bread between the people of their own class will become keener, to such an extent that there will be no room for two competitive races—the one strong and the other weak. To imagine Negroes as district attorneys, judges, senators, congressmen, assemblymen, aldermen, government clerks and officials, artisans, and labourers at work, while millions of white men starve, is to have before you the bloody picture of wholesale mob violence that I fear, and against which I am working. No preaching, no praying, no presidential edict will control the passion of hungry, unreasoning men of prejudice when the hour comes. It will not come, I pray, in our generation, but it is of the future that I think, and for which I work.

"A generation of ambitious Negro men and women, out from the best colleges, universities and institutions, capable of filling the highest and best positions in the nation, in industry, commerce, society and politics! Can you keep them back? If you do, they will agitate and throw your constitution in your faces. Can you stand before civilization and deny the truth of your constitution? What are you going to do then? You who are just will open the door of opportunity and say to all and sundry, "Enter in." But, ladies and gentlemen, what about the mob, that starving crowd of your own race? Will they stand by, suffer and starve, and allow an opposite, competitive race to prosper in the midst of their distress? If you can conjure these things up in your mind, then you have the vision of the race problem of the future in America.

"There is but one solution, and that is to provide an outlet for Negro energy, ambition and passion, away from the attractiveness of white opportunity, and surround the race with opportunities of its own. If this is not done, and if the foundation for same is not laid now, then the consequences will be sorrowful for the weaker race, and disgraceful to our ideals of justice and shocking to our civilization.

"The Negro must have a country and a nation of his own. If you laugh at the idea, then you are selfish and wicked, for you and your children do not intend that the Negro shall discommode you in yours. If you do not want him to have a country and a nation of his own, if you do

not intend to give him equal opportunities in yours, then it
is plain to see that you mean that he must die, even as the
Indian, to make room for your generations.

"Why should the Negro die? Has he not served America
and the world? Has he not borne the burden of civilization
in this Western world for three hundred years? Has he not
contributed of his best to America? Surely all this stands to
his credit. But there will not be enough room, and the one
answer is, find a place. We have found a place; it is Africa,
and as black men for three centuries have helped white men
build America, surely generous and grateful white men will
help black men build Africa.

"And why shouldn't Africa and America travel down the
ages as protectors of human rights and guardians of democracy? Why shouldn't black men help white men secure and
establish universal peace? We can only have peace when we
are just to all mankind; and for that peace, and for that reign
of universal love, I now appeal to the soul of white America. Let the Negroes have a government of their own. Don't
encourage them to believe that they will become social
equals and leaders of the whites in America, without first on
their own account proving to the world that they are capable of evolving a civilization of their own. The white race
can best help the Negro by telling him the truth, and not by
flattering him into believing that he is as good as any white
man without first proving the racial, national, constructive
metal of which he is made. Stop flattering the Negro about
social equality, stop appealing to his vanity, and not to his
good common sense; tell him to go to work and build for
himself. Help him in the direction of doing for himself, and
let him know that self-progress brings its own reward.

"I appeal to the considerate and thoughtful conscience of
white America not to condemn the cry of the Universal
Negro Improvement Association for a nation in Africa for
Negroes, but to give us a chance to explain ourselves to the
world. White America is too big, and when informed and

touched, too liberal, to turn down the cry of the awakened Negro for 'a place in the sun.' "

In his appeal to the conscience of the Negro to be himself, and to create and work toward his own goal, Garvey said:

"It is said to be a hard and difficult task to organize and keep together large numbers of the Negro race for the common good. Many have tried to congregate us, but have failed; the reason being, that our characteristics are such as to keep us more apart than together.

"The evil of internal divisions is wrecking our existence as a people, and if we do not seriously and quickly move in the direction of a readjustment, it simply means that our doom becomes imminently conclusive. For years the Universal Negro Improvement Association has been working for the unification of our race, not on domestic-national lines only, but universally. The success which we have met in the course of our effort is rather encouraging, considering the time consumed and the environment surrounding the object concerned. It seems that the whole world of sentiment is against the Negro, and the difficulty of our generation is to extricate ourselves from the prejudice that hides itself beneath, as well as above, the action of an international environment.

Prejudice is conditional on many reasons, and it is apparent that the Negro supplies, consciously or unconsciously, all the reasons by which the world seems to ignore and avoid him. No one cares for a leper, for lepers are infectious persons, and all are afraid of the disease; so because the Negro keeps himself poor, helpless and undemonstrative, it is natural also that no one wants to be of him or with him.

"Progress is the attraction that moves humanity, and to whatever people or race this 'modern virtue' attaches itself, there will you find the splendour of pride and self-esteem that never fail to win the respect and admiration of all. It is the progress of the Anglo-Saxon that singles them out for the respect of all the world. When their race had no progress or achievement to its credit, then, like all other inferior peoples, they paid the price in slavery, bondage, as well as through prejudice. We cannot forget the time when even the ancient Briton was regarded as being too dull to make a good Roman slave, yet today the influence of that race rules the world.

"It is the industrial and commercial progress of America that causes Europe and the rest of the world to think appreciatively of Americans. It is not because one hundred and ten million people live in the United States that the world is attracted to the republic with so much reverence and respect —a reverence and respect not shown to India with its three hundred millions, nor to China with its four hundred millions. Progress of and among any people will advance them in the respect and appreciation of the rest of their fellows. It is such a progress that the Negro must attach to himself, if he is to rise above the prejudice of the world. The reliance of our race upon the progress and achievements of others for a consideration in sympathy, justice and rights is like a dependence upon a broken stick, resting upon which will eventually consign us to the ground.

"The Universal Negro Improvement Association teaches our race self-help and self-reliance, not only in one essential, but in all those things which contribute to human happiness and wellbeing. The disposition of the many to depend upon the other races for a kindly and sympathetic consideration of their needs, without making the effort to do for themselves, has been the race's standing disgrace, by which we have been judged, and through which we have created the strongest prejudice against ourselves.

"There is no force like success, and that is why the individual makes all efforts to surround himself throughout life with the evidence of it. As of the individual, so should it be of the race and nation. The glittering success of Rockefeller makes him a power in the American nation; the success of Henry Ford suggests him as an object of universal respect, but no one knows and cares about the bum or hobo who is Rockefeller's or Ford's neighbour. So also is the world attracted by the glittering success of races and nations, and pays absolutely no attention to the bum or hobo race that lingers by the wayside. The Negro must be up and doing if he will break down the prejudices of the rest of the world. Prayer alone is not going to improve our conditions, nor can the policy of watchful waiting. We must strike out for ourselves in the course of material achievement and by our own effort and energy present to the world those forces by which the progress of man is judged.

"The Negro needs a nation and a country of his own, where he can best show evidence of his own ability in the art of human progress. Scattering him as an unmixed and unrecognized part of alien nations and civilizations is but to demonstrate his imbecility, and point him out as an unworthy derelict, fit neither for the society of Greek, Jew nor Gentile. It is unfortunate that we should so drift apart, as a race, as not to see that we are but perpetuating our own sorrow and disgrace in failing to appreciate the first requisite of all peoples—organization.

"Organization is a great power in directing the affairs of a race or nation toward a given goal. To properly develop the desires that are uppermost, we must first concentrate through some system or method, and there is none better than organization. Hence the Universal Negro Improvement Association appeals to each and every Negro to throw in his lot with those of us who, through organization, are working for the universal emancipation of our race and the redemption of our common country—Africa.

"No Negro, let him be American, European, West Indian or African, shall be truly respected until the race as a whole has emancipated itself, through self-achievement and progress, from universal prejudice. The Negro will have to build his own government, industry, art, science, literature and culture, before the world will stop to consider him. Until then, we are but wards of a superior race and civilization, and the outcasts of a standard social system. The race needs workers at this time, not plagiarists, copyists and mere imitators, but men and women who are able to create, to originate and improve, and thus make an independent racial contribution to the world and civilization.

"The unfortunate thing about it is that we take the monkey apings of our so-called 'leading men' for progress. There is no real progress in Negroes aping white people and telling us that they represent the best in the race, for in that respect any dressed monkey would represent the best of its species, irrespective of the creative matter of the monkey instinct. The best in a race is not reflected through or by the action of its apes, but by its ability to create of and by itself. It is such creation that our organization seeks. Let us not try to be the best or worst of others, but let us make the effort to be the best of ourselves. Our own racial critics criticize us as dreamers and fanatics, and call us benighted and ignorant, because they lack backbone. They are unable to see themselves creators of their own needs. The slave instinct has not yet departed from them. They still believe that they can only live or exist through the good graces of their 'masters.' The good slaves have not yet thrown off their shackles; thus to them, the U.N.I.A. is an 'impossibility.'

"It is the slave spirit of dependence that causes our so-called leading men to seek the shelter, leadership, protection and patronage of 'the master' in their organization and so-called advancement work. It is the spirit of feeling secured as good servants of the master, rather than as independents, that our modern Uncle Toms take pride in labouring under alien leadership and becoming surprised at the audacity of our organization in proclaiming for racial liberty and independence. But the world of white, and other men, deep down in their hearts, have much more respect for those of us who work for our racial salvation under the banner of the U.N.I.A. than they could ever have, in all eternity, for a group of helpless apes and beggars who make a monopoly of undermining their own race and belittling themselves in the eyes of self-respecting people, by being 'good boys,' rather than able men. Let the white race of America and the world be informed that the best in the Negro race is not the class of beggars who send out to other races piteous appeals annually for donations to maintain their coterie, but the groups within us that are honestly striving to do for themselves with the voluntary help and appreciation of that class of other races that is reasonable, just and liberal enough to give to each and every man a fair chance in the promotion of those ideals that tend to greater human progress and human love. There is no desire for hate or malice, but every wish to see all mankind linked into a common fraternity of progress and achievement, that will wipe away the odour of prejudice, and elevate the human race to the height of real Godly love and peace."

CHAPTER FOUR

Garvey formed a strong branch of the U.N.I.A. in New York City, so that they could lead the other groups and continue the fight for their rights when he returned to Jamaica. Soon after, there was disruption, as two of the officers saw in the organization a means of using the membership's voting strength for Socialists, and another for the Republicans. In this manner they planned to augment their income, and not depend solely on membership dues and collections. This was in contradiction to Garvey's policy that in order to be self-respecting and to deserve the respect of others, no longer must we accept white philanthropy to maintain our leaders and our organization, but must do so on our own. He refused to allow the Organization to be used as a "sideline" for party machines.

On the appeal of most of the members he decided to remain in the U.S.A. and rebuild and expand the work. His former associates, when they could not get the members to follow them, now became the nucleus of an opposition who plotted against him. They had lost their "bread and butter," as they could not show political party bosses a membership list worth the sums they wanted "to swing" elections.

New officers were elected, a women's auxiliary formed, and means of propagandizing adopted. The membership increased rapidly. Across the nation white mob rule was taking a toll of seventy-odd yearly by lynching alone; and hundreds of Negroes lost their lives or were maimed or their properties were destroyed. To counter this there were a few "Better Race-relations Committees." In the lead was the National Association for the Advancement of Colored People, directed by white people and one colored man—Dr. E. B. DuBois, a Doctor of Philosophy, who had been brought up in the comparatively cultured atmosphere of Massachusetts by "good white people," and was the leading intellectual at that time, and so was sponsored as the leading colored American. Membership was of both races. White philanthropists helped them liberally, as they symbolized good race relations, and only came into action after a lynching or a race riot, to protest against such barbarous practices, and to avow that the American Negro was a loyal citizen, and as such deserved equality and equal rights as any other born citizen. Since the death of Booker T. Washington there was no one with a positive and practical uplift program for the masses—North or South.

There was no all-Negro organization with a program or plan for the race beyond equality and citizen's rights. Small individual businesses flourished, mainly in the South, because Negroes were compelled to patronize their own or walk through side entrances of white traders. On the slightest pretext they were thrown into state prisons, and from there farmed out to white planters; the human misery on these farms was appalling. Labor camps used prison labor too, and forced men to work on the highways and state public works. Some white farmers unable or too lazy to use up all their land allowed Negroes to come in and cultivate it on an agreement to share the crop either in money or produce. When harvest time came arrangements were disputed by the farmer, and he usually showed a padded statement of monies advanced during planting time, which was carried on to next year's account. A Negro dare not call a white man a liar in any Southern state; if he did, he would be run out of town or very likely shot dead on the farm, and the sheriff told that the nigger "looked hard" at his daughter. Then the body would be taken to the public square, and souvenirs such as hair, toe- or fingernails cut from it. After this it would be tied to a slowly moving car, followed by the ever increasing mob to a common and burned by the white supremists.

Into this atmosphere traveled Garvey with this message: "No longer must our Race look to Whites for guidance and leadership; who best can interpret the anguish and needs of our people but a Negro? This Organization under God will thrive without the demoralizing effect of existing off the charity of Whites." Among the many things the race needed, and badly too, were self-respect and self-reliance. Henceforth they must think for themselves and of themselves, only relying on their own initiative and ability to right the wrongs being done them. This was the first phase of his campaign to reorient the minds of his people.

He appealed to all Negro newspaper publishers and owners to stop carrying skin-bleaching and hair-straightening advertisements, as they tended to make our people feel that to "be somebody" they must try to look like white people. These businessmen became angry with him. They were well paid for pictorial advertisements; subscriptions cannot "carry a newspaper," and they had no intention to run a paper on sentiment. As the thoughts in the slogan—"Negro, be yourself"—gained more adherents, the tone of the advertisements was changed.

So in every phase of life that subjugated their true self he attacked it. Said he:

Take down the pictures of white women from your walls. Elevate your own women to that place of honour. They are for the most part the burden-bearers of the Race. Mothers! give your children dolls that look like them to play with and cuddle. They will learn as they grow older to love and care for their own children, and not neglect them. Men and women [he continued], God made us as his perfect creation. He made no mistake when he made us black with kinky hair. It was Divine Purpose for us to live in our natural habitat—the tropical zones of the earth. Forget the white man's banter, that he made us in the night and forgot to paint us white. That we were brought here against our will is just a natural process of the strong enslaving the weak. We have outgrown slavery, but our minds are still enslaved to the thinking of the Master Race. Now take these kinks out of your mind, instead of out of your hair. You are capable of all that is common to men of other Races, so let us start now to build big business, commerce, industry and eventually a nation of our own to protect us wherever we choose to live.

A Beggar-Race can never be respected. Stop begging for jobs, and create your own. Look around you and wherever you see the need for factories and business, supply it. Stop begging for a chance, make it yourself. Remember God helps those who help themselves.

Said a colored Southern woman after she had joined the organization, "Garvey is giving my people backbones where they had wishbones." No man had spoken to them like this before. Wherever he went he stirred something in them, so that they could never be the same self-satisfied or happy-go-lucky human beings again. Preachers had told them about the sweet "bye-and-bye," but he was telling them about the "now-and-now." The good book says that "your just reward shall be in Heaven on that great Day"; but Garvey said, "Work for it right here, and get it here, or take it; then the spiritual reward shall surely come."

We are ten million souls in the forty-eight states of this American Union in a majority of ten to one. A majority that legislates and increases its lead with European Immigrants while it limits Coloured ones, so as to maintain its policy of "Keep America white," even as Australia, Canada and New Zealand. We are spoken of as "The Negro Problem"; they say we have not grown up mentally, just a child-race. The indignity of it all! No one hears of a Jewish Problem; yet they too have suffered discrimination and segregation. When a Jew is told he can't do business in the Hub of the commercial area of a city, he reports it to his Jewish Organization, a fund is created, a Holding Company formed, and they buy out the entire business block. He solves his difficulty through Unity and Thrift. A Jew does not go around asking for social equality, decrying the fact that he is not admitted to some of the exclusive clubs of this country, nor can he be President of the United States. He knows the world will knock at his door because he is financially strong and united.

Good white folks have paid our erstwhile leaders to tell us bed-time stories to lull us to sleep like children—that the problem will solve itself as the years go by, with the white population absorbing the Coloured. But I am telling you to wake up! and stay awake! God never intended that you should lose your identity as a Race, but that you must continue to make a distinct contribution all your own to America. Our people are more adaptable than other Races; it is this adaptability that has saved us from extermination. But it is the same characteristic that has made you willing to submerge yourself in another Race. Being collectively slothful too, you accept the easy way out.

The old myths must be cleared away; they are like cobweb in your brains. You blame somebody else for what you yourself fail to do through fear, and lack of forthright thinking. The old belief imposed on you that slavery was caused through the Will of God—exercised in punishment or neglect —still has its baneful effects. You are inclined to submit to wrongs feeling that they are Divinely sent, and should be patiently endured.

Slavery was the result of the needs of the strong to maintain material strength; the weak became the victims because while they enjoyed the bounties of nature around them, they failed to prepare for the Invader. Self-satisfaction weakens a people. That is why slavery is not confined to any particular Race or clime. History records that slaves—by virtue of their experiences and the knowledge gained in captivity in strange lands —have eventually become Masters of themselves, and in time enslaved others. Let us therefore use adversity as others have done. Take advantage of every opportunity; where there is none, make it for yourself, and let history record that as we toiled laboriously and courageously, we worked to live gloriously.

It was said in derision then that every race had a flag except the coon, so Garvey designed a flag for the race of the three colors of red, black and green. He also had an African National Anthem put in verse, and set to martial music; the lines are:

Ethiopia, thou land of our fathers,
Thou land where the gods loved to be,
As storm cloud at night sudden gathers
Our armies come rushing to thee.
We must in the fight be victorious
When swords are thrust outward to gleam.
For us will the vict'ry be glorious
When led by the red, black and green.

Chorus

Advance, advance to victory,
Let Africa be free;
Advance to meet the foe
With the might
Of the red, the black and the green.

Ethiopia, the tyrant's falling,
Who smote thee upon thy knees
And thy children are lustily calling
From over the distant seas.
Jehovah, the Great One has heard us,
Has noted our sighs and our tears
With His Spirit of Love has stirred us
To be one through the coming years.

O, Jehovah, Thou God of the ages
Grant unto our sons that lead
The wisdom Thou gave to Thy sages

ael was sore in need.
e thro' the dim past has spoken,
shall stretch forth her hand
By thee shall all fetters be broken
And Heav'n bless our dear Motherland.

CHAPTER FIVE

As the branches multiplied all over the country, Garvey saw the necessity for a weekly newspaper to convey his message of uplift and present clean wholesome news. Early in 1919 he published the *Negro World*, the official organ of the U.N.I.A. He contributed frontpage articles, no matter where he was. This paper was destined to play a leading part in the Negro Renaissance. As it developed, Spanish and French sections were added later.

Top-page slogans were: "The indispensable weekly, the voice of the awakened Negro, reaching the masses everywhere." After he was forced to leave America an eight-point platform at the head of the editorial page was inserted to show that policy had not changed:

1. To champion Negro nationhood by redemption of Africa.
2. To make the Negro Race conscious.
3. To breathe ideals of manhood and womanhood in every Negro.
4. To advocate self-determination.
5. To make the Negro world-conscious.
6. To print all the news that will be interesting and instructive to the Negro.
7. To instill Racial self-help.
8. To inspire Racial love and self-respect.

In order to counteract misleading and vicious lies about the intentions and behavior of both leader and followers of the organization, the *Negro World* published at different times when necessary, "thirty don'ts" to guide members. Among them were:

20. Always respect authority.
21. Be a good citizen.
22. Vote as the Association will direct for the good of our Cause and the nation.
23. Don't sell your vote.
26. Don't sell your property without getting the advice of your Officers and the Legal Department.
28. Keep your present job, work hard, and save all you can.

This paper brought light and hope to our people in all corners of the world made dark by the deeds of the oppressors. It was carried by trains, ships, smuggled in suitcase linings by seamen and students; concealed beneath garments being worn, or just the frontpage article hidden in a hat or cap lining. Men were lashed and imprisoned for possession of this "seditious publication." Many were given the third degree to tell what it was imagined they knew of the plans for an all-African uprising.

In instances when translations into dialects became risky, then just the tom-tom drums at night would relay the message. The slogan, "Africa for the Africans," thrilled men's hearts, and hope strengthened them into activity. The password for awakened Africans was "Freedom." The glorious career of this paper came to an end in 1933, *The Blackman* succeeding it. Among its editors were T. Thomas Fortune, John E. Bruce and William Ferris, M.A.

In 1918 and for many years after, colored lawyers found it difficult to make a living by their profession. They had the training, but could not get the opportunity to practice freely in the courts; hence they lacked court experience, so necessary for trial lawyers. In the courts they were treated with deft courtesy because of the low rating of their race. Many of them could only afford desk space in a real-estate office, or if one had a room to himself he did part-time manual work, and had a card hung on his door which read: "Busy at court, will be in after four o'clock," or some such explanation for his absence. When he got a little more prosperous he employed a typist to take calls and make evening appointments. The most reliable among these lawyers was James Watson, who was highly thought of in Democratic party circles. Later on he had an office downtown in the suite of a white law firm. Garvey retained him to do the legal work for the organization. Mr. Watson eventually became a municipal judge.

Persons who had relatives and friends in the West Indies and Central and South America wrote telling them of the Garvey organization, and because of his previous activities in these areas hundreds of branches were quickly formed through correspondence. These branches not only functioned as units of a fraternal organization should, but became centers of extensive activities. Summarized reports of these activities and grievances on local conditions were sent to the parent body in New York City.

In response to reports on discrimination on ships against both passengers and seamen, Garvey conceived the idea of getting a ship to carry bananas and other produce to America, and on the return a cargo of manufactured goods. A white fruit company years ago had started with a schooner and became rich. His colleagues vetoed the idea as being too big a proposition. Later on, however, complaints became more insistent, and seamen from Africa came to the office and told them how valuable cargoes were left on wharves to rot if African owners showed any spunk in asking for better prices. After this officers of the U.N.I.A. agreed to form the Black Star Line Company, but they lacked real interest in its progress. The moneys of the U.N.I.A. were used for all promotional work.

In 1919 when the stock-selling campaign was well on its way, two former associates went to the District Attorney's office, and told him all that Garvey was doing uptown, with the result that he was summoned by District Attorney Edwin Kilroe, who told him that he was investigating his activities, and advised him to "close down the Black Star Line." Garvey retorted that he had no intention to do so. Mr. Kilroe sent for him on two other occasions, questioned and cautioned him as before. Garvey became irate, and at a Liberty Hall meeting told the people what he thought of Mr. Kilroe's attitude towards the Black Star Line. For this speech he was taken before the court on a criminal libel charge. He explained that he had been angry and apologized. This ended the court case, but Kilroe warned him "to watch his steps in the future."

It is said that there are more colored churches than white ones in America, according to the population ratio. In the lingering past, religion was thought to be a solace for Negroes—an opiate; so white people subscribed readily to building funds.

Usually prayers were quiet or loud appeals to God for something desired. Few observed the meditative manner of the East and the invocation for spiritual strength to overcome obstacles, and for daily guidance in all things; for who knows beforehand what is good or bad for us? This beggar's approach to prayer created false hopes. As they prayed and hoped for small things, even so they hoped to realize their big desires in the wider aspects of life. Typical of this attitude is the following statement from a young man: "America is our home. The only home we know, and the history of our loyalty to the flag, and our willingness to die for it has been written in deep crimson. Our hopes are high for the ultimate success of the spirit of Liberty."

Hope should be the feeling that after doing one's best one may expect good results. In this instance expectancy should be tempered by historical precedence, contemporary world happenings, human stubbornness and bitterness towards change in the old order of things. In order to break down prejudice one has to be self-assertive in new thinking and living, and thereby force others to change. Because prejudice is largely conditioned by inequalities—poverty and squalor creates contempt and hate on both sides—it warps the minds of men. It retards progress. In its virulent form it saps the vitals of manhood. It takes more than wishful prayer to remove prejudice.

Garvey incurred the enmity of most of the northern colored newspapermen because he condemned their policies of presenting a spread of social activities; no serious reading matter, nor any coverage of international happenings; displays of skin-bleaching advertisements; and referring to our people as "Race-men" and "Race-women."

Among the newspapers that lashed back at him, not on the points he condemned but personal and venomous attacks, was the *Chicago Defender*, published by Robert S. Abbott—a black man. The statements published formed the basis of several libel actions by Garvey in 1919. The Black Star Line won one case in New York, but just a token damage. The other cases in Chicago and New York were listed for the fall calendar.

At the end of the summer Garvey and other officers of the U.N.I.A., on a tour of branches, visited Chicago. A man was sent to decoy Garvey into selling him a stock which he insisted that his wife wanted, saying, "You know how women are, when they want a thing they must get it." Garvey never handled stock books or cash, so he gave him the address where the company's clerk was staying, and forgot all about the incident. That evening while on the platform at a crowded meeting two white men and a colored man came and arrested him for "violating the Blue Sky Law"—selling stock in a company that was not registered in the State of Illinois. It was the first he and many other persons learned of the existence of such a law.

He was released under two thousand dollars bail; but to the great satisfaction of his enemy he had been prevented from speaking to the vast crowd in the auditorium, and humiliated by being dragged off to jail. In court an attorney pleaded his ignorance of the law; he was fined one hundred dollars. Before leaving Chicago he was served a summons for libel, but no particulars were stated by Mr. Abbott. So the attorney said it might be just an attempt to scare Garvey, who gave him a retaining fee and told him to notify him when it came up for trial. The attorney told him that the calendars of the courts were so congested that it might not come up for years.

Early in 1921 he wrote to tell his attorney of his intended trip abroad, who told him he did not think the cases would come up during that period. While he was away his enemies worked hard and succeeded in keeping him out of the country for months. On his return he was told that his cases had gone by default; and in the case of Abbott against him, judgment was taken by default for five thousand dollars, for which Abbott had taken out a body execution warrant. He sought to have the cases reopened but was not permitted to do so. This is an example of the "colored" man's way of striking back at an opponent. "Face a grin, but knife a throat." While Garvey in defiance said: "For me there is no fear, but the fear of Almighty God. Cast any other fear to the winds, Negroes, and go forward to your own creative destiny."

CHAPTER SIX

It was customary for Garveyites coming from out of town and abroad to want to see Garvey personally after transacting business and inspecting the various departments; they just wanted to shake his hand, so that they could tell the folks back home that they had held his hand and that he sent greetings and good wishes.

One day in October 1919, from downstairs came an insistent voice demanding to see Garvey; so he went to the head of the stairs, and said, "You really want to see me?" The answer from the man who had come toward the foot of the stairs was, "You Garvey? Well, I come to get you." Drawing his gun he started firing at him. The first shot went wild, but in that flash he saw the figure of his mother, who motioned him "to duck." He did so, and the second bullet passed so near his temple that the skin was seared. The third bullet hit his leg as he ducked.

The would-be assassin seeing him fall, thought that he was dead and ran, but was caught by the switchboard operator and others who were downstairs; he was arrested and, seeming rather dazed, taken to jail. He gave his name as Tyler. In the meantime Garvey was put in an ambulance and taken to Harlem Hospital. Because of a report that a bullet had hit his head, the newspapers featured him as being in a dying condition.

By the time this news reached Tyler in jail the following day, having slept off his dopey spell, he believed Garvey dead. He told his cell mates that he was "sent to get Garvey"; he had taken something to nerve himself up; now that Garvey was dead he would not take the rap alone; in court he would tell everything. But Tyler never lived to tell who instigated his attack. When the case was called up, the court was told that he had committed suicide by jumping from a second floor window while being escorted by two guards along a corridor. This man came from the South, was unemployed, and had no relatives in the city. Garveyites who went to the morgue to view the body said he looked as if he was sleeping, and showed no signs of being smashed or bleeding, as would be expected on a man jumping from such a height to a paved courtyard. After Garvey was out of the hospital and able to walk around, a committee of members impressed on him the importance of protecting himself against future attacks by carrying a gun. Said he to them, "I am so lost in thoughts at times, that I would not even remember I had the gun when I should use it. Using it is another question, I don't think I could kill anybody. As a boy I couldn't bear to see chickens killed; that is why I never eat them. When I see a chicken trussed up on the table, it reminds me of my people—innocent and carefree in the backyards of the world; then suddenly some are pounced on, caught and carried away to satisfy the greed of others." He sighed at the thought, and said determinedly, "No gun for me; if I am to be killed, then maybe it is my destiny." The committee selected Marcellus Strong, the

Georgia-born switchboard operator, as his bodyguard, and he carried a gun. Strong remained a faithful companion to Garvey. He did not go with him on speaking trips; then the local branches took care of him.

I had heard many conflicting reports about the U.N.I.A. —what it stood for, and what Garvey intended to do—so one Sunday night during the summer I went to Liberty Hall. After the meeting was over, I went and congratulated him on his fine oratory. There were many points he did not cover in his speech; on these I questioned him for the answers; as I told him, I not only wanted to be convinced that he was right, but to be able to argue on my conviction. His answers seemed to call forth more questions, so he made an appointment at his office, where he would have more time to talk, and he could show me around the place.

Discussing international topics was nothing new to me, as my father in his early years lived in Cuba and spoke Spanish fluently, and at one time lived in Baltimore. He bought foreign newspapers and periodicals; on Sundays, I—being the eldest child—had to join him in reading them. He explained that this would improve our knowledge of the world and its happenings outside our small island.

I kept the appointment, and Garvey convinced me on the worthiness of his program, and stressed the fact that the skin-color class system of Jamaica did not exist in America, as all strata of the race were treated as one—the slogan being, "Any nigger is a nigger." Therefore it was necessary for the educated and better able to join with the masses in a strong uplift-and-onward movement.

He showed me around the offices, and asked my opinion. I told him quite frankly that he needed a daily reporting system from each department so that at the end of the day he would be able to tell from the reports how much business was done in each department, and if the treasurer received the moneys. In answer to this he said, "I am placed in an awkward position here; I have to employ all-colored staff, many of whom have never had the advantages of working in business offices; it takes time and patience to train them, and in the meantime I suffer."

He opened a large cabinet in his office and showed me stacks of mail. Said he, "These accumulated while I was on a speaking trip. I haven't the time to help and teach someone to open, sort and put notations on them, before handing the moneys enclosed to the treasurer. You see the awful predicament I am in for lack of qualified honest people."

I promised him I would come in the evenings and inaugurate the system, which I did, and will now describe it, as this played an important part in his first indictment later on.

A bonded mail clerk in the President-General's office received all letters. A mailing slip was pinned to any monetary enclosure, and particulars filled in: date, name, address, amount, whether cash, check or draft; to what department intended; if amount was to be divided among two or more of them, then three slips were attached. The treasurer received all moneys and slips for the Black Star Line, and the chancellor received what was intended for the U.N.I.A. and the *Negro World*. They receipted the totals received. All letters were taken to the Secretary General's department to be answered; if they were not routine, then he consulted with the President-General or the assistant.

The treasurer kept in his safe stock books that were signed by president and secretary, and salesmen had to sign for same, and a record kept of all serial numbers. Cash returns were made to the treasurer, and the secretary rechecked the books. All checks were signed by president and treasurer, on the presentation of a voucher signed by president and secretary. The head of every department sent in a daily report to the President-General's office, with remark column filled in if he had any recommendations to make. In this manner every cent that came in could be easily traced, and Garvey did not handle any money.

He thanked me profusely for what I had done, but said he was unable to check all reports, as he was overburdened with work, and had to be away from the office so often on speaking tours. He had tried to get a secretary, but it was most difficult to get a competent person who had enough strength of character to report discrepancies even if an officer was involved, or to be able to act in any emergency in his absence. After much pleading, I took the job, only to find that because of my ability and capacity for work, I was overworked.

The following year I had to get a gun, as one of the clerks threatened to throw me down the stairs. He had lost a stock book of signed-up certificates and I had promptly reported this to the directors, who acted on the matter. At the trial of the Black Star Line case, it was evident that he had been "planted" there to get information.

At this time Japan was considered the leader of an awakened Asia, striving to throw off foreign domination, and build modern, materialistic states on her own. This threat to white supremacy was called the Yellow Peril by those who saw the potentiality of Asia's numbers, technical training, industrialization, and a possible desire for revenge. Leo Walmsley in an article in the *English Daily Sketch*, November 10, 1919, warned the world of the Black Peril, because in a speech Garvey had said: "We have been used to fight in every war, but the time has come when we will fight for ourselves, we will fight to make the Negro free." This was distorted by reporters, and Leo Walmsley quoted from "a British daily paper," which misquoted Garvey as saying, "I call upon 400,000,000 Negroes to give your blood to make Africa a Republic for the Negro." Then Walmsley goes on to comment:

> Wild words and wild threats no doubt, and of course not to be taken seriously. Why? Who could take the "Nigger" seriously . . . Torn from his home in the African forests, driven in chains to the coast, tortured in the stinking holds of ships, transported to a foreign land, and worked as no animal would be worked, the negro was released from his slavery only to become an object of contempt and racial hatred by the white man.

Instead of a merciless bondage of the body, has been substituted a relentless slavery of the soul, for in the average human estimation the Negro is a moral outcast; and even the lowest type of "white" blackguard is more than a shade higher up the social scale than the best of black men.

To say that the apparent white man is touched with the tar brush is infinitely more insulting than to charge him with stealing from a church poor box.

To say that the Negro has no feelings indicates a complete ignorance of his psychology.

He closed his article with this warning: "Don't under-rate either the intentions or strength of your enemy. Our intentions have never been revenge, but most white people show a guilt complex toward organized Negroes. We are too busy building for ourselves to waste time trying to destroy others. God is our Avenger."

Mr. R. V. Selope-Thema, Secretary to the South African Deputation in London at this time, in reply to Mr. Walmsley's article stated, under the head "Why a Black feels like fighting—Conviction that whites respect nothing but brute force," the following facts:

In South Africa today, under the British flag the black man finds himself dispossessed of his land, prohibited by law to buy, hire or lease land in the country of his ancestors, excluded from participating in the government and affairs of his country; heavily taxed, in spite of the principle of "no taxation without representation," and barred from entering into all the channels that lead up to advancement and civilization.

Against this cruel exploitation he has made constitutional protests both to the South African and the Imperial Governments, but to his horror and disappointment these constitutional protests have not brought about the amelioration of his conditions of life.

It is because the white man relies on his military superiority which modern scientific progress has conferred on him that he has refused or neglected to pay attention to the black man's cry for justice and liberty, and consequently some of the educated black men have been forced, much against their will, to come to the conclusion that what the white man respects, is not constitutional and peaceful appeal, but brute force.

Hence Mr. Marcus Garvey's threatening appeal to the 400,-000,000 Africans to prepare themselves to fight. This "wild threatening language" comes from a broken heart that can no longer tolerate the exploitation of Africa and her peoples.

While he was in Harlem Hospital, Amy Ashwood, a Jamaican friend from Panama, then Secretary of the New York local, removed his belongings from his furnished room to her flat. At the end of December they were married.

The following year, about three months after the event, on his return from a trip, he called Miss Henrietta Davis, Assistant President-General and myself to a conference. He said he wanted us to know before the reporters had it their own way. He had decided to separate from his wife and get a divorce afterwards. He had given the matter deep thought and felt that he was acting in the best interest of his work—which came first in his life—and his own peace of mind. Continued he, "I have to travel up and down the country. I can't drag my wife with me. I can't pay her the personal attention as the average husband. In fact, I have no time to look after myself. My life can either be wrecked because of her conduct, or embellished by her deportment. I must have her sympathy and understanding of every action of mine."

He moved into a flat at 129th Street with an elderly colored member as housekeeper. He offered Miss Davis and I a room to share there; we accepted because we would be better protected at nights coming from meetings.

Later on that year his elder sister, Indiana, wrote to him that she was married, her husband was out of work, would he send for them. He had not seen or heard from her for years, and had thought she was dead. Now she had heard of the famous leader—her brother. She got his address from the *Negro World*, and was anxious to be with him.

When they arrived in New York City, he put her in charge of the flat, and gave her husband a job in the steam laundry of the Negro Factories Corporation. She was just like her mother in looks and disposition—a timid soul, as was her husband. She never dreamed that fame could bring so many exacting duties and so much misery, and grieved silently. After a time she tried to shut it out of her vision by withdrawing to her room when her brother was home; she persuaded her husband to do the same. She showed resentment to those closely associated with his work. To her way of thinking they "were encouraging him in that thing, which will soon kill him."

In 1922 on his return from a tour of the branches, he discovered that both of them had packed up and sailed for Jamaica, without even leaving a note for him. Said he in comment, "At least I won't see her pitying eyes looking at me from the shadow of her room door. I don't want pity. I want help."

In the same year, Garvey, irritated by the tactics of his enemies, all of his own race—and their apings of white people, said, "We are the only people in the world who laugh at the misfortunes of their own, and show no interest in our collective selves."

In another speech he warned the black man. "If Negroes are not careful they will acquire all the low habits of a hustling industrial country, and ruin their character as a people, since the worst in the race is usually given publicity."

As to the future wars he said: "The battles of the future, whether they be physical or mental, will be fought on scientific lines; and the race or people who are able to produce the highest scientific development will ultimately lead the world."

Reflecting on the causes of anarchism he wrote:

Most of the isms that plague the world are the direct result of the crude and unprincipled acts of selfish and unworthy representatives of Government inflicted upon innocent people; who, conscious of their innocence, and cognizant of the injustices done them, resort to measures of their own for justification, that generally result in the formation and promotion of new policies, ideas, or means for the administration of justice, by the overthrow of existing systems. Those who suffer like themselves, eager to obtain what is being denied them, join together and give strength and expression to the new adventure.

CHAPTER SEVEN

Early in 1920 Samuel Duncan, a West Indies-born, naturalized American citizen who left the U.N.I.A. during the split in 1918, wrote a letter dated March 4, 1920, which he sent to all colonial Governors, overseas dominions and consulates of colonial powers.

The following is the text of the letter, so that the reader may be able to realize the enormous injury and damage done, not only to the U.N.I.A. and its allied activities, but to the freedom of travel of colored people:

The West Indian Protective Society of America,
Main office 178 West 135th Street, New York, N.Y.

His Excellency the Governor of St. Lucia,

Sir; I beg to convey to you confidentially the following information and suggestions to the end that peace and good feeling shall continue between His Majesty's white and colored subjects within the British Empire, and especially in the British West Indies.

There is in this city an organization known as the Universal Negro Improvement Association and African Communities League, at the head of which is one Marcus Garvey, a Negro, a native of Jamaica. This organization is not only anti-white and anti-British but it is engaged in the most destructive and pernicious propaganda to create disturbance between white and colored people in the British possessions.

This organization employs as a medium through which to carry on its propaganda a newspaper published in this city and known as the Negro World. So inciting and inflammable and purposely colored are the news and editorial articles in this paper that the authorities in several of the islands have been compelled to take energetic action to deny its admittance to those islands and prevent its circulation among the colored people thereof. It was the known radical attitude and friction creating policy of the Negro World that was responsible for the drastic newspaper ordinance recently enacted in British Guiana, St. Vincent and other West Indian Islands.

Another medium for carrying on the propaganda of the Universal Negro Improvement Association and African Communities League is the Black Star Line whch owns the steamer *Yarmouth* (soon to be known as *Frederick Douglass*). Of greater importance to Garvey and those associated with him in pushing this world-wide pro-Negro and anti-white and anti-British propaganda than the making of money through freight and passengers is the effect and impression that the presence of this ship of the Black Star Line is expected to exert on the colored people of the islands when it calls at their ports.

Yet another and perhaps the most effective way of carrying on its propaganda is through the members of the Universal Negro Improvement Association and African Communities League and stockholders of the Black Star Line who leave this country for the West Indies, and who are expected to stealthily work among the natives and stir up strife and discontent among them. These members and stockholders of the above-named Organization faithfully perform the work that the suppressed Negro World cannot do, and thus sow seeds of discontent among the natives of the island to which they go. The recent bloody strikes in Trinidad, when several persons were killed and wounded, and much injury caused to shipment and other industries can be traced to the subtle and underhand propaganda work of the agencies above referred to.

I venture to suggest that Your Excellency would be serving well the cause of the empire and contributing in no small way to the promotion of peace and good feeling between the white and colored people in the West Indies should you cause to be carefully scrutinized and precautionary measures taken in the case of all colored persons coming into the colony from the United States and the Panama Canal with a view of ascertaining whether such persons are members of the Universal Negro Improvement Association and African Communities League, subscribers to and readers of the Negro World, stockholders of, or in any way connected with the Black Star Line, and upon affirmatively establishing any of these facts to exercise your official discretion as to their admission into the colony.

I have the honour to remain,

Very truly yours,

Samuel Augustus Duncan.

Executive Secretary of the West Indian Protective Society of America, the only society in the United States looking after the interest of colored people of foreign birth.

After this, Jan Smuts, Prime Minister of South Africa, communicated with the necessary authorities immediately to prevent Negroes from the West Indies and America from departing for Africa. The inherited slave complex of telling the master what was happening on the plantation dies hard with some of us.

Our people love to sing; it is said they sang their way out of slavery, through their spirituals, which expressed their sorrow, and the firm belief that God was leading them, as He had led the children of Israel through the Wilderness, and Daniel out of the lion's den. So Garvey outlined a set of meaningful hymns, and Burrell and Ford of the music department put them into proper verse and set them to music.

When sung, the words impressed on the minds of the listeners and the singers the intents and purposes of the organization. So that although zealots and fanatics might arise in their midst in this far-flung brotherhood, which Garvey could hardly prevent, the singing of these hymns would sober extreme utterances.

The ritual used at religious services was most inspiring. The following prayer was chanted, and in some cases recited by the chaplain, the congregation joining in the closing lines:

Almighty God, we beseech Thee to assist us with Thy Heavenly Grace, and to prosper the Godly aims and endeavours of this Association in bringing peace, justice, liberty and happiness to our Race. Grant us wisdom and discretion in all our undertakings, patience under our difficulties, triumph over our enemies, and a happy issue out of all our struggles. Save us, we pray Thee, from the great danger of unhappy divisions. Take from us envy, hatred, malice and whatever may hinder us from union and concord; that as there is but one Body, and one Spirit, and one Hope of our calling, One God! One Aim! One Destiny! so we may be all of one heart and of one mind, united in one holy bond of truth and peace, of faith and charity, and may with one mind and mouth glorify Thee; through Jesus Christ our Lord. Amen.

The letterheads of branches carried this Biblical reminder: "He created of one blood all nations to dwell upon the face of the earth."

The first big event of convention month (August) was the parade. This was carefully planned by the minister of uniformed ranks. All units of branches were uniformed according to regulations and drilled, in order to vie with each other. The police permit was obtained well in advance, and the "Irish cops" enjoyed being on duty, as orderliness was always drilled into the minds of all participants.

The parade was miles long, twelve bands in attendance, all well spaced; the drum majors were magnificent, the admiration of the crowds who lined the route. Mounted legions regulated the marchers under the direction of the Minister of Legion. The officials of the organization rode in open cars, identified by streamers.

Branches, fraternities, churches, etc., carried their identifying banners in front. Other banners were carried, black lettered on white background: "Down with lynching," "Uncle Tom's dead and buried," "Join the fight for freedom," and "Africa must be free." At the head of a Woman's Auxiliary were two women bearing a large banner marked: "God give us real men." The Red, Black and Green flags were dominant, but the Stars and Stripes were there in honor of the principles on which the country was founded.

Hundreds of thousands of people took part in, and watched the parade from windows (for which many had to pay) and sidewalks. The onlookers could not help but catch the spirit of the occasion; they clapped, waved flags and cheered themselves hoarse as thousands of colored men, women and children, smartly uniformed, with heads erect, stepped to the martial strain of good music. Here indeed were New Negroes on the march, with a goal to be reached, and a determined look in their eyes to achieve it.

For months ahead of August a department was created under the guidance of the Registrar of Convention to plan for all phases of activities of the thousands of delegates also visitors to see the parade and the opening sessions. Nothing was overlooked, and the marvel was that the huge crowds could be so well regimented.

The first International Convention of the Negro Peoples of the World held its opening meeting at night at Madison Square Garden—the largest completely covered auditorium in New York. The first half of the program was musical, and the best talent in the race took part. The second half was devoted to speeches. White newspapers estimated the crowd inside and outside as between 22,000 to 25,000 persons; it was like an invasion of the white section. The thousands who could not get in the auditorium just stayed around the adjacent streets, and discussed the day's happenings as something they never thought possible.

The other sessions were held at Liberty Hall for thirty days, strenuous days for the Speaker-in-Convention. The first item on the agenda was reports from delegates on conditions in their localities and territories. For the first time in history all peoples of African descent sat together in brotherly understanding and sympathy to listen to accounts of the awful conditions and handicaps under which they were born, lived and worked. Even this privilege and the results were worth the enormous costs involved.

Spanish and French interpreters helped those who could not speak English fluently. Africans were helped by others to write their speeches in basic English. Committees were appointed to deal with various matters; their terms of reference were investigatory, planning and advisory. This saved time, and the best informed and trained persons were given opportunities to serve in their particular line. The Committee on Africa had to hear certain delegates privately. These had to register under assumed names, for their freedom and lives might be endangered if they openly exposed conditions in their home territories.

The culmination of this work was the Declaration of Rights of the Negro Peoples of the World, which commenced with a preamble, then twelve causes for grievous complaints of injustices, and fifty-four demands for future fair treatment of our people everywhere. the U.N.I.A. held sessions for members only, at which the association's business was discussed, constitutional amendments made, and officers elected.

At this convention the delegates created the following top posts: Potentate, Deputy Potentate, Provisional President of Africa, an American Leader, and two Leaders for the West Indies—Eastern and Western Caribbean areas. To some the office of Potentate was a sinecure. Ostensibly he was likened to the Pope. He was the spiritual head of the organization. He and his Deputy were born Africans. No other Negroes were eligible, and they were to reside in Africa.

There were other duties that these two high officers could be destined to perform, if and when they caught the full significance of the task ahead. These plans were never known or discussed at Executive Council meetings, barely hinted at in Privy Council. Feelers were made to test the individual's courage and capacity to serve Africa under adverse conditions, knowing that peaceful penetration had to be done secretly by men and women on the spot. The Potentate was given wide powers; he could create fraternal and secret orders among tribes as the exigencies of a particular area demanded.

The discussions and decisions reached at the Convention were having grave effects on big world issues. In America at this period the Asiatic Exclusion Act was temporized by a token quota, allotted to Japan, whose migrants congregated in the Pacific states on farms and orchards. Because of their fecundity and thrift they produced crops at less cost, and could undersell the white farmers, whose living standards were higher, and whose family and social life were more costly. Further influx of Japanese en masse was viewed with alarm, especially in California.

Some friends of race equality interpreted their friendship in different ways. The *Nation* magazine voiced the opinion of other friends of Japan in advocating that America should open her Pacific door to Japanese; thinking only in terms of a progressive nation—Japan—the editor omitted any advocacy of opening the Atlantic door to West Indians. The *Globe and Commercial Advertiser*, August 17, 1920, took the *Nation* to task by pointing out the "dangerous implications" of this policy: free marriage and thereby a concession to Asiatics to overrun America and possess it eventually. The editor calmly reasoned out the question. In part he stated:

> The New York *Nation*, under "No more Race Discrimination," proposes to open America to Japanese immigration, and sanctions intermarriage between Japanese and Americans. . . .
> This quotation is for the most part sensible in its statements, but it is questionable in its implications. . . . It does not follow that, because we should be prepared to treat Negroes and Japanese with courtesy and fairness we should regard the

discouraging of colored immigration as silly, or the dislike of racial intermarriage as unsound. . . .

According to Governor Stephens of California, Japanese are entering the United States despite gentlemen's agreements. If given free access they would arrive in much larger numbers. A Yellow group now numbering little more than 100,000 might be millions by 1950. In China and India there are at least a hundred million coolies who could be spared, and who would find better opportunities here than in their own lands. If we accept the logic of free immigration we must accept its ultimate possibilities.

Nor is the question of intermarriage as simple in practice as in principle. . . . Physically, races of any color can amalgamate. Our own South is suggestive of such a possibility. Arabia and India show the mingling of men with different complexions. In Abyssinia color ranges from white to black. Indeed, the question is whether with the presence of a sufficiently large colored population the making of one race of intermediate color or colors can be prevented. History indicates that intermixture has been the habit of the past. Free immigration and free intermarriage thus hold the possibility of an American Abyssinia.

Colored races on whose territories whites have encroached have always protested against encroachment. This encroachment has often been economical in its earlier stages. Even now the Negro viewpoint with regard to Africa is being expressed by the Universal Negro Improvement Association: "We believe in the freedom of Africa for the Negro peoples of the world, and by the principle of Europe for the Europeans, and Asia for the Asiatics, we also demand Africa for the Africans, at home and abroad. We believe in the inherent right of the Negro to possess himself of Africa, and that his possession of same shall not be regarded as infringement on any claim or purchase made by any race or nation."

The writer concluded his article by stating that white America would then be conceding more than the colored races, yellow, brown and black, would concede to them.

CHAPTER EIGHT

The main points of Garvey's speech at Madison Square Garden were:

We Negroes are determined to suffer no longer. For over 500 years we have suffered at the hands of alien races. What is good for the white people is good for us.

For democracy the nations of the world wasted Europe in blood for four years. They called upon the Negroes of the world to fight. After the war we were deprived of all of the democracy we fought for. In many instances in the Southern States colored soldiers in uniforms, returning from the battlefields of Europe, were beaten and a few lynched; before they were demobilized they were mobbed in this land of the brave. But we shall not give up. We shall raise the banner of democracy in Africa, or 400,000,000 of us will report to God the reason why.

I know that America is the greatest democracy in the world; nevertheless, wherever I go, I am given to understand that I am a Negro. We pledge our blood to the battlefields of Africa, where we will fight for true liberty, democracy and the brotherhood of man.

The Negro is not contemplating the initiating of the fighting, but we must protect our interests. We are going in for mass organization. In the past we have worked separately and individually; now we are going to organize.

We are not distributing arms. We are not supplying implements of war. We are preparing the Negro race mentally and physically, and the Negro will win out by evolution.

This speech was interpreted in the press in headlines such as these: "400,000,000 Negroes sharpening their swords for next world war, Negroes called to arms, Negroes urged to take Africa," while delegates assembled in convention mapped out extensive programs of work for the ensuing year to change conditions, not by bloodshed, but by constitutional and enlightened methods. So they sang and meant every word of their hymn:

Shine on, Eternal Light
To greet our souls this day;
Dispel the gloominess of night
And drive our doubts away.

Our longing eyes prepare
When war and strife shall cease,
To view the morn soon to appear
The "New Era" of Peace.

Thy Temple, O our God,
No kingdom can remove;
Made without hands, this blest abode,
The Harbinger of Love.

Of all the gifts that flow
From Thy great throne above,
We ask Thee on our hearts bestow
The gift of "Perfect Love."

My soul the light receives
And dares the Truth to prove,
Not in blind ignorance believes,
But knows that God is love.

Come Love, and give new birth
To man's destructive mind.
Spread where confusion reigns on earth
Goodwill to all mankind.

Shine on, Eternal Light,
Thy penetrating ray
Shall turn the hour of darkest night
Into Eternal Day.

In rebuttal to Garvey's "Africa for Africans," the theme
of colored politicians and others was, "We ain't lost a thing
in Africa." Garvey's retort was, "You have lost everything,
even your manhood." The northern exponents of "satisfaction" were usually born southerners who had run away
from the horrors and uncertainty of life there. In the *New*

York Globe of September 7, 1920, Oscar Walters of the Colored Bureau of the Democratic Party, a southerner living in Harlem, made this statement: "As a property owner, I want to say that the better element is perfectly satisfied with conditions in America. . . . The Negro doesn't know any place on God's earth, but America—and he doesn't want to know any other place."

On the contrary, a minister gives us some of the reasons why the Negro is not satisfied, and exhorts his hearers to continue the fight for full freedom. Rev. G. Miller, pastor of St. Augustine Presbyterian Episcopal Church, Brooklyn, September 1920, spoke from Judges 11, verses 5-6. Subject: "Struggling for Liberty." This sermon was reported in the *Brooklyn Eagle.* He said in part:

> Garvey is the most remarkable man of our times. He may be laughed at and ridiculed, but he has done more to emphasize the restlessness of the black people than any other man. His hopes may not be realized in a millennium, but his spirit is worth more than the compound spirit of the ministers who have attacked him, and who have nothing to do but to fall in with the spirit of those who oppress them. A person is not justified in being less than a man at any time. It is a noble man who will lay down his life for his country. The Black House President is demonstrating to the world that the black people are dissatisfied with their condition, that they know their rights whether they get them or not; that they are not contented to be underlings forever. The manly man everywhere believes in a spirit of independence. Ideas conquer all things, they must precede action. Harriett Beecher Stowe, Wendell Phillips and William Lloyd Garrison did not contend for war, but for ideas. . . .

> The treatment of Haiti at the hands of this Government is something terrible. The United States is not in the League of Nations. Haiti is, yet this country holds sway there. It is not a question, it is a duty, to rise to the occasion. Let us let the world know that the black people of America are not satisfied.

The colored *Norfolk Journal and Guide* of Virginia in an editorial, August 21, 1920, stated:

> We have felt that "no bunch" of paupers ever existed before with more nerve and insolence for capital than the Garveyites, who fill so much of the public eye, and have for some time. The following may be honest but ignorant. . . .
>
> They can't conquer and repatriate Africa and build up and maintain a steamship line between African ports without consulting the Christian Nations which own and dominate Africa and its ports, and Garvey and his lieutenants know that. So do we.

In the *Baltimore American* of August 8, 1920, a contributor under the pen name "Ex-Attaché" stressed the importance and danger of a united Negro world; he wrote:

> Although there seems to be a very general disposition in this country to treat the thirty days Convention of the Negro Race now in progress in New York in the light of a joke, yet it is engaging the very serious attention not only of the Administration at Washington, but also several friendly governments, notably those of Great Britain and France. . . . We are already confronted by the Pan-Asiatic specter, to which we have given the name of the Yellow Peril. We are now being brought face to face with a Black Peril in the form of the Organization of a Pan-African Union of all the Negro tribes and nationalities. . . . It is a species of Christianity quite in keeping with the name of "The Church of Ethiopia," and which in the Dark Continent at any rate, is to such an extent in touch with certain forms of Mohammedanism, and retains so many elements of former Paganism that it does not constitute any obstacle to the cooperation of the blacks of every creed and denomination against those whom they are more and more coming to regard as their common enemy, the whites.

After this convention the world recognized the birth of the New Negro, who said most emphatically: "I am no longer 'a boy,' but a real man. I am now a Negro with a capital 'N,' not just 'a Nigger' to be pushed around! or 'a Coon,' playing the fool to make white folks laugh, but a serious man on my own serious business."

Leading white editors realized this. The Massachusetts *Lowell Courier-Citizen*, September 2, 1920, in an editorial stated:

> Don't make too much fun of these earnest colored people who have a notion of an Africa for the Negro. What reads today like the libretto of an opera bouffe may tomorrow be an act in the great international drama. . . .
>
> The Negro is far from being as hopeless of progress as some of our southern negrophobes would like us [to] believe. It means that, given advantages for development, he might in a century or so create in Africa a style of civilization half or three-fourths as fine as our own. In that event one wonders how many white men would annually be roasted alive in Monrovia and the Congo.

The *World's Work Magazine* had a feature writer—Truman Hughes Talley—devote much time to observing the operation of the organization, by visiting various departments, and talking with officers and employees. The result was two long articles, published in its issues of December 1920 and January 1921. This magazine is published in English and Spanish. As a subhead, the Editor noted:

> The most striking new figure among American Negroes is Marcus Garvey. His significance lies in the fact that he embodies and directs a new spirit of independence among the Negroes. Whatever may happen to his grandiose schemes of finance and politics, he is the best point at which to study what is going on inside the heads of ten million colored people in the United States. They are thinking and doing many things that are unsuspected by the public at large.

The *New York Times*, under the headline "Another Builder," explains the reason for Garvey's fearlessness in its issue of August 3, 1920:

> Garvey's origin probably explains the Empire scope of his ambitions—the quality of his "nerve." All through the West Indies the Jamaican Negro has a reputation for thinking well of himself, and his self-esteem, it must be admitted, is not

without excuse. Between him and the Barbadian Negro honors are about even, when it comes to capacity for racial leadership; but the Jamaican asserts superiority, and it is usually admitted—except in Barbados.

A Berlin report to the Associated Press predicted far-reaching results of the Convention:

> Berlin, December 24, 1920. Both reactionaries and radicals in Germany unite in the opinion that the military education of Negroes in the French army is, in their opinion, a world menace. German propaganda busied itself during the war with tales of the outrages perpetrated by the Negroes. At the same time, the condemnation of France could not be made sufficiently strong because "she took these innocent aboriginal children and slaughtered them in a white man's war."
>
> General Mangin's article in the latest issue of the *Revue des Deux Mondes* demands that France increase her black army and bring pressure to bear on Belgium under the terms of the Franco-Belgian military convention to conscript 2,000,000 natives in the Belgian Colonies.

The *Deutsche Allemeine Zeitung*, the German government official organ, makes the following comment:

> This French Colonial Officer doesn't suspect the results which are already beginning to be apparent from the use of black troops in the World War.
>
> Appreciation of the effects is beginning to dawn on America however. . . . As a result of the first meeting of the International Negro Improvement Association in New York, the slogan was adopted, "Africa for the Africans." The speakers at this convention await a new world war within the next twenty years. Then the African Negro will fight neither under the banner of France nor of England, but under the banner of liberty to conquer the African continent themselves while the white races are otherwise engaged. In the meantime, the leaders will continue their propaganda. In this connection, it is to be remembered that at the beginning of this year, their own publication, the *African and Oriental Review* in London, advised the co-operation of the Africans and the Asiatics.

Albert Guérard, a Frenchman writing in the March 1925 issue of *Scribner's Magazine*, revealed the thought behind France's attitude when he stated: "Native troops have always been used by France, and by all Colonial Powers. There is something soothing to the moral sense, in the thought that if Negroes had to be killed at all, they had better be killed by men of their own Race; besides it is cheaper."

M. Guérard in closing his article admitted the Nordic's supremacy in scientific destruction of human beings, which justifies Garvey's feverish and persistent warnings to our people to "be prepared." He stated: "A few white scientists can do today more harm than a million armed blacks. . . . When it comes to atrocities, the supremacy of the Caucasian, and particularly of the Nordic, is beyond challenge."

In commenting on the 1920 convention, the editor of *The Monitor* analyzed the plans and work of Garveyism as a social phenomenon. Under the head "The Garvey Movement," he wrote:

> Whatever one may think about it, or how fantastical it may seem, the fact that a man has sufficient genius, magnetism, or what you will to assemble a convention of 20,000 people of African descent to formulate plans for a great Pan-African empire or republic, is an unparalleled and unique social phenomenon which demands serious consideration. History has presented similar social movements, among other ethnic groups, but not among the African group. That this widely separated people—for the Garvey Movement is far-flung and embraces members of our race not only in the United States, but in the British West Indies and Africa—should be influenced by the spirit of unrest and dissatisfaction with certain conditions of exploitation of which they have been, and are yet victims is by no means strange. It only proves the unity and solidarity of the human race, and the demand for justice is fundamental with mankind and that ultimately it is bound to assert itself.

That Marcus Garvey has been able to interpret this demand for justice and self-determination on behalf of thousands of the black race to the extent that he has, shows that the time is ripening, if not already ripe, for the development of an international race-consciousness which can be turned to good account, or ill, for it has both these possibilities in world business, commerce, and politics. Granting that there are many impracticable and fantastic ideas connected with it, granted that the man who is its moving spirit may be a fool, fanatic or dreamer, it must be conceded that the so-called "Garvey Movement" is a tremendously significant social phenomenon which may have an importance and influence beyond imagining. Into what it may grow and develop who can say?

The *Philadelphia American* in its issue of September 11, 1920, asks this question:

WHY SO MUCH MARCUS GARVEY IN PUBLIC PRINT?

There has appeared almost daily in the public press for the past month something about Marcus Garvey, the African Communities League, the Universal Negro Improvement Association and the Black Star Line. Why all this hysteria? What has Garvey done, or what is he doing? Some of the papers give facetious accounts, some burlesque, some are vindictive, but all of them more lie than truth. We are advised that our chicken-hearted Attorney General of the United States, A. Mitchell Palmer, has been disturbed in his pleasant dreams and has dispatched two of the best Secret Service men attached to the Department of Justice to shadow Garvey day and night, and make a complete record of everything he says and does and everywhere he goes. Photographers snap him on every corner. All the machinery of justice and annoyance has been let loose on Garvey and his associates. Why all this consternation? Have not Africa and the Africans the right to organize a Communities League? Will anybody deny the Negro's right to uplift and improve himself by organization? If the Black Star Line sees fit to incorporate, purchase and build ships to engage in the business of transportation upon the sea, whose business is it? Nobody questions the right of the White Star Line, the Red Star Line, nor would they raise a single objection to the Green Star Line. But everybody seems excited about the Black Star Line.

In an article published in the Literary Digest, September 4, 1920, entitled, "The Purple-Robed Champion of 'Africa for the Africans'," this sedate and presumed intellectually edited weekly descends to the level of the most of its color-fobia, scurrilous and defamatory contemporaries, and with bristling bitterness and ridicule in almost every line, seeks to belittle the efforts of Garvey and his associates. In this article is published a supposed interview with Garvey by one Michael Gold, representing the New York World Magazine, during which interview Gold is supposed to have asked Garvey the following question: "Do you think the white nations of the world will tolerate a Negro Empire? Garvey replied: We are four hundred million strong." This question seems to indicate the source of all their nervousness. Garvey is far more practical in his real ideas than most people think. These journals are engaged in "shadow fighting." Whether Garvey is serious about his African Colonization idea or not, matters little. We are all familiar with its failures heretofore. The principle upon which the three organizations founded by Garvey rests is sound and practical, and while we may not agree with his modus operandi, we see nothing wrong in the united effort of persons of African descent to repel wrong and oppression here and elsewhere. Nobody questions the Irishman's right. In fact he is secretly assisted in his revolt against the English Government.

We think that the principle of Garvey's Movement is all right. He has no doubt, in our mind, successfully concealed his real object from the sight of his detractors; so that they have mistaken the citadel and are shelling the woods. Make them work overtime, Garvey."

CHAPTER NINE

In order to help pay for the fourth ship of the Black Star Line, which was to be renamed the S.S. *Phillis Wheatley*,

Garvey planned a trip to Central America in February 1921.

He took an express train from New York City down through the South to Key West, Florida. His next stop was Havana, Cuba, where he was received by President Menocal, and the large and enthusiastic membership packed the meetings to hear him. He journeyed by train right through the island, speaking at large towns, such as Morón, Camagüey, Nuevitas, Barnes and Santiago, looking after divisional matters in the day, and interviewing prominent persons on behalf of the West Indian population. From Santiago he traveled by the *Kanawha* (later the *Antonio Maceo*) to Kingston, Jamaica. Early on his journey Garvey had caught a cold from the sudden change in temperature; he suffered from pressure on his chest, and a doctor whom he consulted in Kingston diagnosed the symptoms as asthma.

The neglect of the men had caused damages to the boiler tubes of the ship. He wanted to pay off some of them, and take on new ones; but the ship was under American registry, so he had to take them before the American Consul, prefer charges through the Captain, who was not the type of man who could control his men, as they did not respect him, and he did not want them to "gang up" against him. The Consul adopted the attitude that Negroes had no business trying to run ships anyhow, and if they wanted to break it up, well, why should he stop them. With this combined attitude Garvey was powerless under maritime regulations. The more he argued, the more animosity he created. He just had to pay the enormous bills for repairs and shore leave allowance for the officers.

He took another ship to Port Limón, Costa Rica. His arrival meant a holiday for all West Indian workers on banana farms and those loading ships. The fruit company, seeing the inevitable stoppage of work, contributed their goodwill by providing an excursion train from Port Limón to San Jose, the capital, stopping at big towns on the way. It was a festive season for the time he was there. Halls could not hold the crowds that came to see and hear him. After he left, native Costa Ricans had a better respect for West Indians because at last "Los Negroes" had a leader.

He went on to Bocas-del-Toro, where he had a wonderful reception, and the admiration of the Spanish people. Among the many who welcomed him in poetry and song was John Smith of Changuinola who wrote a poem with the opening lines:

Blest be thou of Afric's Race,
Ye son of the Isle of Springs!
Blest, thrice blest, 'tis echoed back
The woods of the Homeland ring.

While here he was informed that he would not be allowed to land on the Canal Zone, American territory; furthermore, he would not be permitted to reenter the United States of America. All this information was substantiated. So he hired a launch, at the risk of his life, which took him to Colón, while the American authorities watched at the wharves where ships came in. This increased his popularity even more; white Americans came to the meetings to see "that smart guy." He spoke right through to Panama City. Where Liberty Halls could not hold the crowds, he spoke at theatres, and bullrings; even those were packed to overflowing. In all the Spanish-speaking countries, many natives attended the meetings, some out of curiosity, others readers of the Spanish section of the *Negro World*; therefore it was necessary to have Spanish interpreters for parts of his speeches.

He returned to Jamaica where the same American Consul he had encountered previously refused to visé his passport for his return to America. He wrote his fellow officers asking them to make representations to Washington officials on his behalf; as head of the company and other allied organizations, it was imperative for him to return to look after their business. During the two months of waiting for the visé, he traveled and spoke in all the parishes of Jamaica, resuscitating and setting up branches of the U.N.I.A. From here he went on to British Honduras, where he was the guest of Mr. and Mrs. Isaiah Morter—ardent members of the organization. After his speeches people joined the local branches in large numbers. The Black Cross Nurses under the capable training of their head nurse were later recognized by the government for their splendid work.

From Belize he went to Guatemala, landing at Puerto Barrios. He went up to Guatemala City. The fruit company here also facilitated their workers in having an enjoyable time. He returned to Jamaica, where he wrote the Secretary of State setting out his reasons for the urgency of his return to America. While waiting for an answer the American Consul was transferred, and finally he got the visé from the newly appointed Consul. He could not secure an early passage to America, so he had to go back to Puerto Barrios and took passage on a "banana boat" to New Orleans.

While in Jamaica a boyhood friend asked him to accompany him to the Easter Races to see his horses run. Urging him, he said, "I know you love horses, and it would be a day off from your worries." This remark brought back memories of the time he used to spend with a bachelor uncle. He went to the race track, which to many in the tropics is just a day's outing. Ladies go there to show off their finery; the Governor and his wife are usually present. When he had forgotten about it, and was engrossed in his worries and perplexities, the colored press featured him as being an habitué of the race track, squandering the Black Star Line's money. At the trial in New York City, a government witness also referred to the incident in this manner. And he was speaking of a man who had denied himself recreation, because the only race in which he had any real interest was his own race. They had been so heavily handicapped for so long that they were known as "non-starters"; he had to give them day and night training, even to place them.

On arrival at New Orleans, he was detained, and got in

touch with Washington officials, and his associates; he was eventually allowed in. The necessity then arose for him to become an American citizen, so he took out his "first papers," which signifies one's intention to become a citizen after a probationary period.

Before leaving Jamaica he wrote a long letter to the *Daily Gleaner* (June 2, 1921) on his impressions of the people, and suggested remedial measures of reform as follows:

If Jamaica is to be saved, if Jamaica is to take her place among the progressive and successful nations of the world, then we must have a change of policy. Jamaica is void of that national spirit that should characterize every country, such as the nationalist spirit of Canada, Australia, India, etc. Everybody in Jamaica seems to be looking to the "Mother Country" for everything. . . .

Those of us who have been trained refuse to admit that we are children. We feel that we are quite competent to handle the affairs of our country, and now all that we ask is a chance; but if we don't get a chance, we should take a chance, and I am here advising the people of this country to adopt a more aggressive attitude in handling the affairs of the island. . . .

Jamaicans—as I see them—worship too much that which comes from abroad, and from anywhere. If a thing, a man, or an animal is imported, it is supposed to be better than the native product. How silly! I recommend that the poorer classes of Jamaica—the working classes,—get together and form themselves into unions and organizations and elect their members for the Legislative Council. With few exceptions, the men in the Council are representing themselves and their class. The workers of Jamaica should elect their own representatives and if the Government here will not pay the Legislators, as is done in England and America, then the Unions and Organizations should pay these men, so that they can talk out without caring whom they offend. The Legislators in Jamaica should be paid at least five hundred pounds per annum. If this was done you would have a better class of Legislators and more independent ones. Poor, honest men like

Messrs. Wint, Lightbody, Young and Smith can't afford to waste four and five months annually away from their work and paying high living expenses without feeling it; that suits the wealthy Legislators of today. . . .

The people of Jamaica want advanced religion now. The religion that will prepare them for heaven by having them live clean, healthy, happy and prosperous lives down here. No hungry man can be a good Christian. No dirty, naked, civilized man can be a good Christian. No shelterless civilized man can be a good Christian for he is bound to have bad wicked thoughts; therefore, it should be the duty of religion to find physical as well as spiritual food for the body of man; so when your preachers ignore the economic condition and moral depravity of the people, they are but serving themselves through preachings and not representing the spirit of God. . . . I feel that Jamaica wants a political awakening, and it should come from within, and not from without. . . .

During his enforced stay in Jamaica, a white minister of the gospel and a few other gentlemen of means wrote letters to the local paper against what they called "Garvey's propaganda." A correspondent on the subject, who signed himself as "Vic—the Roman," in a letter dated June 9, 1921, to the *Daily Gleaner*, offered an alternative program to the British government's in the development of the Confederation of the West Indies, Nigeria, Sierra Leone and the Gold Coast by West Indian Negroes:

Very few of your correspondents seem to grasp the significance and magnitude of Marcus Garvey's dream and his efforts to make that dream materialize. Why is it so few attempt to examine the Movement in the light of comparative history? . . .

Is it not constantly being told you, because you are black, that you had better go and plant? . . . However as Jamaicans you and I are expected to be hypocrites to pretend that this intangible, yet ever present barrier does not exist—we must harp upon the glorious tradition of fairplay and justice and golden opportunities we enjoy (in dreams mostly) in this ancient and loyal colony. . . .

Garvey aims at pulling the scales from the eyes of all Negro peoples, that they may see light and truth. Cecil Rhodes, Alfred Beit, Sir Harry Johnston, and several others, have made Africa their field to wealth and fame, and they had no more right to its natural resources than the man of the North Pole; then why should not Garvey and any other ambitious Negro? If the energetic, far-seeing, progressive, determined Negroes of the world back Garvey he will succeed in making Liberia a great and prosperous country. . . .

Our hope is, if the British Government throws open Sierra Leone, the Gold Coast and Nigeria to development by Negro citizens of the Empire, giving them full citizenship rights, equal opportunities and salaries with the white citizens, there would be splendid chances for them to do in these portions of British Africa the very things Garvey is asking their co-operation to accomplish in what is now a foreign country. British Negro enterprise would build and own railways, steamship corporations and shipyards, build roads and bridges, towns and cities, own and operate electric light and power plants, telegraph and telephone systems, banks, insurance companies, newspapers, churches and the thousands of big and little things that make for a progressive and prosperous people— like the Canadians and the Australians; and Negro brains and energy and ability would be conserved to the Empire and enhance its greatness. The Confederation of the West Indies, along with the actual removal of the color bar would also bring greater chances for employment and the development of skilled ability and talent in the individual would surely be a stabilizing factor with the Negro population. . . .

The men who dare are the men who do; the men who do, get results—whether it be floating a steamship company as did Samuel Cunard, planning a trans-continental railway system like Donald Smith, Lord Strathcona, expanding and adding to the glories of an Empire as Cecil Rhodes, or remodelling a nation as Cavour and Bismarck—the present day conditions demand a change. Garvey is daring the path millions fear. Since he dares, he may achieve his end, and the results may be—even though some jeer and scoff at it now—the foundation of a powerful Negro State.

CHAPTER TEN

In August 1921 the Second Convention, in New York City, was heralded by a monster parade which was preceded by a prayer meeting in the morning conducted by the Chaplain General.

The Fifteenth Regiment Band lead the parade. This regiment is known as the "fighting 15th," because of the glorious achievements of its Negro soldiers overseas. The first mass meeting was held at the Twelfth Regiment Armory at 62nd St., which overflowed with the crowds. Resolutions were passed and cables sent to Mahatma Gandhi, sympathizing with him in his efforts for a free India; Eamon De Valera, in his fight for Irish independence; and to King George V of England, stating that nothing would please the Negro peoples more (except the freedom of Africa) than the emancipation of Ireland, India and Egypt, so as to prevent future world wars, and bring peace among freedom-loving peoples. The banners in the parade also expressed those sentiments. Said Garvey in his opening speech: "If sixty million Anglo-Saxons can have 'a place in the sun,' I don't see why four hundred million Negroes can't have a place—a big place too—in that same sun."

The other sessions were held at Liberty Hall, at which all delegates reported. Then followed discussions under the following heads: religion, politics, industry, commerce, education, social welfare, propaganda and humanity. They protested against the recruitment of ex-servicemen by Spanish Consuls in London and New York City in the Foreign Legion to fight the tribes of Morocco.

At one of the sessions Mrs. Stokes, a pacifist, was allowed to speak. The *New York World*, August 20, reported under the following headline—Negroes refuse to indorse Bolshevism: "One thousand Delegates in the Convention of the Universal Improvement Association which claims to repre-

sent the 400,000,000 Negroes of the world, last night heard
Rose Pastor Stokes proclaim the glories of Bolshevism at
Liberty Hall. . . ." When she asked for an indorsement of
the Soviet form of government, however, they declined to
commit themselves. In an interview with the *New York
Globe* reporter, Garvey said, "We will fight for any nation
which guarantees us political status." In answer to a *New
York Times* reporter, he said, "We have much to accomplish before the time is ripe for mass migration, but it is
bound to come. Maybe fifty years or eighty years, who
knows? The wars of the future will time our evolution."

It was decided that the Potentate should hold a Court
Reception during this convention, the main purpose of
which was to train and demonstrate better social behavior
than formerly, and to show respect and recognition within
our own race. It took months of preparation by a subcom-
mittee, working under the Registrar; from time to time
mimeographed instructions were sent to all branches, who
formed similar committees. Men's and women's meetings
were addressed by medical men, specialist nurses and social
service workers. So that behavior would stem from clean
living. Even the details of showing invitees how to answer
their invitations were not omitted. Among the many brief
replies had been this one: (alongside the R.S.V.P. were)
D.S.C.C. (damn sorry can't come).

The hall was transformed into a magnificent tropical setting, with lighting effects and appropriate music. Each dig-
nitary was timed to arrive according to his rank, and an
anthem or appropriate music played until he was seated.
Potentate Johnson—resplendent in his uniform—inspected
the Guard of Honor. Young ladies were presented, and
honors conferred on persons who had served the race faithfully and well. Titles were: Knight Commander of the Nile,
Distinguished Service Order of Ethiopia, and the Star of
African Redemption. After the ceremonies, supper was
served; guests were seated according to rank. Then followed

the grand Ball, with all the courtliness of training, natural gift for dancing and love of music.

While the campaign against Garvey was bitter, its tactics to ridicule him crystallized into gross exaggeration, which to those who knew him, and to reasoning minds, made the authors themselves ridiculous in their mischief. When he was kept out of America and forced to use ships for speedy travel, they reported him as "cruising on his yacht." They further described him as "drinking, feasting, smoking and reclining on soft cushions with a harem around him." The description was almost identical in many newspapers, so it must have originated from one source. He never ate chicken, duck, turkey or pork; his favorite dishes were ham and eggs and roast beef. He ate sparingly of lean meats because, he said, "A full stomach slows up my thinking machine." He did not drink liquor; his "quenchers" were fruit juices, "Virginia Dare," and other cider drinks. He never smoked until he contracted asthma; then he used asthma cigarettes when necessary. He enjoyed a piece of plain cake, also homemade ice cream. In the summertime, assisted by Strong his bodyguard, he used to experiment with all sorts of fruits and flavors to produce a "Garvey Special." I was only called in to sample the mixtures; Strong was tolerated because he would do as he was told; but I, being "full of arguments and contradictions," gave him a chance of freedom in the kitchen. He really enjoyed himself, stirring and tasting his mixtures. He never wrote down his quantities, so on other occasions, in attempting to produce a similar flavor, he would turn out something different; this only delighted him, and once he said, "Too bad I never had the chance to learn chemistry." But would he have had the required patience?

In reporting the Court Reception, one of New York's big dailies dropped all semblance of truth, and dipped its pen in the same ink that most of the colored newspapermen usually used, when it stated in its issue of August 11, 1921: "There were diamond necklaces, any one of whose stones would have felled Goliath, which reached from the nape of the wearer's neck to her knees; feathers which towered to the ceiling, feathers which trailed to the floor. Uniforms and gold laces in dazzling array. . . . Each Knight received a new sword, whose hilt gleamed with diamonds, sapphires and rubies." Perhaps that reporter was competing with his colored colleagues for the liar's medal, and this was a published entry.

Garvey filed many libel suits in the courts against newspaper publishers and writers for the most vicious attacks on his character, but these cases were held back on the court calendars for "the law to get him." Besides, in the minds of white judges, the character of a colored person is assessed by the standard character of his race. What appreciable amount of damages can he suffer from the lying statements of another member of his race? A rich Negro, an educated Negro, is still just another Negro.

In order to get the help of European colonial powers in his campaign to get rid of Garvey, DuBois called a Pan-African Congress, in Paris, timed with the opening of the Second International Convention of the Negro Peoples of the World, in New York City. He sent out a press release as to number of delegates and the purpose of the conference. The following are extracts from the leading New York City newspapers:

The *New York Tribune*, September 6, 1921, with this headline reported:

> Garvey plan for Colored State repudiated by U.S. Delegates.
> Paris, Sept. 5.—Thirty American Colored men and women, Delegates to the Pan-African Congress in session here today, headed by Dr. W. E. Burghardt DuBois of New York, repudiated the plan of Marcus Garvey, Provisional President of Africa, of "Africa for the Africans."
> Dr. DuBois said, the Colored Americans cannot withstand the African climate. We cannot oust the European, and do not desire to do so.

The *New York World* of the same date stated:

> At Sunday's session of the Pan-African Congress, M. Diagne, Negro Deputy from Senegal, and M. Candace, Negro Deputy from Guadeloupe, decried the "Africa for Africans" slogan, and denounced Garvey.
>
> Dr. DuBois, one of the best known Negroes in the United States declared the African redemption plan was a chimera. The Colored American could not stand the African climate. He said, "we cannot oust the Europeans from the Dark Continent, and we do not desire to do so."

The *New York Sun* of the same date, under the headline "Africa for the Africans, not Negro slogan," stated:

> France's two Negro Deputies do not agree with Marcus Garvey's contention of "Africa for Africans." . . . If I were asked to choose, the Deputy said, I would reply, "I am black, but I am French first!" Bellegarde, the Haitian Minister, who is here for the Negro Congress, corroborated the attitude of the Colored Deputies.

The *New York Herald* of the same date repeated the statement made by Dr. DuBois and added:

> Senator Aubert summed up the attitude of the Congress, when he declared, "Rather than return to Africa, and remain Negro, I prefer to remain a Frenchman."
>
> Garvey's "Africa for Africans" scheme was side-tracked by a suggestion that the League of Nations be asked to remove the color line in all member states.

The editor of the *Rochester Weekly* of New York, commenting on this statement, wrote: "They demand social equality . . . it is a mistake; intelligent colored people know it; Justice is what all men want . . . work for that."

In order to understand the strange and unreasonable way of thinking of the intellectuals of our race, we may examine the analysis of Dr. Woodson, given in a statement to the press on the psychology of Negro leadership issued during Negro History Week, and reproduced in the *Negro World*, February 7, 1931:

Washington D.C.—In their own as well as in their mixed schools, says Dr. Woodson with respect to Negro History Week, Negroes are taught to admire the Hebrew, the Greek, the Latin and the Teuton and to despise the African. The thought of the inferiority of the Negro is drilled into him in almost every class he enters, and in almost every book he studies. If he happens to leave school after he masters the fundamentals, before he finishes high school or reaches college, he will naturally escape some of this bias, and may recover in time to be of service to his people.

Practically all of the successful Negroes in this country, says Dr. Woodson, are of this type, or that of Negroes who have had no formal education at all. The large majority of the Negroes who have put on the finishing touches of our best colleges are all but worthless in the uplift of their people. If after leaving school they have the opportunity to give out to Negroes what traducers of the race would like to have it learn, such persons may earn a living, but they never become a constructive force in the elevation of those far down.

The explanation of this is a simple problem. The schools and colleges of this country are so conducted as to produce this result. For example, an officer of Howard University, thinking that an additional course on the Negro should be given there, called upon a Negro Doctor of Philosophy of the faculty to offer such work. He promptly informed the officer that he knew nothing about the Negro. He did not go to school to waste his time that way, he went to be educated.

Edward Johnson, former Dean of Shaw University Law School, agreed with Dr. Woodson, and said that, as far back as 1891, he was emphasizing the importance of Negro history in the schools and had written books on the subject.

Africans in America were quite disgusted with the statements of Dr. DuBois in Paris, and four of them representing different territories in Africa, wrote to the newspapers, which published their comments. In part they stated in repudiation: "Dr. DuBois and his Associates, when they state that Africa is not for Africans, are unworthy of membership in the Negro Race, and should be eliminated from any consideration at the hands of the Masses of the colored people of the U.S.A."

We read of M. Diagne again in August 1930 in a news release from Paris, under the caption, "African defends slavery, white Laborites oppose." It read:

> Paris.—M. Blaise Diagne, Negro member of the French Parliament from Senegal, French West Africa, in a labor convention at Geneva, recently, defended forced labor in Africa, holding that this was necessary for the welfare of the natives. . . .
>
> M. Diagne, who represented the government, was vigorously opposed by M. Jouhaux, Socialist, and head of the French Labor Delegation, as well as by M. Bromley, head of the English Delegates, both white.
>
> The clash between M. Diagne and his opponents came when the labor delegates proposed that a clause be inserted to the effect that forced labor, under whatever form, even if it be "in the public interest," be completely suppressed at once. M. Jouhaux replied that he valued as much as any other the work that France is doing for her African Colonies, but that he also desired to weed out all defects.
>
> Albert Thomas, Laborite and member of the MacDonald Cabinet, then proposed that forced labor be abolished in five years. Deputy Diagne proposed that the delay be increased to ten years, but the commission accepted the amendment of Albert Thomas.
>
> Forced labor has been defined by the commission as "all labor or service exacted of any individual under a penalty and for which the individual did not offer himself of his own free will."

The following comments—from white journalists on Garvey and his convention speeches—contrast with his colored rivals. "The Drifter," a columnist in the *Nation*, August issue, wrote:

> We Americans are too race conscious to appreciate the riches that lie hidden in Negro songs and Negro speech. Perhaps the American Negro himself is too eagerly seeking recognition of his equality to wish recognition of an art much of the splendor of which lies in its primitiveness. The Negro

too, is becoming standardized on second-hand white models, and it is a pity. But there is nothing less second-hand than such speech as this of Marcus Garvey, who describes himself as President General of the Universal Negro Improvement Association and Provisional President of Africa:

"Some people, some foolish white men and ignorant Negroes—believe that Negroes should not talk big. Brother, I want to ask you where do you get that idea from? Where do you get that notion from that Negroes should not talk big? This is the time, this is the age for big talk. Talk on, Lloyd George, I can hear you; I can hear you talking for the rights of Englishmen. Talk on, Charles Evans Hughes, talk on, Warren Harding; I can hear you talking in the name of 90,000,000 white Americans. You would be untrue to your race if you did not speak for them. Talk on, Sonnino, talk on, Orlando. I can hear you talking in the interests of millions of Italians. Talk on, Ishii, I can hear you talking in the interest of 60,000,000 Japanese. I say, talk on, New Negro, talk without stopping; talk on, talk on, and let there be a free Africa; and if anyone dares to stop you, use the power that God Almighty gave you to battle your way through the world."

In an article in *The World Tomorrow*, September's issue, Worth Tuttle gave this impression of Garvey:

Until I met Mr. Garvey, I was a bit supercilious. I found him surprisingly unassuming, even modest, with a very rare use of the perpendicular pronoun. His bearing is that of the educated West Indian Negro, who, neither pathetically humbled nor pathetically arrogated by the burden of prejudice in the United States, meets the white man on his own ground. He is a forceful speaker, with a sincerity in his voice that is convincing.

In accounting for Garvey's daring and boldness, it should be noted that the traits of an islander—regardless of race— are inherent in him; besides, the tropical islander is a natural migrant; he is brought up to know that his land space grows smaller and smaller by erosion from the sea that washes its shores, the flood rains, and primitive hill cultivation. It is ingrained in him that in order to make a better living, he must adventure forth unaided into strange countries, even among people who speak different languages; and wrest from them and their environments all he can to satisfy his needs and ambitions, and make a place for himself and his children. Thus, he develops a rugged, dogged determination and courage.

CHAPTER ELEVEN

When the Conference on the Limitation of Armament assembled in Washington D.C., Garvey sent a letter, dated November 11, 1921, on behalf of the 400,000,000 Negroes of the world. He reminded the delegates that although they were called together by the President of the United States to discuss the problem of armaments, there were other important questions the settlement of which was essential to ensure perpetual peace in the world:

> . . . At the Versailles Peace Conference, the Statesmen who gathered there made the awful mistake of legislating for the disposition of other people's lands (especially in Africa) without taking them into consideration. . . . The mistake is now apparent. . . .
>
> Peace not founded on real human justice will only be a mockery of the Divine invocation, "Peace, perfect Peace." I trust your Honourable Conference will not fail to take into consideration therefore, that there are four hundred million Negroes in the world, who demand Africa as their rightful heritage, even as Europeans claim Europe, and the Asiatics Asia. I pray that your Conference will not only be one of disarmament, but that it will be a Congregation of the Bigger Brotherhood, through which Europe will see the rights of Asia; Asia and Europe see the rights of Africa, and in turn Asia and Africa see the rights of Europe; and accordingly give every Race and nation its due, so that there can be peace indeed.

The Secretary General of the Conference replied November 17, acknowledging receipt of the letter, and stated: "I am charged to express to you our appreciation of the interest and support which you have been so good to evince."

Writing in his column "Today" in the *New York American*—a paper which describes itself across the top of its pages as "a paper for people who think"—Arthur Brisbane commented on the conference, and pointed out:

> The wise of the earth, including this Government, listen politely to soft words of the Japanese delegates at Washington. Consider a remark to the Japanese Ambassador by the late Gladstone of England, who was no fool: "Why should I pay attention to what you say my dear Friend, when what you do sounds so loud in my ears?"
>
> Nobody threatens Japan, Korea is her slave, China is her farm, the rest of Asia doesn't count. Europe is seeking no quarrel on that side of the Pacific Ocean. Yet Japan spends half her total income getting ready for war.

People who think were not being fooled into complacency while progressive nations prepared for defensive, and even offensive action in their own interests.

There is an African-West Indian proverb which says: "Stone at river bottom, can't feel sun hot." This saying holds good in its application to the behavior of the strong toward the weak, and treatment by powerful nations of colonial peoples, who are smarting under scorching conditions. The dispersed Jews, feeling the indignities and cruelties inflicted on them when they had no nation, organized a quota system to finance the building of their national homeland. A report from Europe, April 23, 1921, stated: "Dr. Alexander Goldstein, Chief Rabbi in Bulgaria, announces that every Jew in Bulgaria will give a tenth of his capital and income towards the fund for rebuilding the National Home in Palestine."

Garveyites all over the world had a greater task, as their subscriptions started when the sleeping race had to be awakened, right through to the development of our people to national consciousness and its attendant responsibilities.

The following news item from League of Nations headquarters in Geneva is another illustration of the aptness of the foregoing proverb. The people under the Mandatory System were suffering all the ills common to those subjected to the will and pleasure of rulers. Yet in 1921 the Commission reports favorably to the League of Nations:

> Geneva, Aug. 7.—The Mandate Commission of the League of Nations today finished its study of the reports of mandatory countries. It found that the clauses of the covenant of the League of Nations and the Peace Treaty relating to mandates had been generally respected by Mandatories, including the clauses calling for suppression of slavery and prohibition of traffic in alcohol.

Sir Harry Johnston, commenting on the exposés made at the convention by the African delegates, admits the truth of the appalling conditions in East Africa, in a newspaper report as follows:

> CONDITIONS IN EAST AFRICAN PROTECTORATE INVITE REVOLUTION. London, Sept. 12, 1921.—An indictment of British treatment of Negroes in British East Africa is made by Sir H. H. Johnston, writing in "The Observer." Many of the assertions made before the Negro conference in New York, he says, were "wild and windy"; but it behooves our Colonial office to see plain justice done to the 4,000,000 of black and brown people in this colony and protectorate. Numerous instances of bullying, flogging and torture are cited by the Writer.
>
> The natives, he says, are slowly coalescing, Bantu with Nilote, Mohammedan with Christian and pagan, Somali with Galla, with hitherto despised Negro in their common hatred of the invading white man, owing to the exceptional cruelties which have stained the white man's record during this period of 15 years. These are not cruelties of soldiers, or policemen, of government servants of any kind, but of individual settlers, British or Boer in origin.
>
> Not only have murders, light-hearted murders, of natives taken place all too frequently, not only have revolting cruel-

ties been committed, but when the white delinquents are brought up for trial white juries acquit them or white judges inflict trivial penalties or rebellious public opinion forces a Governor to revise sentence. I doubt if capital punishment for murder has ever been imposed on a white man in East Africa.

Again, in the great war, thousands and thousands of native porters were compulsorily enrolled by our government or by the military authorities in the unhappily styled "Protectorate," and the arrangements for their commissariat, their medical treatment, their lodging and clothing have been miserably inadequate, with the result that some 23,000 to 25,000 of them (it was reported) died during the pursuit of the German forces.

The survivors have retained tongues and the power of speaking; some, even, had been educated and when "Dora" (Defence of the Realm Act) took her hand off the mail service they have stammeringly told the world outside Africa something of their preventable sufferings and even of singularly callous and sometimes cruel treatment at the hands of the military authorities.

Now the culminating incident is this: Some months ago there occurred at Nduru, in British East Africa, cases of flogging and torture, so severe that according to a medical officer's report, in some cases, "the flogged natives died from the torture and flogging." These crimes were seemingly committed on a European's plantation. The Europeans, in what is now termed a "colony," apparently take the law into their own hands and administer punishment as they please.

Of a truth is this African adage: "Backra (whiteman) don't love Quashie; him give him basket to carry water, then flog him."

Failing serious criticism of Garvey, his flea-like rivals took to calling him "a clown strutting around in gaudy uniforms." The facts are that all the members of the Executive Council of the U.N.I.A. wore academic gowns at special mass meetings and in parade only. The Potentate, and the Provisional President of Africa (Garvey) had uniforms with matching hats; the Potentate's was more elaborate than

Garvey's as he was higher in rank. These were full-dress uniforms and only worn in parades, and at the opening of conventions.

It is strange that the High Exalted Ruler of a Lodge, to the Standard-bearer in uniforms and regalias, on parade, never seemed ridiculous to those critics. Was it because they were copying white folks?

The wearing of uniforms and robes of office by Garveyites had a deep significance and psychological effect. Had Garvey landed in Africa he would have discarded the uniform and European attire for tribal gowns, to become a part of the masses, and thus impress them, while satisfying his inner longing for Africanization. James H. Robinson writing in the *Christian Century*, June 8, 1955, stated:

> Marcus Garvey captured the imagination of thousands, because he personified the possibility of the fulfilment of a dream latent in the heart of every Negro. I remember as a lad in Cleveland, Ohio, during the hungry days of 1921, standing on Central Avenue, watching a parade one Sunday afternoon when thousands of Garvey Legionnaires, resplendent in their uniforms, marched by. When Garvey rode by in his plumed hat, I got an emotional lift, which swept me up above the poverty and the prejudice by which my life was limited.

CHAPTER TWELVE

Dr. DuBois, in his relentless fight as the intellectual leader of the "Garvey must go" crusade, was persistent and bitter. He had entré to white magazines, and exploited these sources and personal contacts to the fullest advantage.

In an article in the February 1922 issue of *Century Magazine*, he described Garvey as "a little fat black man, ugly, but with intelligent eyes and a big head." According to the racial beauty standard of white people, this is a disparaging reference, used to ridicule a man; but as it comes from the pen of a colored man, it is he who looks ridiculous, for he belongs to a race whose standard of beauty must be measured by the likeness of its majority. Therefore "black" is the logical reference; besides, "colored" suggests adulteration—displeasing to equatorial Africans.

Contrast a southern white reporter's description of Garvey in the *News and Observer* of Raleigh, North Carolina, October 26, 1922, who stated:

> He is a trifle heavy set, and the racial characteristics of his face are very marked. His cheek bones are high, his eyes are beady black. His voice rather high-pitched, and his words come rapidly, reminiscent of French or Spanish that they speak in the West Indies, where he comes from. His delivery is free from accent of any sort. It is a neutral voice, high-pitched.

Each race should see beauty in itself. All do, except some of the colored people in the Western world—who by propaganda are taught to think in terms of white superiority in all things—seen and unseen. The impressions of a Chinese lady from the interior, seeing a white man for the first time, are interesting. She stated:

> The door was suddenly opened and a tall male "foreign devil" stood there smiling all across his face. To my horror, his head, instead of being covered with human hair—black and straight—like other people, had on it a fuzzy red wool. His eyes were blue, and his nose rose up like a mountain from the middle of his face. Oh, a frightful creature to behold, more hideous than the God of the North in the temple. The foreigner made as if he would take my hand. I looked at it—large and bony, with long red hairs and black spots on it. My flesh shrank. I placed my hands in my sleeves and bowed.

Africans in the interior, seeing a white man for the first time, regard his pale skin as devoid of pigmentation, therefore leprous. The white man was created in a mold giving him pale skin, thin lips, aquiline nose, and silky hair, to enable him to live in the cold regions of the earth. The black man was cast in a different mold, giving him black skin, thick lips, broad nose, and frizzly hair, so that he could live easily in the hot tropical clime. If white people had been made to withstand the intense rays of the sun in West and Central Africa, they would have occupied the entire continent, after they had exhausted the natural wealth of Europe; because they would have been able to exploit its rich resources by themselves; then all of Africa would have been a white man's paradise.

In the same article Dr. DuBois misinterpreted Garvey's race-pride program as race-baiting, which, he said, sentiments of white superiority and human inequality were fanning into flames—a danger to America where, "Races are living together. They are buying and selling, marrying and rearing children, laughing and crying." He closed his article with his challenging question: "Which path will America choose?"

America did choose to get Garvey out of the country. But after that the New Negro forced DuBois to change his way of thinking, to the point that during the "Red scare" he was arrested and charged with "un-American activities." The charges were not substantiated, so he was freed, but up to 1957 in his 90th year he was denied passport for foreign travel.

American and foreign statesmen were now weighing a colonization plan for Africa, which would rid them of heavy war debts, and provide a haven for colored surplus population. The *New York Times*, April 17, 1922, reported:

Berlin, April 6. (Associated Press.)—Could the United States dispose of her surplus colored population by distributing it among the former German colonies in Africa under some agreement with the present European mandatories?

This question arose today in the course of a conversation with Dr. Heinrich Schnee, former Governor of German East Africa, in connection with a special despatch from Washington published in Berlin attributing to Senator France a suggestion that the Allied debts to the United States could be redeemed by the transfer of the former German colonies in

Africa, now controlled by Great Britain, France and Belgium, to the United States. Senator France is reported to have declared that such a transfer would need as a complement a joint international plan for reconstructive development.

Assuming that the Senator means the transfer of the mandatory powers, and not annexation, the scheme would seem both feasible and desirable, provided United States control would mean a continuation of the American open door policy, admitting the co-operation of all nations, said Dr. Schnee.

This, he added, would be exactly opposite to the present regime, which excludes all but the nationals of the occupying powers. We still hope that our colonies, now held in trust by the Entente powers, sometime will be restored to us.

Doubtless the German African colonies would be able to support thrice the present native population. Indeed there is room there for 50,000,000 colored people now, and there will be more room as development progresses. German East Africa, Southwest Africa, Togoland and the Cameroons aggregate an area of more than a million square miles, rich in natural wealth and abounding in the raw materials the world sorely needs. Moreover, most of them have zones suitable for white settlers, but their tropical coast line regions are entirely suitable for colonization by millions of colored people.

The largest zone, East Africa, consists of 389,000 square miles, about the size of Alabama, Georgia, the two Carolinas, Florida, Virginia, Mississippi and Louisiana combined, and has a population of less than eight millions. Next is Southwest Africa, with 326,000 square miles, and only about 90,000 population; while the Cameroons has 809,000 square miles and a population of 2,500,000.

As a colonizing power, I have the greatest regard for the United States. I was able to observe American methods while Governor of Samoa. Their sanitary achievements in Panama deserve the highest praise.

As regards the attempt to colonize Africa with the surplus American colored population, this would in a long way settle the vexed problem and, under a plan such as Senator France has outlined, might enable France and Great Britain to discharge their debts to the United States and simultaneously ease the burden of German reparations which is paralyzing economic life.

This colonization of such vast areas in Africa would have meant the carrying out of Garvey's program by the American government; the colored politicians and intellectuals realized this, and with parasitic desires to use the cause of the "oppressed masses" for their own selfish gain, as well as for vote-catching, they vigorously opposed Senator France's proposals.

CHAPTER THIRTEEN

In the fall of 1919 Garvey's enemies goaded him on to acquire a ship for the Black Star Line. Tonnage was still high, and it was extremely difficult to get qualified colored officers for an ocean-going vessel. All these facts were ignored, and their slurs were to the effect that he was only trying to get enough money to go back to his "Monkey Island."

The average person regards a ship as a truck, which can be put in a garage until one obtains an honest driver; not so with a sea-going vessel; it is a world unto itself, and is governed by maritime laws. A marine expert was employed part-time to advise and negotiate all matters pertaining to the operation of the ships; a marine lawyer was retained to look after legal work involved. The ships were under American registry, except one—Canadian. American seamen are the highest paid, and best rationed in the world. Every applicant has first to be taken before the Shipping Master at the port of embarkation, who examines his seaman's passport and records of qualification and service before he is "signed on." The captain, who is in full charge of the ship, attends to this; and the officers of the company have no say; they pay the bills.

The change of name and registry of a ship—say from American to Nicaraguan—can only be obtained when bonds and guarantees are posted; then it is up to the good-will of the authorities to grant same, as they know too well that this means a great monthly saving in wages, subsistence, rations, and above all more sympathetic understanding and control by the Consuls on behalf of the company.

Passenger ships do not make money for the line; the freight ships do. Most of the big white companies are subsidized by their governments to carry mail on their passenger ships. As soon as a ship is acquired, and when it is undergoing repairs, a "skeleton crew" has to be kept on board. When cargo is contracted for, if the vessel does not sail on schedule, the company is liable to pay heavy demurrage. Ships are inspected periodically, in order to get a certificate of seaworthiness and insurance. Before a ship leaves port on a voyage, the port authorities see that everything is in order before granting a clearance permit, permits for the ports to which it is destined, and a clean bill of health.

The S.S. *Yarmouth*, renamed the *Frederick Douglass*, was the first ship acquired. The purchase price was $165,000, of which $135,000 was paid. Captain Cockburn, the first master of the ship, later a government witness at the trial, admitted that he received $1,600, part of $8,000 divided between five of them to induce Garvey to purchase the ship for the line; and Leo Healy—the agent for the vendor, also a government witness—said he knew at the time that the vessel was purchased that it was not worth $100,000.

This ship made three trips to the West Indies and Central America. The second trip the cargo consisted of whisky, which had to be taken out of port on schedule, as prohibition laws were coming into effect. It is alleged that Captain Cockburn was compensated by the shippers to get the cargo away. The ship sailed, and was supposed to have developed engine troubles. The boatswain at the trial testified that the captain stopped the ship, and ordered cases of whisky put

on tugs at sea. The captain brought the ship back to port
with the balance of the whisky cargo, and thereby put the
officers of the company into thousands of dollars of litiga-
tion, besides bills for repairs, which some of the seamen on
board said could have been avoided. That captain's pay was
$400 per month and $10 per day allowance when in port.
When the company was able to dispense with his services he
became a real estate broker.

A river boat was acquired at a cost of $35,000, which ran
excursion trips on the Hudson River. In this transaction the
vendor did not give the correct age of the vessel, until a
down payment was made, and a search of the records made
by the lawyer, which revealed that it was older than represented.

The S.S. *Kanawha* was purchased for $60,000 and re-
fitted for passenger service at a cost of $25,000. This ship
was to be renamed the S.S. *Antonio Maceo*, and used for
intercolonial service to link up the larger ships of the line.
The first captain to take her out was Adrian Richardson—a
man who obtained his captain's licence after he was employed by the Black Star Line. Allegedly he exercised no authority over his men, drank and played card games with them.
The engine was a twin-screw one; with no sober men on watch,
her boilers were allowed to become overheated and dry,
which caused a great deal of damage. Enormous repair bills
were incurred; it is alleged that commissions were paid by
repairing firms. Captain Richardson was a government witness at the trial, and he seemed delighted with himself at the
part he played. He appeared to want a chance to get Garvey
outside the court to do to him physically what he thought
he had helped to do to him spiritually.

Early in 1921 arrangements were made with the United
States Shipping Board to purchase a large ship from them
for the African trade. Vice-President Thompson was left in
charge of the administration of the company's affairs when
Garvey went abroad to help raise funds. Garvey sent in
moneys for stocks sold, and was informed by Thompson

that the company had acquired the ship, and $25,000 had been paid on it.

After five months, when he was permitted to return to the U.S.A., he found that no ship had been turned over to the Black Star Line, and that only $5,000 had been lodged with the Shipping Board by a man named Silverstone, a broker, who Thompson said had been given $25,000. Silverstone asked Garvey not to investigate the matter, as negotiations were at a delicate point. In November Garvey wrote to the Shipping Board, and was informed by them that $22,500 was on deposit for the S.S. *Orion*. In December the Massachusetts Bonding Company wrote the Black Star Line demanding payment of $11,000 borrowed from them through Thompson; then Garvey learned that this amount was used to make the $22,500 deposited with the Shipping Board. He started an investigation into the whole affair, preparatory to taking legal action to recover the sum of $13,500 balance from Silverstone, and to prove to what extent Thompson was negligent or implicated in handing over to Silverstone the large sum of money, and in trying to cover up the deficit by borrowing from the bonding company. But to his amazement, instead of getting help from the District Attorney's office in the matter, he was indicted in January for using the mails to defraud.

During the years of the company's operations, stocks were sold at $5 each. About $800,000 was collected. Despite the protection white shipping companies had, they lost money in the operation of their ships. Naming just a few, the United States Shipping Board heads the list with a loss of billions of dollars. On the Hudson River alone there were 120 ships tied up belonging to the government. The Green Star Line went into the hands of receivers. The Polish Navigation Company's ships were sold for debts.

The indictment was faulty, as the corporation had active officers who took part in its administrative work as recorded in the minute book, and whose daily reporting system showed that all moneys received were turned over to the

Treasurer and disbursed by him. In February Garvey and the following officers were indicted: Orlando Thompson, Vice-President; George Tobias, Treasurer; and Elie Garcia, Secretary. They were released on bail of $2,500 each pending trial.

The District Attorney sent his agents with a van and took away all books and records, not only of the company, but some belonging to the U.N.I.A. and the *Negro World*; when Garvey remonstrated with them, they defiantly threatened him with contempt of court charges. As stockholders did not volunteer information against the officers, the District Attorney used the company's records to send out tricky questionnaires to them. Very few answered, for they were members of the U.N.I.A. and knew that the shipping company was only incidental to the program. The stocks were never placed on the general market, only confined to organization members.

Hurrahs went up from the enemy camps at his indictment in 1922. Now they maligned him with impunity. (The District Attorney had a colored man named Amos to do what he could not, and would not do.) Some of the shipping-company employees became careless in their work; they were being egged on and promised "protection" if they became government witnesses. Garvey had to be on tour most of the time, speaking to the people whose loyalty and devotion was a source of inspiration and encouragement to him. However the pressures increased and the preparation for the convention had to be made, demanding more of his personal attention than before. Thought he, if the trial was rushed, and the outcome adverse, what would he do? And what would happen to the organization, since treachery was so well recompensed? He must have some one who had the right to be his personal representative—to act on his behalf, and on his instructions. A secretary would only be brushed aside as an employee, and dismissed too. He must get a wife. He wanted a born American, so as to please the people. The duty of sharing his turbulent life might have been

requested of Miss Davis; he admired her, as she was dignified, charming, and an able speaker; but she was older than
he, and he had hopes of having a son to carry on his name.
There were other eligibles among the membership, but they
lacked the sum total qualities of what he wanted for a wife
now—a stand-in, in an emergency. Again he turned to me,
and very adroitly put the onus on me, stating that it was in
my power to help the organization in this crisis. He had
already obtained a divorce, so we were married July 27,
1922.

The Black Star Line being the most vulnerable point on
which Garvey could be attacked, all labored it, to destroy
him. Some used the ships' officers, over whom Garvey had
no control, to carry out their intentions. In 1921 when the
S.S. *Kanawha* reached Cuba, Garvey discovered that the
chief engineer had been using salt water in the boilers and
conniving with the captain to cause damages to the ship, so
as to collect off repair bills; so he had the captain sign him
on as Purser, thus hoping to be able to save the company
further loss. On his arrival in Kingston, Jamaica, the United
States State Department, through its Consul, acting on
malicious lies that Garvey was organizing Negroes against
white people, threatened reprisals if Garvey's name was not
removed from the crew list. This prevented Garvey from
acting as an officer of the ship, and protecting the ship's
expenditures.

Garvey had Lloyd's Surveyor at Kingston examine the
ship and make a report, in which the Surveyor stated "that
the engine and boilers were badly corroded from sea-water
. . . such a condition could only be brought about through
sheer neglect." With this report Garvey presented a twelve
page complaint to the American Consul, charging the captain and chief engineer with destructive mismanagement,
and asked permission to dismiss them for "incompetence,
neglect and conspiracy." Consul Latham dismissed the
charges against the men as "absurd."

The $22,500 deposited by the Black Star Line with the

United States Shipping Board was never returned to the stockholders and creditors. In 1928 the U.S. Senate authorized its return, but the House of Representatives failed to pass the necessary concurring measure.

Anthony Silverstone never had to account for the $13,500 which Garvey believed he took.

CHAPTER FOURTEEN

After the painful, heart-breaking experiences that Black Star Line officers had trying to operate the first ship, Garvey as president of the line, if he were a cautious businessman, would have counseled his directors not to acquire any more ships for a time, even for the good of his own peace of mind; but he never considered himself, and felt that as he was pioneering in business for the entire race, he could not bow to obstacles that were manmade and not the acts of God. He would keep pressing on, ever trying to overcome them, appealing to the race that it show to the world that Negroes could sail the seas in their own ships. For, argued he, "all the material wealth that a Coloured person acquires can never compensate him for the loss of human dignity and all its attendant abuses."

Colored people are not inclined to take orders from their own; this was one of the handicaps under which the businesses of the Black Star Line and the Negro Factories Corporation suffered. Garvey pointed out the reasons, and stated that only political autonomy could entirely eradicate this attitude by civil disciplinary laws. He wrote:

The Negro in Western civilization, because of his environments that force upon him a complex inferiority, is the most stubborn individual to discipline within the race. He has but little, if any, respect for internal racial authority. He cannot be depended upon to carry out an order given by a superior of his own race. If the superior attempts, in his presence, to enforce the order he is undermined and accused of "putting on airs." If the order is entrusted to a lieutenant he in turn, changes the order to suit himself and endeavours to constitute himself the superior individual.

In my experience, as head of the largest serious Negro organization in the world, I have found that to every hundred orders given to be executed for the absolute good of the organization and the race, not 2 per cent of them have been carried out in their entirety. This lack of obedience to orders and discipline checkmates the real worthwhile progress of the race. This accounts for the Negro's lack of racial nationalistic ideal. The only cure for him is his removal to an atmosphere entirely his own, where he would be forced under rigid civil and other discipline to respect himself and his own racial authority.

It was suggested by some writers that Garvey should have invested the Black Star Line's money in real estate in the Northern states of the U.S. The U.N.I.A., parent body and local branches, owns real estate, not only in America, but all over the world. Liberty Halls, office buildings, business premises and houses in America totalled circa 1924 more than half a million dollars. During Garvey's incarceration in Atlanta, the New York local's Liberty Hall was mortgaged by some of the officers for $32,000 to pay fake claims for "back salaries" of their colleagues, whose judgments were obtained by default, because the cases were not defended.

The main purpose of the formation and promotion of the Black Star Line was to acquire ships to trade between the units of the race—in Africa, the U.S.A., the West Indies and Central America, thereby building up an independent economy by business, industry, and commerce, and to transport our people whither they will—on business or pleasure, without being given inferior accommodation, and not subject to questioning or refusal of any sort of accommodation.

His efforts were not merely to find a good investment for people's money—let others do that; but his was the task to

pioneer in shipping to remove the disabilities that hamper
their trading contacts one with the other for mutual success.
His whole concept of uplift, betterment and progress for the
race was always planned to coordinate all units—all working, subscribing, and struggling forward for their common
good and well-being.

That his overall program for African redemption and
economic independence would be costly, year after year, he
knew only too well; but surely an entire race could subscribe, even meagerly, to its implementation.

In emphasizing the urgency of his pleas in 1920 he por-
trayed the Negro worker in the Northern cities of the
U.S.A. as an industrial makeshift, when he wrote:

> The Negro's prosperity today, limited as it is, is based upon
> the foundation laid by an alien race that is not disposed to go
> out of its way to prepare for the economic existence of anyone
> else but itself; therefore our present prosperity, as far as em-
> ployment goes, is purely accidental. It is accidental today, as
> it was during the war of 1914–18 when coloured men were
> employed in different occupations they never occupied be-
> fore—not because they were wanted, but because they were
> filling the places of men of other races who were not available
> at that time. Negroes are still filling places, and as time goes
> on, and the age grows older, our occupations will be gone
> from us; because those for whom we filled the places will
> soon appear, and as they do, we shall gradually find our
> places among the permanently unemployed. Therefore the thing
> for the Negro to do, is to adjust his own economic present in
> readiness for the future.
>
> A race that is solely dependent upon another for its eco-
> nomic existence sooner or later dies. As we have in the past
> been living upon the mercies shown us by others, and by the
> chances obtainable and have suffered therefrom, so will we in
> the future suffer if an effort is not made now to build our own
> economic structure.

While they sought economic independence he warned
them as workers to beware of being used by the Commu-

nists and trade unionists to further their own ends. He stated:

> I am advising the Negro working man and labourer against the present brand of Communism or Workers' Partisanship as taught in America, and to be careful of the traps and pitfalls of white trade unionism in affiliation with the American Federation of white workers or labourers. . . .
>
> White Unionism is now trying to rope in the Negro and make him a standard wage worker, but it is not as good as it appears on the surface. The danger is that when it becomes generally known that he demands the same wage as the white worker, an appeal or approach will be made to the white capitalist or employer to alienate his sympathy or consideration for the Negro, causing him in the face of all things being equal to discriminate in favour of the white worker, as a race-duty and obligation. The Negro Workers' general position to which he is relegated is the uncertainty of being "the last hired and the first fired."
>
> The danger of Communism to the Negro, in countries where he forms the minority of the population, is seen in the selfish and vicious attempts of that party or group to use the Negro's vote and physical numbers in helping to smash and overthrow, by revolution, a system that is injurious to them as white underdogs, the success of which would put their majority group in power, not only as Communists, but as white men. Fundamentally what racial difference is there between a white Communist, Republican or Democrat? On the appeal of race interest the Communist is as ready as either, to show his racial ascendancy or superiority over the Negro. . . .
>
> Since they are so benevolent let them bring about their own reforms, and show us how different they are to others. We have been bitten too many times by all the other parties. . . . Negroes have no right with white people's fights and quarrels, except, like the humble, hungry, meagre dog, to run off with the bone when both contestants drop it, being sure to separate himself from the big well fed dogs by a good distance, otherwise to be overtaken, and then completely outdone.

While Garvey's colored rivals were working overtime to get him out of the way, our people, not only in the South, but in the Northern industrial cities were being chased and killed, simply because they were competing with white labor. All this gave Garvey greater justification and urgency for ships, factories and a national homeland. In an article to the *Negro World*, and reproduced in the *Philosophy and Opinions* under the head "Will Negroes succumb to the white man's plan of economic starvation?" Garvey stated, in part:

Protests against black cabarets were heard in all sorts of places in London recently. The Chairman and organizer of the Variety Artistes' Federation sent the Clerk of the London County Council a protest against the licence for a cabaret being granted if Negro artistes were to be imported to act in it. Said they: "We have no objection to white American artistes coming to England. In fact ninety per cent of those who come here join our federation. There are also in England Negro turns that behave themselves and keep their places. But we view with the greatest apprehension a cabaret where black artistes would actually mix with the white folk at the tables."

While the prejudiced whites in England are depriving Negroes of the right to earn a livelihood, in the United States of America the same methods are employed, but on a larger scale, and the plan of economic starvation is more vigorously and rigidly pursued. Who would have thought that the white man in America would have sought to compete with Negroes even in the occupation of picking cotton, but the following news article speaks for itself:

"Caruthersville, Mo., March 2, 1923.

"A carefully organized campaign of intimidation has driven more than 2,000 Negro workers from the cotton fields of Southeastern Missouri within the last thirty days, according to complaints made to local officials here. Negro leaders charge that threats and warnings were sent to the Negroes by white laborers fearful of losing their jobs by the influx of Negroes into the recently reclaimed section. Ambrose Young, Negro, appealed for protection after he had received several warnings, 'Nigger, get to hell out of here; this is a whiteman's country,' was one notice delivered by five hooded men. Young says, the next night I found another note on my front porch weighted down with a cartridge box, which said, 'Nigger, if you cannot read, run; if you cannot run, you are as good as dead.'"

What happened at Caruthersville, Missouri, is what is happening throughout America. For instance:

"South Bend, Indiana, Sept. 12, 1923.

"South Bend, once a haven for escaped Negro slaves from the South, is witnessing an exodus of Negroes as the result of a rumor of a threatened race riot. A number of letters addressed to several Negro leaders on the west side of the city caused the flight. Approximately 2,000 Negroes—men, women and children are said to have fled, some leaving their belongings."

Shortly after this occurrence at South Bend, Indiana, a similar occurrence took place at Johnstown, Pa., an industrial center, where there had been a great deal of unemployment. The unemployed whites were waiting for an opportunity to run the employed and unemployed Negroes out of town, so as to brighten their prospects of employment. The opportunity presented itself when two policemen were shot in one of the labor districts of the city. It is apparent that white labor leaders seized upon the opportunity of getting the Mayor to take immediate action, which he did not fail to do. The result was that thousands of Negroes were driven out of town by order of Mayor Joseph Cauffiel, with the following declaration as his ultimatum, which cannot be mistaken:

"Johnstown, Pa., Sept. 15, 1923.

"I don't care what authority I have; for their own safety, and for the safety of the Johnstown public, the Negroes are going out of this city. Most of them are out, and the rest of them are going fast. If the rest of them don't get out soon, I'll arm the police and send them into the colonies to walk the Negroes out at the point of a gun."

Similar occurrences have taken place in East St. Louis, Tulsa, and other industrial centres, accompanied by bloodshed and the burning of Negro homes and belongings, and is happening weekly, as the reaction sets in, in the American labour market. . . . In a short while, except where the Negro has created for himself a job, and a haven of refuge, he will be a drifter.

It had been the policy of the organization to allow its members freedom of choice in religion and politics; the officers of the local branches directed their own political activities. In 1924 however, feeling the full onslaught of concerted opposition pounding at the organization from all sides, a Committee in Convention decided that a political party could exert more influence by the power of the vote than propaganda could accomplish.

The convention acted on the committee's findings, and the Universal Negro Political Union was formed, under the Chairmanship of the American Leader. The general principles were "men and measures." It demonstrated this by having on its ticket Republican candidate Coolidge for President, and for the 21st Congressional District of New York, Royal Weller, Democrat, instead of Negro Dr. Charles Roberts, who was opposed to the U.N.I.A. Garveyites in their respective localities decided who best served their needs and aspirations in legislatures.

On the death of Lenin in 1924, Garvey sent a cable to Moscow, on behalf of the Negroes of the world expressing sorrow at his passing. For despite the fact that he felt convinced that his race should not participate in Communists' activities in the U.S.A. or be used by that party, yet Nikolai Lenin as a leader of the masses of Russia deserved respect for what in all sincerity he tried to do for them. Said he, "The masses need peace, bread, liberty and land."

CHAPTER FIFTEEN

Liberty Halls, wherever located, served the needs of the people—Sunday morning worship, afternoon Sunday Schools, public meetings at nights, concerts and dances were held, especially on holidays and Saturday nights. Notice boards were put up where one could look for a room, a job, or a lost article. In localities where there were many members out of

work during the winter the Black Cross Nurses would organize soup kitchens, and give them a warm meal daily. The
Legions would make portable screens for a corner of the hall,
where men who could not be temporarily housed with fellow
members, could sleep on benches at night. In the freezing
winter days stoves had to be kept going to accommodate the
cold and homeless, until they "got on their feet" again. One of
the "stovewarmers" later won some money in a sweepstake,
and went to Jamaica to spend it. Another owned a fleet of
buses; they, like others, forgot the organization that succored
and inspired them.

Many preachers felt that the U.N.I.A. was depleting their
membership, and in revenge they informed their local police
and political bosses that Garvey was preaching hate. Once
on a tour of the South, he arrived in New Orleans to be met
by a despondent looking delegation, who told him that a
colored preacher had caused the police lieutenant to order
that "Garvey must not speak in town."

He decided to speak. No one was to take a gun or black-
jack to the meeting. The Legions were to stand at the doors
and see to this. Only members were admitted. The choir
led them singing hymns and spirituals. As the singing
progressed, the lieutenant led twelve of his men—heavily
armed—into the building. Up the aisle they filed towards
the platform. The lieutenant asked in a commanding voice,
"Which one of you guys is Garvey?" Garvey walked to the
edge of the platform and said, "I am Garvey."

"Did you get my message that you were not to speak here
tonight?" queried the police officer, and Garvey in reply
said, "Yes, Lieutenant, but I have a message for you to tell
the white folks of this city. I have been longing to talk to
them, but as they can't attend my meetings, and I can't
attend theirs, we never get a chance to understand each
other. This misunderstanding has been the cause of most of
the trouble in the South. Let me tell you what the New
Negro under the leadership of our Organization wants." He
paused, and saw the white men listening attentively, so he

said, "Gentlemen, please sit down. I have reserved these front seats for you."

They sat down, and he proceeded to trace the Negro from Africa, in the hellholes of ships to America, their contribution to its wealth during and after slavery. Surely, said he, "the right to work and live peacefully here should not be denied him? The New Negro does not hanker after your women, and we are asking you to leave our women alone [smiles]. We have the same pride as you have in keeping your Race pure and prosperous." He went on to explain more fully his program, and closed by saying, "I hope that instead of hindering our plans, you will leave us alone to work out our own destiny."

He spoke for over an hour, like a machine gun finding its mark, at the end of which the police officer said he sure liked the way he talked, and was sorry the whole town did not hear him.

"Mouthagram" can cover more distance among colored people than telegram; so the news of this incident spread throughout the South, which was won over to Garveyism. White people, too, wanted to see and hear this man. Some felt that his African program would take away their best workers, and thus create a scarcity of skilled, reliable men and women. One of the most curious was the Imperial Wizard of the Ku Klux Klan—the largest white organization in America, commonly called "The Invisible Empire," with headquarters in the state of Georgia. He expressed a desire to see that "King George Nigger," and got a message through to the local office of the U.N.I.A.

The K.K.K. excludes Roman Catholics and Jews from their membership; and is organized to keep Negroes in subjection, through their rabid race purity idealism, which most Roman Catholics and Jews inwardly share. However the former have their exclusive organization—the Knights of Columbus, and the Jews are protected by their faith-bound religious-economic society. The only exclusive Negro organization was the U.N.I.A.

The whole atmosphere of the South reeked of fear and hate. The poor whites, especially, feared the rising prosperity of the Negroes in the states where the latter are in the majority; their brutal efforts to keep them down keeps themselves down economically, as they limit their expansion, fearing that "Negroes will get something out of it." Their minds become so warped with animus that their dictums regarding colored people are silly and lack reasoning. For instance, a Southern white woman will refuse to sit beside a colored woman on a bus or train, yet she will get a black mammy to wet-nurse her baby, as she does not want to spoil her figure and miss social engagements. The colored woman is thus forced to neglect her child; yet she feels honored to be chosen to mother a white one. Later in life that white boy may exhibit his latent love for that woman—whose breasts he suckled and whose arms nestled him in his infancy—by forming a liaison with a colored girl and produce a mulatto child. On the other hand he may be weak enough to be so influenced by conventional prejudices as to join in lynching his black mammy's son. This has happened.

The "hooded Terrors" enveloped in long white gowns, white hoods, carrying torches at night, terrorize and lynch our people, often setting fire to their homes. A wooden cross is carried in the lead of their nocturnal marches, as a symbol of their Christianity, by which they crucify a people. Many lynchers do not wear masks, and the K.K.K. disclaim the high annual number of lynchings as being their work.

Lynching is a practical demonstration of racial hysteria; it is actuated through fear, a guilty conscience, or a retributive foreboding. White people envy the husky colored man for his strength, his laughter, when he should be sad, his endurance through every hellish condition; hate grows into frenzy, and presto! a mob is formed to kill him at the slightest provocation. "Let's string him up to a tree! Riddle his body with bullets, and get souvenirs; then pour gasoline on him and give him 'a hot farewell.'" The charge against the victim for attempted rape is timeworn and hardly ever true. What sane colored man living in the South would do such a thing, knowing the consequences? Arthur Brisbane, the noted columnist for the *New York American*, one of Hearst's publications, explained: "The fact is that the mob, at a burning, are not human beings at all, but, as Professor Shaler shows in his book on the Mob, they are wolves with the spirit of the pack ... and nothing else."

Into this atmosphere, in June 1922, Garvey went to see the Imperial Wizard. There are many doors before one sees the "Exalted Ruler," but he was met at the outer door, and ushered into an office. It is said that once a Jew knocked at that door, and was told he should know better than to come there. Said the Jew apologetically, "I only came on business; I wanted to see the fellow who buys the white sheets."

Garvey had a long talk with the Assistant Imperial Wizard, telling him of race relations in the West Indies and the northern states, finally of his efforts toward colonization in Africa, which impressed the white listener, as a new and candid approach to the old question.

To his surprise his enemies in the North interpreted his bravery as cowardice; yet most of them were afraid even to visit relatives in the South. The startling news was flashed that Garvey had become a member of the K.K.K.; some said he had formed an alliance. Both accusations were ridiculous and wicked. The implications were that he would encourage the Klan to brutalize Negroes, and cause them to want to leave America for Africa. At no time of his life did he plan mass migration, or forced or coerced migration. His definite plan had always been select colonization by pioneering people, with the means to establish themselves, and the initiative to help build up the colony.

Clarence Darrow, eminent white criminal lawyer, addressing a gathering of Negroes in Washington, D.C., at the "Suburban Garden," in 1928, commended the New Negro in his fight for full freedom; he pointed out:

If there is any class of people to whom whites owe a debt of gratitude it is the Negro; but it is a debt they never will pay, and they have no intention of paying it. . . .

You have only been a little way out of slavery. You could not do much in the beginning without the aid of men who wanted to help you. But now you are pretty well able to look the world in the face, and make your own plans, and do your own work; and I for one, am rather glad that you will be compelled to do it; because it will give you strength, courage and energy. You will know that what you have got belongs to you. . . . You have got to make the fight for full equality yourselves; you have got to win by your own efforts; you haven't got much money, but you need every cent of it for important movements. . . .

I know and believe that you are in a winning fight, but it is long and slow, it needs every bit of your courage and independence, and judgment to conquer . . . it will come about in no other way, for people who cannot make a fight for freedom, are hardly fit for freedom if they get it.

CHAPTER SIXTEEN

Before the Third Convention assembled, William Pickens of the N.A.A.C.P. toured the states, speaking at meetings denouncing Garvey and his African program. Thousands of handbills marked, "Garvey must go," were distributed. But all this only gained more sympathy for him among the masses. As an impartial observer said, "If Garvey must go, then who is to take his place? The time they spend chasing Garvey, they ought to start something that we all can follow."

The parade was grand as usual, as was the opening meeting at the Seventy-first Regiment Armory. During the convention Pickens went on with his campaign. In a letter to the *New York Times*, August 10, 1922, three Africans told him what they thought of him, and his kind:

As natives of Africa who are proud of our country, our hearts were made to bleed on last Sunday at Shuffle Inn at the assault upon Africa, our Motherland, by one Dean William Pickens, who, from his complexion, is a descendant of Africans. We never realized how far Western civilization had demoralized the Negro until we heard the address of this supposedly educated Negro. He spoke of Africa as a heathen land, where life is not safe on account of cannibals.

We wish to inform the good professor that life and property are safer in Africa, but for the white usurpers, than in any part of the United States. Cannibalism in Africa is all fiction. While we appreciate any help offered us by those of the Western world who have had certain advantages of school, Africa would be better off without such Negroes as Dean William Pickens, and we trust until such have had a change of heart toward their Motherland they will remain forever in this Western world.

Africa shall be free, for within her borders has arisen that spirit which shall not exhaust itself until Africa is free and her people are in possession of the land.

We have no ill-will toward this Dean William Pickens. We can only pity him and his kind, for they have been blinded by this Western civilization. They imagine they have, when they have not; they think they see, when they are as blind as a bat.

> M. M. Martin,
> Sierra Leone, West Africa,
> Austin Dafora Horton,
> Sierra Leone, West Africa,
> V. Quashie Lawson,
> Gold Coast, West Africa.

Contrast the race-destroying activities of DuBois and Pickens, to the importance white people attach to Garvey and his program:

Johannesburg, S.A.—A Garvey paper published here and known as the African World, has created a furor among the whites.

Its platform of "Africa for the Africans" has created consternation both here and in England. The government has
been asked to suppress it. . . . The avowed aim of the African
World is to "free Africa from the incubus of European control," and to "instil the psychology and traits of Zaghlul Pasha
in the African race." In its third issue, published on June 13, it
has the barefaced impudence to refer to "the imperishable
message" of His Highness Marcus Garvey, Potentate of the
Universal Negro Improvement Association. . . .

To detect and demolish the specious fallacy of the "Africa
for the Africans" argument is child's play to the European
mind.

The following letter from Cape colored people to the
South African *Blackman* appealed to peoples of African
descent abroad to unite and help them:

We, the Cape Coloured citizens of the Borough of Oudt-
shoorn and district, herewith tender our heartiest thanks to the
Editor of "The Black Man" for publishing from time to time
articles for the enlightenment, advancement and welfare of
our non-European races. May those in authority and responsible for the publication of this brave little journal prosper and
be successful in all their undertakings for the good cause. May
the Almighty deem fit to instil in your mind the keen insight,
fortitude and clear judgment which will render possible the
building up of our poor and oppressed race.

Ye dusky sons of Africa, though distributed far and wide
over the face of the Universe, hail! The soil of Africa calls. In
the past we have been ignorant enough to allow aliens to
dominate us. . . .

Today we find that instead of religion dominating the influence of the powers that be, they have become slaves of pagan-
ism. Nevertheless the dawn is breaking. Shall we hear the
call and stand together once and for all, regardless of the
different social sects, which more or less retard the progress of
our noble race? To you who claim Africa as the origin of your
birth shall this call go unanswered? You have proven yourselves men to fight the battles of your oppressors in the past.
Why can't you show the same majesty of manhood and co-

operate with those who are trying to show the European nations their wrongs and evils upon the subject races?

Africans! The time for dreaming is past. Now is the opportune time to join your efforts with those who have dauntlessly faced the common foe. Throughout the Union of South Africa this pest and insult will ever strike your face: "Europeans only!" Europeans only! Until we succeed in removing this degradation to the race, rest assured that no real and formidable progress can be laid down. Remember that it is you who delay this progress of our race. It is you—the man who is doing well in bad times; you who live on the sweat and blood of the struggling, remember where your children will be when you are dead and gone.

God bless glorious Africa!

During the convention a well-known Bible society offered to present each delegate with a Bible; put to the vote the house declined the kind offer as the delegates already had Bibles. It was recommended that they be sent to sections of the South, and circulated among those obsessed with race and religious prejudices. This was done as a protest, to "let them know we are not Atheists. We are not rejecting God's Holy Book, but we disapprove their brand of Christianity," said Rev. Diggs, a Baptist pastor.

The substance of the discussions at the session is expressed by R. T. Brown, editor of the *Negro World*.

Africans at home, like Africans abroad, have grown weary and tired of that false brand of Christianity, which teaches humility and subjection to the white usurper and exploiter, who at the same time is demonstrating an aggressiveness and overlordship that is bewildering and disillusioning. What Africa needs at this time are men and women, who counting the cost are willing to venture forth, in pilgrim fashion, to spread the gospel of Unity, with Infinity, and At-one-ment with Universal Mind. Men and women who are charged with the impelling urge to rouse their kinsmen from the slumber of ages, and work such a transformation in their souls, and in their bodies too, that the world shall acclaim them.

One of the highlights of the sessions was a message from the King and Queen of Abyssinia, which the *New York World* reported, August 29, 1922:

Liberty Hall was the scene of a wild demonstration lasting ten minutes yesterday, when a message from the King and Queen of Abyssinia was read to the convention of the Universal Negro Improvement Association. Men threw up their hats and women their hand-kerchiefs. Marcus Garvey, usually the personification of dignity, led in the cheering.

The message was delivered to the convention by H. H. Topakyn, Persian Consul General, who represents Abyssinia in this country. When the part of the message was reached in which the King and Queen invited members of the association to "come back to the homeland" the delegates yelled themselves hoarse. Parts of the message delivered by the Persian Consul General, particularly pleasing to the delegates were:

"During a recent audience with these venerable and distinguished Rulers of a great historic land, I spoke of this approaching convention. The exalted Ruler quickly caught, as we do, the significance of this gathering, and with visible emotion he said:

" 'Kindly convey our greetings, congratulations and best wishes to the assembly. Here their race originated, and here it can be lifted to its highest plane of usefulness and honor. Assure them of the cordiality with which I invite them back to the home land, particularly those qualified to help solve our big problems and to develop our vast resources. Teachers, artisans, mechanics, writers, musicians, professional men and women—all who are able to lend a hand in the constructive work which our country so deeply feels, and greatly needs.

" 'Here we have abundant room and great opportunities and here destiny is working to elevate and enthrone a race which has suffered slavery, poverty, persecution and martyrdom, but whose expanding soul and growing genius is now the hope of many millions of mankind.

" 'Thus the King of Abyssinia speaks and thus the thoughtful all around the world speak, for the black man is showing his grit and conquering genius today as never before in his history, and future ages will witness his higher ascent in the

realm of science, law, literature, religion, industry and economics, and his growing contributions to the world-wide
structure of liberty and civilization.' "

The convention unanimously voted thanks and cabled congratulations to the King and Queen of Abyssinia.

Marcus Garvey was re-elected Provisional President of Africa. In his speech of acceptance he said:

"This is the most troublesome office in the world, declaring
for freedom of Africa, when at this time it is coveted for its
gold and other mineral wealth. It is like being elected to a
powder house. Before many years roll by I hope we will have
a real and active President of the Republic of Africa, whose
affairs will be administered from New York, the United States
of Africa, instead of New York, the United States of America."

Following up the proposal of Senator France that America take over the former German African Colonies and
colonize them with colored Americans, the delegates in
convention sent a delegation to the League of Nations at
Geneva, Switzerland, asking that body to permit the
U.N.I.A. to take control of the colonization. The delegation consisted of: Marke, Deputy Potentate; Sherill, American Leader; O'Meally, West Indian Leader; and J. Adam of
Haiti, secretary and interpreter. *L'Illustre*, October 14,
1922, had a picture of them seated at a conference table.

The Persian Delegation, as member to the League, presented the petition on behalf of the Negro peoples of the
world. The next year G. Marke was sent back to press the
petition's appeal; but the big colonial powers side-stepped
the issue by adopting a new rule that nationals can only
submit their grievances and petitions through their own
governments.

A *New York Post* reporter in an interview with the organization's Secretary General, August 14, sums up the
other activities of this convention:

AFRICA FOR THE AFRICANS

This is the fundamental tenet of the Universal Negro Improvement Association which opened today, the fourth week

of the annual convention at Liberty Hall, 120 West 138th Street. This slogan sums up all that the association is attempting to do, and to it can be traced all the discussions in the convention since it opened on August 1.

The desire to secure Africa for the Negro race explains the action of sending delegates to the League of Nations to represent the Negroes when the discussion of the African Mandates takes place; it explains in part the opposition which has met Marcus Garvey; it explains the association's attitude on lynching.

All these, and many other subjects have come up for discussion at the meetings, and in the final analysis all the discussions have been based on the hope and expectation that in the distant future there will be a strong Negro state in Africa.

In the matter of lynching, the feeling of the association, as explained by Robert L. Poston, Assistant Secretary General of the Association, speaking for Mr. Garvey, is that legislation such as the Dyer anti-lynching bill will do little good, whereas the representations of a strong foreign power, such as it is hoped there will be one day will do much good.

Liberia, the Negro Republic of Africa, has also been much discussed at the convention, and the decision has been reached that Negroes in this country should aid in the proposed loan from the United States to Liberia. This country gives the race a real foothold in Africa, the speakers at the convention declared, and to allow its destruction means the abandonment of the hopes of "African redemption."

CHAPTER SEVENTEEN

In order to speed up legal action to support the "Garvey must go" campaign, a long letter dated January 15, 1923, was written to Hon. Harry M. Dougherty, United States Attorney General, Department of Justice, Washington D.C., by eight prominent Negroes, namely:

Harry H. Pace, President of the Pace Phonograph Co.

Robert S. Abbott, Editor and Publisher of the *Chicago Defender*.

John E. Nail, President of Nail and Parker Inc., Real Estate Agents.

Julia P. Coleman, President of Hair Vim Chemical Co.

William Pickens, Field Secretary of the N.A.A.C.P.

Chandler Owen, Co-editor of *The Messenger*.

Robert W. Bagnall, Director of Branches of the N.A.A.C.P.

George V. Harris, Editor of the *New York News*.

The letter contained twenty-nine paragraphs giving reasons why the Attorney General as Chief Law Enforcement Officer should use his "full influence completely to disband and extirpate this vicious movement [U.N.I.A.]" and that he vigorously and speedily push the government's case against Marcus Garvey for using the mails to defraud. They closed the letter by stating: "we sense the imminent menace of this insidious movement, which cancer-like is gnawing at the vitals of peace and safety—of civic harmony and interracial concord."

What appalled and puzzled Garvey all his life, as death-thrusts were made at him was that there was no act too low that his enemies—of his own race—would not stoop to; thereby sacrificing the prestige of the race in order to destroy his leadership. They demonstrated the old "crab-in-the-barrel" psychology: If I can't be on top, I will pull the other fellows down as they climb. That is why "good white people" had to select a leader for the race, and take care of him.

In December 1926, while Garvey was in prison, this same Harry M. Dougherty, now a former Attorney General, along with others, was tried on charges of conspiracy to defraud the government in connection with the transfer of alien property. The trial was held before Judge Julian Mack, and resulted in a hung jury. In February the following year, objections having been made to Judge Mack, a new judge and a new trial was ordered for Mr. Dougherty. Compare this to Judge Mack's denial to Garvey for another judge in his trial to follow. We are reminded of the Nordic philosophy: "The black man has no rights that a white man is bound to respect."

Messrs. Randolph and Owen in their magazine, *The Messenger*, June 1924, gave a clue as to why Mr. Owen signed the notorious letter. They stated:

> Exit the Agents of Injustice.
>
> Good-bye Mr. Dougherty and farewell Mr. Burns. Peace be with ye. We are glad you are gone, and sorry you stayed so long. At last the government is rid of these two gentlemen of the political underworld. Mr. Dougherty, the erstwhile United States Attorney General, is notorious for his crooked, shady, political dealings.

In an attempt to counteract the wrong impressions created by the subversive letter to the Attorney General, Garvey held a mass meeting at Carnegie Hall, in midtown New York City. It was packed to overflowing; white people attended too, as it was well advertised in white newspapers, and by circulars distributed in the white sections. Items on the musical part of the program were: Ethel Clarke, Soprano, singing Eckert's "Swiss Song," and Cavallo's "Chanson Mimi"; The Black Star Line Band, in smart uniforms, playing the "Overture" from *Rigoletto* and *Mirello*; New York Local Choir, fully robed, singing "The Bridal Chorus" from *The Rose Maiden* and "Gloria" from Mozart's *Twelfth Mass*; The "Perfect Harmony Four" in the "Sextet" from *Lucia*; Basso Packer Ramsay singing Handel's "Hear me, ye Winds and Waves." On the second half of the program were speeches by the officers of the organization and himself. Subjects were: "The future of the black and white Races," and "The building of a Negro nation."

Garvey did many acts of kindness to relatives of his enemies. When asked how he forgot the past so easily, he said: "I have to forget such injuries; if I kept them fresh in my mind, the added ones would be harder to bear. I never encourage hate—it is consuming and weakening. Hateful thinking breeds negative action, which retards the positive work I have to do. If I tried to hate all the people whom I know are doing all they can to destroy me, I would be so busy hating and avenging that I would have very little time for good constructive thoughts and actions."

Garvey has been accused of hating mulattoes, but when Robert Bagnall of the N.A.A.C.P. described him thus—"Of unmixed stock, squat, stocky, fat and sleek, with protruding jaws and heavy jowls, small bright, pig-like eyes and rather bull-dog like face"—is it any wonder that Garvey should lash out at him and others like him, who see no comeliness in unmixed stock, and say: "These bastards hate the Negro blood of their mothers, and endeavour to build up a society based on colour of skin, and not on achievement and worth."

In an article to the *Negro World*, written August 1923, from the Tombs prison, Garvey exposed the Pink Tea Set, the Colonial Club, the Blue Vein Society, and the N.A.A.C.P.'s policy in 1916 to employ only persons of light complexion because, they said, "this was better for business." In this article he emphasized the policy of the U.N.I.A. in this regard as follows:

> To draw together into one universal whole all the Negro peoples of the world, with prejudice toward none. We desire to have every shade of colour, even those with one drop of African blood in our fold; because we believe that none of us, as we are, is responsible for our birth. In short we have no prejudice within the Race. . . .
>
> For long we have been made to believe that the nearer we approached the white man in colour the greater our social standing and privileges. . . . We have been trying to get away from pride of race, into an atmosphere of colour worship, to the damaging extent that the whole world has made us its laughing stock. . . . But now we have reached the point where the entire race must get together, whether we are light, yellow, black or what not, and build up a mighty race. . . .
>
> God made us in His own image, and He had some purpose when He thus created us; then why should we seek to destroy that identity? Let us not divide ourselves in castes. To change

our race is no credit. The Anglo-Saxon does not want to be a Japanese and the Japanese does not want to be a Negro; then in the name of God, and all that's holy, why should we want to be somebody else?

There is no white man that could be as aggressively proud of his race as Garvey was of his own; and when that identity was ridiculed, or persons mistreated or discriminated against because they were black, he became fighting mad, to vindicate the injured and the aggrieved. Everything he said or did denoted action, and speed to span the centuries of racial inactivity and hibernation; in his zeal he never counted the costs in dollars and cents.

In 1922 he published the *Negro Times* as an evening newspaper, and although it was a drag on the funds of the organization, he kept publication going until 1924. Said he, "The benefits our people derive from daily interpretation of national and world events will more than compensate for the monetary losses."

Impractical! Yes, he was, because he was obsessed with the idea of speeding up the awakening and education of the minds of our people and teaching them to think independently. Every one must be geared to the need and speed of his work, or they would be brushed aside or ignored. Every circumstance or incident, even if adverse, was used to illustrate and dramatize the urgency and dire necessity for militant advocacy of the cause of the oppressed.

Irrepressible, extravagant, even fanatical, he was dynamic in speech and action. He had a message to deliver to all his people everywhere—a redemptive, soul-searching, yet practical, comprehensive program for his race's way of life, to prepare them really to live as real men, and be partakers in the fullness of the earth, through their own efforts and diligence.

His aim was to preserve and develop the Negro personality, for, said he, "We have got to teach and show the world that different races and creeds can live on this earth, with envy and malice toward none, in the fair exchange and trading of the world's goods, and an acknowledgement of merited equality, not only before the law, but under God."

As he traveled throughout the states of the Union, and observed the varying degrees of suffering and abuse that the masses of his people were still being subjected to, his mind was constantly agitated to find new outlets and opportunities for his work, as his enemies blocked his progress; but the changed attitude of the masses to their local problems, and the forthright manner in which they were tackling them in unity and love, gave him impetus to carry on in the face of untold and often unseen opposition.

No longer was his people seeing through the eyes of the white race, and speaking the white man's thoughts, which kept the black in his low, restricted status, and the white in his high estate; no longer was the collective creative spirit of the race warped or largely crushed by the indoctrination that "nothing good can ever come out of the Negro race." They were no longer a hypnotized race under the spell of the white man's material and military power like the zombies of Haiti—living, but not being. Oh no; they had cast off the spell; they no longer believed that God had cursed them when He made them black, but that God blessed them when He gave them such an enduring color, and such a wonderful physique. Indeed the most rewarding freedom is the freedom of the mind.

I will digress to explain how my legal training came about, which fitted me to better serve the organization; and how destiny, fate or a chain of circumstances brought it about. As a high school girl, I was being taught to play the piano, because music and music appreciation were considered a cultural finishing to a girl's education. I had no ear for music, and have always felt that whatever I do, I must excel in it. So I was able to reason with my father to let me do shorthand and typewriting instead. He agreed, but warned me that it was only to be used to take notes when I was being trained as a nurse in England—this was his plan for me after I had taken the Cambridge University School Certificate Examination. I finished the course, received a prize, and an offer from the legal firm to which my teacher was attached, for a beginner's post. My father graciously declined the offer. At home he said, "I do not want any daughter of mine to be exposed to the wiles of men in an office."

He died suddenly from a stroke. Our lawyer suggested to my mother to send me to his office as a clerk; in that way I could also look after my father's estate. I remained there four years, and finally could attend to every legal phase of the work, including that of a fire insurance agency. However, I became restless and decided to go to England; but when everything was ready, the ships would not take women passengers because of submarine warfare. I then decided to go to America in 1918. My mother was so upset that she had a conference with our minister and the lawyer in hopes to dissuade me, as I could not stay with her people: They all passed as white. Our lawyer argued that I should remain and become a lawyer, as America was no place for my type (the exodus was to come later). I promised them to return in three months if conditions were unbearable. I really wanted to see this land which was, according to my father's description, one mixed of opportunity and restrictions.

CHAPTER EIGHTEEN

May 21, 1923, in the U.S. Federal Court, in New York City was held the trial of the four officers of the Black Star Line. Judge Julian Mack presided over the jury. Each defendant was represented by an attorney. As the trial formally opened, Garvey through his attorney made application that the trial judge declare himself disqualified to try the case on the ground that he was a member of or a

contributor to the N.A.A.C.P.—an association, whose officers were actively opposed to Garvey and his movement.
Judge Mack admitted his connection with the N.A.A.C.P.,
but denied bias. The motion was denied, and the same judge
proceeded to try the case.

After the first two days of the trial, Garvey's attorney
came to our flat after court, and said he was acting on
advice, and in Garvey's interest; as his lawyer he advised
him to plead guilty of the technical charge; he had reason to
believe that he would be fined and admonished in regard to
future activities. Garvey was surprised at the suggestion,
and told him he did not seem to understand the motives
behind the prosecution. After a lengthy argument on the
matter, which brought out other facts, Garvey felt that his
attorney was being used innocently to trap him, and asked
him to withdraw from his court defence. In leaving, the
lawyer warned, "It will go hard with you." Garvey retorted,
"I will prove to the jury that I am not guilty of any
fraud."

He tried to get another attorney, but it was almost impossible, as he wanted one whose politics were Republican;
besides, no one could study the case overnight, and many
were warned "not to handle the Garvey defense." After a
week he retained Mr. Armin Kohn to advise him after
court, and to question him as a witness.

Party politics plays an important part in the state judiciary, for though judges are elected, the politicians pick the
candidates. The customs of this system are at times reflected
in the federal judiciary. Mr. Edward J. Flynn, formerly
Democratic Leader in the Bronx, stated in his book, *You're
the Boss*, "Political leaders have always maintained, not
only in New York, but throughout the entire United States,
that they have the right to speak on behalf of a client, to a
Judge on the Bench. Ethically it is wrong; but practically
the custom has always existed, and it would be difficult to
eradicate."

Among the renegades from the black race, the one whom

the prosecutor listed as his star witness, "to testify against Garvey," was J. Eason—the first American U.N.I.A. leader. Under impeachment at the 1922 convention, in his defense he said: "I am no saint; when the President-General is talking about saints he is not referring to me; I must confess I love women; I am broke out with that; but when it comes to love for my people, no one can lift an accusing finger at me." Eason forced the U.N.I.A. to pay him back salary on the maximum scale. He campaigned throughout the country against Garvey and the organization that he had sworn to protect even with his own life. After one of these denouncement meetings in New Orleans, in January 1924, he was shot to death in an alley. The prosecutor said he had rendered valuable service.

Most of the government's witnesses were ex-officers or ex-employees of the corporation or the organization; many of them had been dismissed—the officers suing for salaries they had never earned. Their major roles were to irritate Garvey, mock, ridicule and threaten him. In his efforts to retaliate in cross-examination he became unnerved, having to restrain himself; all this lengthened the trial into almost four weeks. In the meantime the prosecutor's henchmen circulated all sorts of rumors, such as that Garveyites had guns on them, which justified searching them daily, and allowing only a few of them in the courtroom. The climax came when a supposedly anonymous letter was sent to the District Attorney's office, stating that one of Garvey's men was "going to get the Judge." The letter was released to the press, with the consequent exaggerated headlines. Bomb squad men and secret service police were now in daily attendance at court. After this, Hugh Mulzac, a former captain of the Black Star Line, and a government witness, reported to the prosecutor that he was threatened by Charles Lennon not to testify against Garvey. The trial judge asked the jury to withdraw, and sentenced the man to two months imprisonment, and to be held for Grand Jury action in $10,000 bail, despite the fact that Lennon denied the charge, and said he was being taunted and called "one of Garvey's fools."

The entire attitude of the prosecution is summed up in the District Attorney's plea to the jury: "Gentlemen, will you let the Tiger loose?" It was clear he was not prosecuting the officers of the Black Star Line, only Garvey. The morning after his summation, William Pickens of the N.A.A.C.P. came into the courtroom, just before the judge entered; he shook hands with the prosecuting attorney, patted him on the back, and glared at Garvey. Amos, the colored agent of the Department of Justice, remarked to a U.S. Marshal, "See. I have started my fireworks." His daily loud remarks and jeers at Garvey were most irritating. On one occasion he remarked loudly to attorney Johnson: "So you are defending Garvey."

Garvey addressed the jury at length; so did the other attorneys. H. Lincoln Johnson on Garcia's behalf, closing his plea, in a voice vibrating with emotion, said:

> Gentlemen, you can't have any idea what it means to be a Negro in these days—the ignominy of it. You can't have! If every Negro could put every dime, every penny, that he has earned into the sea, and if he might get in exchange the knowledge that he was somebody, that he meant something in this world, that he had gained the respect of the world, he would gladly do it. The black man does not live, who does not hope that his children may be established in a settled business, who does not pray that this hideous curtain of hell and hate may some day be lifted from them.

The judge charged the jury. After they were out eleven hours, they were called in and a second series of instructions given them, without their request, the intent of which is evident:

> Some men feel that having given their view in the beginning, it is an indication of their firmness of character, their sound judgment, if they stick inalterably to it. . . .
> Now the effect of a disagreement, whether it be as to one

count, two or three or four of them, as to any particular count, means that as to such count or as to such defendant, or both, as to which you may disagree, the government is put to the expense, the public is put to the loss of time, and the Court and the Jury, and the witnesses, and the Defendants are put to the expense of having to go through the whole thing again.

The jury again retired, and in less than thirty minutes returned with a verdict of guilty against Garvey alone.

The judge said he would not pass sentence for a few days. Making the startling claim that Garvey had arms and ammunitions stored in Liberty Hall, and was a menace to society, the prosecutor asked that Garvey be held in custody and not be granted bail. Garvey, in protesting his innocence to the court, said: "I am disappointed that your Honour has taken into consideration the remarks made by the Prosecutor, for whom I have nothing but contempt. His statements are utterly false, and this trial has been a conspiracy to ruin Marcus Garvey. . . . I am satisfied to let the world judge me innocent or guilty."

The judge remanded him in custody; then several detectives, bomb squad men and uniformed policemen closed in on Garvey and pushed him toward a freight elevator; he was conveyed in an armored car to the Tombs prison.

Government raids were made on Liberty Hall, and the offices of the organization, but not even a pistol or a cartridge was found. Newspapers had already carried scare headlines of the prosecutor's allegations. Not many reported the result of the raids.

On the 21st of June he was escorted to the courtroom heavily guarded, and Judge Mack pronounced the sentence of five years imprisonment, $1,000 fine, and the costs of the case. His attorney gave notice of appeal, and his motion for bail was promptly denied. Garvey was hustled back to prison.

The four defendants had against them two indictments, each of which contained counts for various offences involving use of the mails to defraud, and each of which contained a count charging conspiracy to commit the substantive offence. All of the defendants were acquitted of the charge of conspiracy, and Garvey was acquitted of all the charges in both indictments except the charge contained in the third count of the second indictment, that on or about December 13, 1920 "for the purpose of executing said scheme and artifice Garvey placed in a post office of the Southern District of New York, a certain letter or circular enclosed in a postpaid envelope addressed to Benny Dancy, 34 W. 131 St., N.Y.C."

For the appeal he was represented by Kohn and Nagler, attorneys, and George Gordon Battle and Isaac Levy of 37 Wall St., counsel. In their brief and Bill of Exceptions, which charged to the court ninety-four errors, we note the following:

> The Court erred in refusing to comply with the request of the Plaintiff-in-Error to restrain persons attached to the Court from giving out to the press, news prejudicial to the Plaintiff-in-Error.

> The Court erred in not declaring a mistrial after the Prosecutor referred to the Plaintiff-in-Error as a "liar" in the presence of the Jury, upon the Prosecutor requesting the Plaintiff-in-Error to turn over to him certain papers, which papers the Plaintiff-in-Error stated had previously been turned over to the Prosecutor.

> The Court was unduly severe in its repeated admonition of Garvey. Time and again the Court appears to have sustained objections that were never made. Time and again the Court suggested to the Assistant District Attorney that an objection would be sustained.

> The attitude of the Assistant District Attorney toward Garvey during the trial was improper. The Assistant District Attorney had no just right to interrupt Garvey in his examinations, except by proper objection to the Court, or to address remarks directly to Garvey. . . . The whole situation was one that tended unduly to prejudice the defendant in the conduct of his case and to suggest an atmosphere of antagonism on the

part of the Court and the Assistant District Attorney that necessarily was reflected in the attitude of the jury.

There is not a scintilla of evidence competent or otherwise to establish the mailing of the indictment letter "A." The only exhibit offered in support of the mailing of the indictment letter under the Dancy count is the front and back of an envelope.

The envelope was offered in evidence on the testimony of Dancy that he recognized it. It was offered by the Prosecuting Attorney as follows: Mr. Mattuck; I offer the envelope in evidence on the ground it bears on the back a stamp "Black Star Line" and it is a reasonable assumption that envelope contained matter from the "Black Star Line." . . .

This case called for the finest discrimination on the part of the jury, and the most scrupulous consideration of the facts. It required the jury to be constantly awake to the danger that it might be influenced by consideration outside of the record. It was a matter in which every juryman had an intimate personal interest. While it is important that the Government should protect a class from the alleged schemes of their accepted leader, it is even more important that the people whose just aspirations Mr. Garvey represents should be left with the feeling that their leader has received a fair trial. It was peculiarly a case where the rights of the defendant should have received the utmost protection. . . .

In the claim that the jury was actuated not alone by prejudice, but by passion, we do not mean to imply that it was actuated by a purpose to commit an injustice against the individual Garvey. But we do mean to assert that the testimony was such as was calculated to make a most potent appeal to the feelings, the passions, and prejudices of the jury, and to put them in the position, not of administering justice in the case of an individual, but of dealing with a general situation, represented to them as one fraught with great danger and many evils. It is as if Gandhi were to be tried by a jury of Englishmen for his leadership of the people of India. It is as if DeValera were to be tried by a jury of Ulsterites for his leadership of the Irish people. It is as if a Zionist were to be tried by a jury of Moslems for his plans and activities in the

establishment of a homestead for the Jews in Palestine. It may
be that the system of laws prevailing in the jurisdiction where
such a case might be tried would permit only such a trial. But
it does undoubtedly present a situation where the courts must
be careful to scrutinize the result so as to determine whether
the jury was guided by law, or was carrying out what it
conceived to be a social or political remedy, determined by its
own selfish interests.

In all these movements money is necessary. In all these
movements great promises are held forth. No one who does
not put himself in the place of the stricken and afflicted
people to whom the appeal is made can understand or sympathize with the enthusiasm of the leader, and the trust and
confidence of the masses. To treat such a situation as this
indictment does, as a matter of dollars and cents and monetary
fraud, and to judge it as one would judge a criminal transaction, or a speculative mining enterprise, is to warp the facts,
and to commit a travesty upon the truth.

No movement for the redemption of a people has succeeded
in making money. The American Revolution was conducted at
a financial loss. During the years that the Revolution was
fought, and before the Constitution was adopted, and the
finances of the country placed upon a stable basis, any jury
would have been justified in convicting the abettors of the
Revolution and the Fathers of the country for a money fraud,
when they induced people to invest in the loans upon the
promise of repayment. It will not do to say that these matters
were disposed of by the verdict of the jury. For that verdict is
so inconsistent with the acquittal of all the defendants on all
the other charges, that it cannot be defended as a verdict in
accord with the facts and the law. The only explanation that
can be made is that the jury proposed somehow to see that
Garvey was stopped. The jury did not believe in Garvey and
his movement.

CHAPTER NINETEEN

Soon after we were married he borrowed $400 of my early savings, to meet an emergency for the organization: A good speaker attached to the N.A.A.C.P.'s antilynching campaign, decided to join the U.N.I.A. if he got an immediate advance of $400 to remove his family from St. Louis to Cleveland, Ohio. He changed his mind after he received the amount.

The day before being sentenced his attorney advised him to make a will, which he did. The following is the full text:

I MARCUS GARVEY, being of sound and disposing mind and memory, considering the uncertainty of this life, do make, public and declare, this to be my LAST WILL AND TESTAMENT as follows, hereby revoking all other and former wills or codicils by me at any time made.

FIRST, after my lawful debts are paid, I give, and bequeath all my personal, real, and mixed properties including household effects, and chattels at 133 West 129th Street, New York City, New York, also all Bonds in the Universal Negro Improvement Association, and all wages that may be due me by the said Universal Negro Improvement Association for services up to the date of the termination officially of my service, and further all increments thereto appertaining to an Insurance Policy in the New York Life Insurance Company of New York, made payable to my estate, to my wife Amy Jacques Garvey, and said wife Amy Jacques Garvey is to be the only Beneficiary under this will and testament.

SECOND, That my wife AMY JACQUES GARVEY shall have all and exclusive rights to all the writings and speeches of MARCUS GARVEY and shall couple them and use same to her desire to the exclusion of all others.

THIRD, all my financial interest in all books, pictures, and pamphlets shall be included in this my bequest to AMY JACQUES GARVEY. She shall receive all monies, gifts, and considerations intended for me, and hold same as her own personal property.

On my death, the said AMY JACQUES GARVEY shall bury me out of the funds of my Insurance Policy as by her discretion, and all gifts at such funeral by the Universal Negro Improvement Association shall be accepted by AMY JACQUES GARVEY to be disposed of to her discretion.

FOURTH, I hereby appoint AMY JACQUES GARVEY to be Executrix of this my last will and Testament.

IN WITNESS WHEREOF, I have hereunto subscribed my name and affixed my seal, the 20th day of June, in the year of Our Lord One thousand nine hundred and twenty three.

                              Marcus Garvey.
                              Testator.

WITNESSES
  John E. Bruce,
  Florence A. Bruce,
  H. Vinton Plummer.

Subscribed by MARCUS GARVEY, the Testator named in the foregoing Will, in the presence of each of us, and at the time of making such subscription, the above Instrument was declared by the said Testator to be his LAST WILL AND TESTAMENT, and each of us, at the request of the said Testator, and in the presence of each other, and in his presence, signed our names as witnesses thereto.

Name John E. Bruce Residing	258 W. 139th Street, N.Y.C.
Florence A. Bruce	258 W. 139th Street, N.Y.C.
H. Vinton Plummer	56 West 135th Street
June 20, 1923.	243 West 136th Street.

While in the Tombs he continued to send his frontpage articles to the *Negro World*, but these were now hand written, so they were brief. The following paragraphs are taken from two such messages:

> I trust you are not over worried and distressed over my continued confinement without bail; other than to realize that all those who make efforts to serve humanity are bound by the same laws of suffering and injustice.
>
> I fully calculated the cost of service to my Race, and know

that what is being done to me is only a part of the price I must pay for daring to arouse the consciousness of four hundred million Negroes. It is not likely that our African jails of the future will be as massive as the one in which I now have my residence, but there will be improvements I hope for the accommodation of those who will be in for good, and those who will be waiting their "turn of justice."

A few days ago my attention was drawn to the new slogan —"Keep Africa for the white man." In this slogan lies the plan of doom of our Race. Because I attempted to combat the sinister effort with the retort "Africa for Africans" I find myself where I am. Keep your spirits high, and yield nothing in the fight we are making to emancipate our Race, and free our Motherland.

With God's choicest blessings,

I remain, your obedient servant.

In his second message, June 20, 1923, he again thanks the people, and commends me to them in these words:

I take this opportunity to return thanks to you for the splendid interest you have manifested in me during the trial of my case. I bear with me the kindliest feelings toward you. I commend to your care and attention my wife, who has been my helpmate and inspiration for years. She has suffered with me in the cause of service to my Race, and if I have any sorrow, it is on her account, that I cannot be with her at all times to protect her from the evil designs of the enemy; but I commend her to your care and keeping, and feel sure that you will do for her as much as you have done for me. Her tale of woe has not been told, but in my belief that truth will triumph over wrong, I feel sure that a day will come when the whole world will know the story of her noble sacrifice for the Cause I love so much.

While in prison he wrote a few verses of a song, "Keep Cool," and sent it to Arnold Ford, Director of the U.N.I.A. Music Department, who set it to a lively tune. The opening lines are:

> Let no trouble worry you,
> Keep cool! Keep cool!
> Dont get hot like some folks do,
> Keep cool! Keep cool!

We made several applications for bail. Each time the trial judge refused to recommend same, so Garvey was kept in the Tombs for three months. When the Judge left for Europe on vacation, we tried again and were successful, but the bond was set at $15,000. The officers of the organization, the trial lawyer and I contacted the leading bonding companies in the city. Some said, as they heard the name, "Sorry, just can't touch it." Others said frankly, "If we carried this man's bond, we would be blacklisted." We tried the smaller companies, one of whom, at an interview promised to take it up, if we could put up part of the money in cash.

The onus was now on us: He could be free as soon as we raised that cash. Feverishly we phoned, sent special delivery letters, and traveled to members, who responded splendidly. We arranged with the lawyer to fix a time with the bonding company to post the bond in court; to our utter dismay, we were told that the company had changed its mind. Said the lawyer to us dolefully, "You will have to raise every cent of it in cash; that is the only way we can get him out." We had to go right back to the members, and raise the full amount of $15,000; and that is how he was released from prison pending his appeal, after three months' confinement.

The following is the first speech he made on his release, which proves his dauntless spirit. The subject was: the future as I see it.

> It comes to the individual, the Race, and the Nation, once in a life time to decide upon the course to be pursued as a career. The hour has now struck for the individual Negro as well as the entire Race to decide the course that will be pursued in the interest of our own liberty.

We who make up the Universal Negro Improvement Association have decided that we shall go forward, upward and onward toward the great goal of human liberty. We have determined among ourselves that all barriers placed in the way of our progress must be removed, must be cleared away, for we desire to see the light of a brighter day.

The Universal Negro Improvement Association for many years has been proclaiming to the world the readiness of the Negro to carve out a pathway for himself in the course of life. Men of other Races and nations have become alarmed at this attitude of the Negro in his desire to do things for himself, and by himself. This alarm has become so universal that organizations have been brought into being here, there and everywhere for the purpose of deterring and obstructing this forward move of our Race. Propaganda has been waged for the purpose of misinterpreting the intention of this Organization; some have said that it seeks to create discord and discontent among the Races; some say we are organized for the purpose of hating other people. Every sensible, sane and honest-minded person knows that the Universal Negro Improvement Association has no such intention. We are organized for the absolute purpose of bettering our condition, industrially, commercially, socially, religiously and politically. We are organized, not to hate other men, but to lift ourselves, and to demand respect to all humanity. We have a programme that we believe to be righteous; we believe it to be just, and we have made up our minds to lay down ourselves on the altar of sacrifice for the realization of this great hope of ours, based upon the foundation of righteousness. We declare to the world that Africa must be free, that the entire Negro Race must be emancipated from industrial bondage, peonage and serfdom; we make no compromise, we make no apology in this our declaration. We do not desire to create offense on the part of other Races, but we are determined that we shall be heard, that we shall be given the rights to which we are entitled.

For the purpose of creating doubts about the work of the Universal Negro Improvement Association, many attempts have been made to cast shadow and gloom over our work. They have even written the most uncharitable things about our Organization; they have spoken unkindly of our efforts, but what do we care? They spoke unkindly and uncharitably about all the reform movements that have helped in the betterment of humanity. They maligned the great movement of the Christian religion, the great liberation movements of America, France, England, Russia; can we expect then to escape being maligned in this, our desire for the liberation of Africa, and the freedom of four hundred million Negroes of the world?

We have unscrupulous men and organizations working in opposition to us. Some trying to capitalize the new spirit that has come to the Negro, to make profit out of it to their own selfish benefit; some are trying to set back the Negro from seeing the hope of his own liberation and thereby poisoning our people's mind against the motives of our Organization; but every sensible far-seeing Negro in this enlightened age knows what propaganda means. It is the medium of discrediting that which you are opposed to, so that the propaganda of our enemies will be of little avail as soon as we are rendered able to carry to our peoples scattered throughout the world the true message of our great Organization.

Men of the Negro Race! let me say to you that a greater future is in store for us; we have no cause to lose hope, to become faint-hearted. We must realize that upon ourselves depend our destiny, our future; we must carve out that future, that destiny; and we who make up the Universal Negro Improvement Association have pledged ourselves that nothing in the world shall stand in our way, nothing in the world shall discourage us; but opposition shall make us work harder, shall bring us closer together, so that as one man the millions of us will march on toward that goal that we have set for ourselves. The New Negro shall not be deceived. The New Negro refuses to take advice from anyone who has not felt with him, and suffered with him. We have suffered for three hundred years, therefore we feel that the time has come when only those who have suffered with us can interpret our feelings and our spirit. It takes the slave to interpret the feelings of the slave; it takes the unfortunate man to interpret the spirit of his unfortunate brother; and so it takes the suffering Negro to interpret the spirit of his comrade. It is strange that so many people are interested in the Negro now; willing to advise him how to act, and what Organization he should join; yet nobody was interested in the Negro to the extent of not making him a slave for two hundred and fifty years, reducing him to industrial peonage and serfdom after he was freed; it is strange that the same people can be so interested in the Negro now, as to tell him what organization he should follow and what leader he should support.

Whilst we are bordering on a future of brighter things, we are also at our danger period, when we must either accept the right philosophy, or go down by following deceptive propaganda which has hemmed us in for many centuries.

Many so-called leaders of our Race tell us that everything is well, and that all things will work out themselves and that a better day is coming. Yes, all of us know that a better day is coming; we all know that one day we will go home to Paradise; but whilst we are hoping by our Christian virtues to have entry into Paradise we also realize that we are living on earth, and that the things that are practised in Paradise are not practised here. You have to treat this world as the world treats you; we are living in a temporal, material age, an age of activity, an age of racial, national selfishness. What else can you expect but give back to the world what the world gives to you, and we are calling upon the four hundred million Negroes of the world to take a decided stand, a determined stand, that we shall occupy a firm position; that position shall be an emancipated race and a free nation of our own. We are determined that we shall have a free country; we are determined that we shall have a flag; we are determined that we shall have a government second to none in the world.

Men may spurn the idea, they may scoff at it, the metropolitan press of this country may deride us; yes, white men may laugh at the idea of Negroes talking about government; and let me say to you also that whatever you give, in like measure it shall be returned to you. The world is sinful, and therefore many believe in the doctrine of an eye for an eye, a tooth for a tooth. Others believe that revenge is God's; but at the same time we are men, and revenge sometimes springs up, even in the most Christian heart.

Why should man write down a history that will react against him? Why should man perpetrate deeds of wickedness upon his brother which will return to him in like measure? Yes, the Germans maltreated the French in the Franco-Prussian war of 1870, but the French got even with the Germans in 1918. It is history, and history will repeat itself. Beat the Negro, scoff at the Negro, deride the Negro, it may come back to you one of these fine days, because the supreme destiny of man is in the hands of God. God is no respecter of persons, whether that person be white, yellow or black. Today the one race is up, tomorrow it has fallen; today the Negro seems to be the footstool of the other races and nations of the world; tomorrow the Negro may occupy the highest rung of the great human ladder, as civilization moves in cycles.

When we come to consider the history of man, was not the Negro a power, was he not great once? Yes, honest students of history can recall the day when Egypt, Ethiopia and Timbuktu towered in their civilizations; towered above Europe, towered above Asia. When Europe was inhabited by a Race of cannibals, a Race of savages, naked men, heathen and pagans, Africa was peopled with a Race of cultured black men, who were masters in art, science and literature; men who were cultured and refined; men who, it was said, were like the gods. Even the great poets of old sang in beautiful sonnets of the delight it afforded the gods to be in companionship with the Ethiopians. Why, then, should we lose hope? Black men, you were once great, you shall be great again. Lose not courage, lose not faith, go forward! The thing to do is to get organized; keep separated and you will be exploited, you will be robbed, you will be killed. Get organized, and you will compel the world to respect you. If the world fails to give you consideration, because you are black men, because you are Negroes, four hundred millions of you shall, through organization, shake the pillars of the universe and bring down creation, even as Samson brought down the temple upon his head and upon the heads of the Philistines.

So Negroes, I say that through the Universal Negro Improvement Association there is much to live for. I have a vision of the future, and I see before me a picture of a redeemed Africa, with her dotted cities, with her beautiful civilization, with her millions of happy children going to and fro. Why should I lose hope, why should I give up, and take a back place in this age of progress? Remember that you are men, that God created you lords of this creation. Lift up yourselves, men; take yourselves out of the mire, and hitch your hopes to the stars—yes, rise as high as the very stars themselves. Let no man pull you down, let no man destroy your ambition, because man is but your companion, your equal; man is your brother; he is not your lord; he is not your sovereign master.

We of the Universal Negro Improvement Association feel happy; we are cheerful. Let them connive to destroy us, let them organize to destroy us, we shall fight the more. Ask me personally the cause of my success, and I say opposition; oppose me, and I fight the more; and if you want to find out the sterling worth of the Negro, oppose him, and under the leadership of the Universal Negro Improvement Association he shall fight his way to victory; and in the days to come— and I believe not far distant—Africa shall reflect a splendid demonstration of the worth of the Negro, of the determination of the Negro to set himself free and to establish a government of his own.

CHAPTER TWENTY

The Tombs prison is, as its name implies, an unhealthy place; this had its effect on Garvey's asthmatic condition. His doctor recommended a change in the warmer states. Much to the delight of the people out west he planned an itinerary that took him through the following states: New York, Pennsylvania, West Virginia, Ohio, Indiana, Missouri, Kansas, Colorado, Wyoming, Idaho, Washington, Oregon and California.

He took me along, as the people in the Western states were anxious to see and hear me. We spoke in the cities and some of the towns where large branches prospered. In most cases members from smaller branches journeyed to the cities to hear him.

I used to contribute articles to the *Negro World*; on this trip I wrote a series describing the places, the industries that gave our people employment, the handicaps and insecurity of their lives, and just how necessary it was to have united action to help overcome such conditions. Everywhere we went Garvey spoke to overflowing audiences; at times he had two meetings in succession. When Garvey came to town, it was a gala day. Sometimes a reception committee had a small band outside the railroad station; on his arrival they would strike up "God bless our President." Some carried banners such as: "You can't keep a good man down" and "Hail, the conquering hero comes." Each Branch had its own novel way of receiving and entertaining him. The local offices often had the mayor or a prominent white politician to either chair the mass meeting or give the welcome address.

We stayed in California about two weeks, traveling through San Francisco, Oakland, Los Angeles, going as far south as San Diego. We went on location at one of the studios of Hollywood, and saw how motion pictures were being made. People came from far and near to see him, tell him their woes, or just to give him a hearty hand shake, and say, "God bless you, carry on."

We returned by the southern route—Arizona, New Mexico, Oklahoma, Arkansas, Mississippi, Alabama, Georgia, South Carolina, Virginia, Washington, D.C., Maryland, New Jersey and New York. The people received and heard him in true southern style. While in Alabama we went to Tuskegee Normal and Industrial Institute—primarily to pay homage to the late Booker T. Washington, at the monument erected to his memory in front of the chapel. However, we stayed two days in order to see and learn how the youth were being trained. There are 115 buildings and 2,300 acres of farm land, 300 of which were given to the Negro Veterans' Hospital—an institution in itself. Dr. Carver, the scientific wizard on the staff of the school, was the most interesting person to talk with, for notwithstanding his marvelous discoveries, he lived humbly, and was gracious and charming to all.

At the first mass meeting after our return to New York, I was not on the program, but my series of articles had created so much interest and enthusiasm, that—just before Garvey appeared as the last speaker—the audience clapped and called out, "We want Mrs. Garvey." I rose, and when their cheering had died down, I had caught their infectious spirit, and responded with a speech, that came to its climax in a call to rededicate their lives for service to all. Before he spoke he said smilingly, "Now I have a rival, but I am glad she is my wife."

He asked me to take over a page of the *Negro World*, which I did, giving the woman's viewpoint on all subjects of news. But my editorials were mostly on international subjects. I conducted this page for three years, and the fourth year I concentrated on feature articles.

He had no time to read through newspapers and magazines; this was one of my many assignments. I used to cut out clippings, date and identify them, underline significant statements, and pin on my comments. Whenever I thought his mind was clear and receptive, I gave them to him. Quite often he handed them back to me saying, "You tell me what they are all about," settling himself in an armchair, or getting into bed, if the time was after a night meeting. On topics of international or national importance which warranted discussion we often differed on points; and then we would argue—until we could compromise, or until he would say, "O.K., 'Mopsie' you win. Now let's get some sleep, for we know not what tomorrow will bring." He used this news material for his speeches and frontpage articles. Sometimes he sought my opinion before going to press, but he would not let me put my blue pencil through his copy where I found superfluity. Said he, "I am writing for the masses— people who have not been accustomed to serious reading matter—I must hammer in what I want to impress on their minds."

He could not speak from notes; they handicapped his ready flow of thoughts. He was always the last speaker at big public meetings, so as to hold the crowds who wanted to hear him. To facilitate reporters from big white dailies, he had the high points of his proposed speech typed, and given to them when the meeting was in progress. He memorized only the outlines of very important speeches. The *Negro World* employed expert shorthand writers, who also served at conventions and conferences. The fluency of his speeches lay in the fact that he had something to say, something which touched him so deeply that it constituted an outpouring from his heart and found response in his hearers. Wherever he went to speak he first got all the information on conditions; this he weighed in his mind while sitting on the platform waiting his turn to speak, and inhaling the perfume from his kerchief. He also studied the faces of his audience; in this way, and by use of illustrations which they understood, he was able to reach them with his message. He could speak for more than an hour without searching for words.

The organization had many brilliant speakers, but most of them could not interpret international happenings as they affected our people. Some were too lazy even to study local conditions, as they traveled from state to state and from city to city, in order to be able to speak on conditions, not with just a passing reference but with deep understanding and pronouncement. Mainly, they studied set speeches, and delivered them with all the natural expression of pathos and humor of an emotional people. In this way many of them swayed delegates to vote them into highly paid offices, but afterwards when called on to speak without preparation they flopped or, often, excused themselves from speaking at all. Unfortunately, too, these speakers would not write for the newspapers, and most newspapermen for the cause were not good speakers.

There is a big difference between a hired speaker and a speaker dedicated to a cause. The latter is so keen, that he can sense hostility in an audience, even if it is in the thought-wave of a person without any outward demonstration of it—which in fact there could not be in a Garvey meeting because the unanimity of the crowd would not countenance hostile expressions. Sometimes hired spies are there; then the speaker must be gifted enough to swing his speech deploring the baseness of the Judases within the race, when all should be serving to build instead of helping to destroy.

During our trip from New York to California, the statements in a leading white magazine contrasted so violently with that of a colored newspaper that I made them the subject of one of my articles, and Garvey used them in his speeches. One Midwestern newspaper stated: "The white man has made many concessions that it was thought he would not make. What is needed, is to teach the Negro to measure up to meriting the concessions he demands."

This was the suggested program for our people. On the other hand reenslavement was proposed by H. L. Mencken, then dean of American writers, in the December 1923 issue of *Smart Set*—called the aristocrat of magazines—published in New York City. Under the heading, "The crime of January 1, 1863," he surveyed the conditions of colored people from the time of slavery to the present, and came to a brutal but frank conclusion:

> The present parlous condition of the late Confederate States, with the native blackamoors emigrating to the rolling mills, illicit distilleries and jazz-palaces of the North by the hundred thousand, will probably give some pause to the surviving proponents of the old doctrine that chattel slavery was economically sound. Was it? indeed! Then try to imagine Georgia under chattel slavery, getting into the appalling economic condition that it labors under today. One of the leading bankers of the state is authority for the estimate that the departure of field-hands will cost its cotton growers $20,000,-000 this year. Certainly they never suffered any such staggering loss under slavery. The slave may have been an indifferent workman, but he at least did some work.

The truth is that the plan of remedying the acknowledged evils of slavery by abolishing it altogether was as extravagant and imprudent as the plan of cutting off a man's head to cure his headache. As a matter of historical fact, it was not adopted with any such nonsensical intention; it was adopted simply as a device of harassing and punishing the confederates. Unluckily, it set a precedent which still harasses and punishes all of us. . . .

If, as was widely held at the time, chattel slavery was full of defects, then the obvious remedy was to search them out and remove them. Most of them had been detected and cured 1,500 years before by the Romans. For example, the custom which allowed a slave-owner to separate a slave family. A few simple reforms of that sort, most of which would have been supported by the overwhelming majority of Southerners, and the slaves would have ceased to fret under bondage. As everyone knows, the complete freedom that was suddenly thrust upon them demoralized them almost unanimously, and brought upon them a host of woes. Before ten years had come and gone, the white Southerners, in self-defence, had to take their liberty away from them, again by extralegal devices—this setting another evil precedent. In most parts of rural Georgia today the black field-hand is almost as much a slave as his grandfather was on December 31, 1862. He is not permitted to exercise any of the common rights of citizenship, he is deprived of equality before the law by being denied a trial by his peers, and now the alarmed cotton-growers are even trying to take away from him his right to free movement. The only right that remains to him is the right to acquire and hold property. This right was enjoyed by all slaves under the Roman Empire; many of them grew far richer than any Southern Aframerican is today. In addition these Roman slaves got honest justice in the courts, and many of them were permitted to travel. The free Aframerican is thus worse off than they were. More important still, his vain efforts to obtain his theoretical rights have caused him to be disliked intensely; the Roman slave was popular, and often rose to positions of public eminence. . . . These blackamoors shiver when they hear the word SLAVERY, though the thing itself would unquestionably rescue them from most of their current troubles.

They'd rather be "Free" chained to an upright rail with a pyre of fat pine-knots under them, than "Slave" in a comfortable cabin, with plenty of hog-meat in the smoke house and no tax bills to pay.

The energies dissipated to destroy Garvey were badly needed to help build up our race and counteract racial reactionaries.

The phrase "Back to Africa" was a label tagged on to the U.N.I.A. in ridicule, as it implied mass migration, even good-riddance to undesirables. In a convention speech he explained the loyalties and rights of our people:

> To fight for African redemption does not mean that we must give up our domestic rights for political justice and industrial rights. It does not mean that we must become disloyal to any government or to any country wherein we were born. Each and every race outside of its domestic national loyalty has a loyalty to itself; therefore, it is foolish for the Negro to talk about not being interested in his own racial, political, social and industrial destiny. We can be as loyal American citizens or British subjects as the Irishman or the Jew, and yet fight for the redemption of Africa, and complete emancipation of the Race.

Then he made the following prediction:

> Out of the unsettled state and condition of the world will come such revolutions that will give each and every Race that is oppressed the opportunity to march forward. The last world war brought the opportunity to many heretofore subject races to regain their freedom. The next world war will give Africa the opportunity for which we are preparing. We are going to have wars and rumours of wars. In another twenty or thirty years we will have a changed world, politically, and Africa will not be one of the most backward nations; but Africa shall be, I feel sure, one of the greatest commonwealths that will once more hold up the torchlight of civilization and bestow the blessings of freedom, liberty and democracy upon all mankind.

CHAPTER TWENTY-ONE

In May 1924, Dr. DuBois became so indignant and impatient that Garvey had not "gone" yet, that he issued this edict to his readers in the same month's issue of the magazine *Crisis*, the organ of the N.A.A.C.P.:

> The American Negroes have endured this wretch all too long with fine restraint . . . but the end has come. Every man who apologizes for, or defends Marcus Garvey from this day forth, writes himself down as unworthy of the countenance of decent Americans. . . . Garvey is without doubt the most dangerous enemy of the Negro Race in America and the world.

Many Communist workers tried to infiltrate into the ranks of the U.N.I.A., and in so doing studied the leader and the movement. Among them was Robert Minor who, covering the convention of 1924 for his paper, the *Daily Worker*, gave us insight into what black intellectuals, particularly Dr. DuBois and George Schuyler, thought of Garvey and his movement; he gave the following considered opinion:

> The Negro intellectual, George Schuyler, writes in irony: "Like an inspiration from heaven, the idea dawned upon him (Garvey) one evening at dinner, and absently thrusting the remainder of the pig foot into his overall pocket, he sat for hours in his favorite trash box" etc., etc., and "still Mr. Garvey enjoys the enviable record of collecting more money in a given time than any other Negro. Nor was this from the idle, self-satisfied, wealthy, upper class Negroes. No, Sir! It came from the great masses; the washerwomen, porters, maids and other hard-working people. That in itself shows whom this great man was looking for."

This is intended as the most biting sarcasm. But the careful reader will catch two important points: First, Garvey is irresistibly associated with "overalls." Second, Garvey's followers are invariably classed as "hard-working people," such as washerwomen, porters and hod carriers, day laborers, etc. When we discover this, we get a key to the Garvey organization, which is not the key its enemies intended to give us.

And out of the sarcasm of the intellectual and genteel Negro leaders who despise Garvey, we get another key in the constant references to "his five year semester in geology in the Federal University of Leavenworth," to use again the language of Mr. Schuyler, who finds a subject for humor in Mr. Garvey's sixty days in the Tombs (prison), and the government's consent "to board him and furnish exercise at Leavenworth for five years."

I would think long before I would dispute the judgment of the Negro scholar Dr. DuBois about Garvey and his organization. . . . But I get a different reaction from that intended by Dr. DuBois. I am obliged to look beyond the details at the apparent fact that a government which hates and despises the Negro masses, a government which hates the working classes, and which has never been unforgiving to grafting schemes, that such a government does not find a friend in Garvey.

And above it all towers the fact that the Universal Negro Improvement Association, the largest organization of Negroes in the world, is made up almost entirely of the working class.

I am waiting for some Negro leader who has organized more Negroes than Marcus Garvey has organized, to criticize Garvey, and I frankly confess that if such a leader has been given a longer term in Leavenworth than Garvey received, I will listen to him more attentively.

The lickspittles of capitalism in Washington do not love Marcus Garvey. This alone ought to make any one of the working class think twice before condemning the man. His enemies say the government condemns Garvey for using questionable financial methods for the purpose of fleecing the masses of uneducated Negro workers. But I don't think the Teapot Domers at Washington have any objection to the fleecing of the Negro masses.

I think their solicitude is based upon something else. The fact that Garvey is organizing many thousands of Negroes of the class that is destined to take over the earth, and make a militant demand for a sweeping international liberation of colonial peoples, seems to me to be a more likely reason why Messrs. Coolidge, Dougherty and, yes, Mr. Hughes of the State department, have interested themselves in Garvey.

I heard Garvey speak last night. He is one of the most powerful personalities that I have ever seen on the platform. He is of the rare type that history finds rising in every unsettled period to express new currents among the masses of men. For weal or woe, Garvey is of the stuff that Leaders (or every powerful misleader) are made of. Not the kind of leaders who rise in times of quiet and fit their environment as a fashion model fits the gowns of the day; but the kind of leaders that rise in times of storm and stress, who do not fit their environment, who look and feel and act out of place in the order of the day—who are called uncouth, who are jeered as misfits, and yet who may form the heads of the battering rams which smash down the walls of their environments.

Eric Walrond, in an article in the January 3, 1929, issue of the magazine *The Independent*, points out that DuBois's persistent attacks on Garvey had not had the desired effect on colored people. On the contrary, like a rubber ball, the harder he was hit, the higher he soared. Reasoned Mr. Walrond:

Garvey out on bail, while DuBois asked for his repatriation, held his Fourth International Convention of Negroes in New York, from August 1 to 31; to which came three thousand Negroes from various parts of the globe. Undaunted, unswerved by the enemy's fire, by an uncanny turn of Fate, Garvey—so far as the black masses are concerned—is still at the helm. Steering the Negro Ship of State, and doing it with the old characteristic fire and spirit. Forever hitting at the high spots of the old international Negro problem. It is natural that he should excite the wrath of Negroes like DuBois in America, and Herbert George DeLisser in Jamaica—men who put national above racial consciousness. Yet, through some Divine mystery, Garvey is the Moses of the black masses. Instead of diminishing, his power is growing daily. It is one of the anomalies of the complex racial problem of the age.

CHAPTER TWENTY-TWO

The Fourth Convention was preceded by a parade that had the people wondering how a man out on bail could retain the love and confidence of his followers. Paintings of the Ethiopian Christ, "Man of Sorrows," and a black Madonna and Babe, were borne in the parade by robed choristers. The opening mass meeting was held at Carnegie Hall. The Rev. Van Richards, Chaplain to the Senate of Liberia, was among the prominent Africans in the parade and at meetings. The miraculous success of Garvey, despite all his enemies did to malign him and smash every practical effort of his, was past understanding. Now there was a chance perhaps that he might win his appeal. What then? He would be able to apply for his final papers for citizenship, and could not be deported.

On the fifth of August, while the convention was in full swing, he was arrested again, this time for allegedly filing incorrect income tax returns for the year 1921, when he had been kept out of America for five months. His attorney succeeded in obtaining bail for him at an additional $2,500. Did that lessen the prestige of Garvey because the colored press called him a fraud and a jailbird? People joined the organization by the thousands when delegates flashed home news of what was happening in New York City. They felt it was an affront to the race, and a deeply laid plot by many, using various means to destroy and disperse their organization. Thus the work went on with renewed vigor, and a rededication to Garveyism, regardless of what happened to Garvey the man. A white reporter, summing up the attitude of the man-on-the-street wrote: "Everybody is talking about Garvey—Garvey good, or Garvey bad—it is Garvey."

At one of the sessions of this convention, a letter was drafted and later sent to President Coolidge requesting an official investigation into conditions in Haiti as described by the members of the Haitian Delegation. The *New York American* reported as follows:

> Theodore Stephens, speaker for the Delegation from Haiti, spoke to the Delegates at length in an impassioned plea for assistance on the part of the Universal Negro Improvement Association on behalf of the "down-trodden Islanders."
>
> It is sad to state, Stephens proclaimed, "that the American Government, through its many representatives in Haiti, has, and even now is, in defiance of the protestations of the whole country, still violating and ignoring many of its prescriptions."
>
> The Haitian charged that the construction which had been forced upon the people at the point of the bayonet, was being violated by American officials, and that the Commander-in-Chief of the American forces, assisted lately by a High Commissioner from the American Government, rules supreme—hiding his hands and responsibilities behind the shadow of a sham President, who himself was born of a French father, and therefore not eligible to the office he now holds.
>
> Marcus Garvey yesterday addressed the Convention, urging that travel should be encouraged among the leaders of the Colored race to better fit them for leadership. "Lack of progress of the Negro in America," Garvey stated, "is due greatly to the fact that the American Negro leader is handicapped in the knowledge of world affairs. As a rule he is known only in his own community, and he indignantly rejects the idea of reaching out beyond his own little sphere. This very lack of knowledge has been the chief cause for the opposition to the U.N.I.A. in its program of international expansion in industry, commerce, and politics for the Negro."

Another subject which had far-reaching effect was the convention resolution that though God is a spirit, as we all know, nevertheless when we visualize Him, He must be in our own image and likeness. Remarked an old woman from Alabama, "No white man would die on the cross for me." A delegate from Mississippi said, "The Man of Sorrows ain't nothing else but a Colored Man"—to which many said, "Amen, brother." Rev. J. Barbour of Abyssinia referred to

John caught up in the grand Council of God on the Isle of Patmos, describing Christ as "a black man with feet that shone as polished brass, hair of lamb's wool, and eyes with flame of fire." Said a delegate from Boston to a newsman at the end of the session, "We haven't let God down. We have elevated Him in our minds, as the Spiritual Perfection of our sinful human selves."

The discussion became one of the general subjects of religion, which the chair ruled should be discussed at another session. When this subject did come up, and was thoroughly aired by both clergy and laity, the pious and the worldly, it was decided that, as there are Moslems and other non-Christians who are Garveyites, it was not wise to declare Christianity the official religion of the organization; but by establishing the Temple of God in each heart, and letting our every word and action be motivated from that Source, we could reach a state of inner serenity so as to enable us to establish on earth the Fatherhood of God and the Brotherhood of Man—a belief which is the basis of recognized religions. Christians who were not members of a church could join the African Orthodox Church; but all church members should bear this in mind: that God is everywhere, not just in churches on Sundays; that attendance at church was for Christian fellowship, and rededication to righteous living.

Many of the colored newspapermen viewed this declaration on the image of God with disfavor. They ignored the fact that it was a subject exhaustively discussed in the convention and decided on. To them, "The black Kluxer now wanted Colored folk to worship a black God." But the white influential newspaper, the *New York Journal*, revealed in its editorial the following:

> Marcus Garvey, President-General of the Universal Negro Improvement Association, offers one reasonable suggestion. He says, "God tells us to worship Him in our own image. We are black, and to be in our image, God must be black."

He insists, therefore, on a black God for colored people, with black saints, and in addition demands the whole of Africa for the colored race.

Mr. Garvey's idea of adapting God to the racial color is not entirely new. Missionaries in Africa long ago showed divine personages with black faces in order to make it easier to convert the Africans. Their primitive minds could not in a hurry get used to the idea of a white-faced divinity.

Today, on the edge of the Mediterranean, in Northern Africa, you might see a famous holy image, jet black, offering comfort to many dark-skinned Christian mariners. The color pleases them and doubtless does not annoy any divine being.

Similarly, good missionaries among the North American Indians, in their preaching, emphasized those parts of the Old Testament telling of the Lord's battles and victories, and the great number KILLED on each occasion. They realized that Indians would be converted to a victorious FIGHTING god much more easily than to any peaceful, forgiving deity. Men WORSHIP what they RESPECT and what they consider to be fairly good imitations of themselves.

As to the blacks OWNING AFRICA, that's surely reasonable. It's their country.

Incidentally they have owned it, all except a few thousand years, for endless centuries. Even in Egypt, where the Ptolemies were merely "new rich" and the Egyptians rank intruders, the black race ruled once. Their traits are proved in the Ethiopian face, the thick lips, high cheek-bones of the Sphinx. Mr. Garvey says, "When the white men were living in caves, we Negroes gave them a civilization that they have snatched away from us." There may be something in that. Some historians agree, in part, with Mr. Garvey.

But civilization belongs to him who has it, and knows how to use it. The Japanese seek to take it from us and improve on it. Honor to them, if they make a better success of it.

CHAPTER TWENTY-THREE

Between 1922-24 the K.K.K. had gained a large following in the North in reaction to the influx of thousands of colored southerners who had left the Bow-weevil cotton farms, and established themselves in the northern industrial towns and cities, where they had greater opportunities to work in factories and plants, better educational facilities, and "good times."

The *New York Herald* of Sunday, March 18, 1923, in its magazine section carried a page of pictures of northern Klansmen in full dress. Under the caption, "Ku Klux Klansmen Coming into the Open," the news article stated:

> The remarkable and unusual photograph reproduced above, shows hooded members of the George Washington Klan as they attended services last Sunday night, their identity concealed, at the Grace Methodist Episcopalian Church in Newark, New Jersey. . . . The Klansmen were welcomed by the Minister, the Rev. Paris E. Greenly, who introduced "The Exalted Cyclops" to the Congregation. . . . The Klan is gaining ground substantially in West Virginia, Maryland, New York and Northern States. The Department of Justice has no intention of moving against the Klan now. President Harding has manifested no special interest. Assistant Attorney General Crim sent the Attorney General, before he became ill, the names of more than three hundred Federal employees, who belong to the Klan, and recommended that he ask the President to dismiss them from the service. That report is still on the desk of the Attorney General.

In Washington, "Protectors of white neighborhoods," after service at United Brethren Church—one thousand men and women singing "Onward Christian Soldiers," with 300 automobiles and carrying homemade weapons—marched on homes of Negroes in the northwestern section of the capital. The pictorial section of another Sunday paper showed a Klan wedding in Youngstown, Ohio.

There are different kinds of Kluxers; some wear masks, others do not. Some lynch Negroes, others starve them economically. Some are registered members, others are active sympathizers. Here is an example of the admiration of the K.K.K. for the prosperous Jew: At Fairfield, Illinois, September 1924, 15,000 white people participated in the Ku Klux Klan festivities in honor of Manny Steiner, local Jewish merchant on his fiftieth business anniversary. The Rev. H. G. Markley, pastor of the Presbyterian Church, and Secretary of the local Klansmen, made the principal address.

Rev. Caleb Ridley, a white man, addressing an audience in Convention Hall, Tulsa, Oklahoma, August 11, 1921, said that the Klan was organized "to protect the weak, innocent and defenceless from the outrages of the violent, the lawless and the brutal." But, said he, "A white man is a white man, whether he lives in New Jersey, Indiana, Oklahoma or Georgia; and a white man's job is to see that civilization comes under the dominion of no inferior race, so long as he lives."

The Call, in its issue of May 19, 1923, sarcastically suggested university courses in the art of lynching:

> The charming tale of the lynching-bee at Columbia, Missouri, the seat of the University of Missouri, with students as enwrapped and approving spectators of the glorious deed, brings to mind a suggestion which we have often wanted, but have lacked opportunity until now, to make. We refer to the idea, wholly and proudly our own, that the art of lynching be made a regular part of the curriculum in the colleges and universities of this country. Every reason, at once of commonsense and of idealism, would seem to support the recommendation. Here is lynching, a well-recognized and thoroughly established institution of our American life. Patriotic citizens are again and again called upon to join lynching parties, and do their share in stringing up nooses, piling faggots, and shooting roasted corpses. It is inevitable, in lack of proper training, that the process should frequently be carried out in bungling and halting fashion. Hence the advisability, nay the necessity, of education in the art! Let every freshman in every

institution of higher learning be made to take "Lynching 1," as a required course. Instruction should include the history of the practice, its unique relation to the democratic ideals of American life, its justification from legal and ethical standpoints, together with a survey of the best approved methods. Higher courses for juniors and seniors should take up special points as how to roast the victim slowly, how best to torture women, laboratory tests for securing the maximum of pain and ignominy. Specimen "Niggers" for practice tests could undoubtedly be secured in abundance from Georgia jails and Florida peonage camps. That the students would welcome an innovation of this kind is shown impressively by what took place at the University of Missouri, on April 29 last. We might add that we have not copyrighted this idea, but pass it on gratis to our seats of learning East and West.—Unity.

The Communists now conceived a plan whereby they could play Garvey against the Klan, then worm their way into his organization. They had handbills distributed just before the August 1924 convention, challenging him to declare against the Klan if he was not in alliance with them. Garvey's answer was that since the Communists were organized to overthrow governments, and establish their own system, it should be very easy for them to uproot the Klan. They infiltrated in some of the branches, and secretly sent delegates to the convention, who moved a motion that the organization, in the interest of its members, should declare war on the Klan. The majority of delegates were in jitters: What would happen to them and their homes, when they went back South, if such a resolution was carried? Since the government would not suppress what was accepted as a legitimate organization, Garvey and his followers would be committing suicide to declare war on them. Yet the Communists expected him to take their bait and order his members to don black hoods and gowns and go into action. Tactfully he was able to put through a motion that was mild yet not compromising, condemning the alleged atrocities committed in the name of the Klan. After this incident, the

Communists revealed their true intentions in the *Daily Worker*, August 9, 1924:

> The reason for our working with the Universal Negro Improvement Association, is because we desire to win over the masses, organizationally and ideologically following this Association for the Communist program. . . . It is our task in working amongst the masses found here, to supplant the present weak, and hesitant leadership, with a virile, class conscious, and aggressive Communist leadership. We are aiming to win over these Negro masses to fight under a genuine revolutionary leadership, to fight for the Negro Workers on a class basis. In the course of our propaganda and activity in this field we will not hesitate to expose and mercilessly criticize all those, whether it be Garvey, or any other of the present leaders, who stand in the way of the achievement of our fullest program—the Communist program . . . under the leadership of the world Communist Party International.

The *Black Despatch* later warned our people about being used as tools by Communists. The editor pointed out:

> Communism offers graver dangers to Negroes, than to white people. . . . We are sure that those in control of the established order would, in case of open physical conflict use the Negro as an object lesson for recalcitrant white folk. We should be slow to lead the mass of black folk to a slaughter house in attempting to replace the social and economic balance wheels of the nation.

Communism was one of the many insidious oppositions Garvey had to combat; but the rectitude of his pleas gave him moral arguments that his opponents dared not dispute on their merit for fear of expressing the selfishness and personal hate that underlay their attacks, so they countered with subversive stratagems within and without the organization. His life was so closely meshed with the fate of his race, that every trial or triumph of his, was symbolic of the crucible through which the entire race was passing. He was the living dynamo that motivated the Negro masses of the world in thought and action. The statesmen of imperial powers realized this. Their financial, industrial and commercial supremacy depended on the raw material and mineral wealth of Africa. If they could silence him, it would take years before as powerful a duplicate could be found to create equally forceful activities and concerted action at the periphery, as at the center of the Negro world. Asia was slipping from their grasp, so Africa must be held at all costs. Thus the "Garvey must go" campaign had the backing of forces with millions at stake, and the prestige of European supremacy in the balance. But the minds of the masses were fully awakened and producing local leaders. Ideas cannot be destroyed once they have become the ideals of millions of people.

CHAPTER TWENTY-FOUR

In May 1920, the Executive Council of the U.N.I.A. decided to send a delegation to Liberia to negotiate with the government regarding colonization over there. It was difficult to get passports in a hurry, which was necessary since they wanted a reply for the August convention; so only Elie Garcia was able to go, as he had a Haitian passport. He was given the rank of commissioner and empowered to negotiate all business.

In a letter dated June 8, 1920, addressed to Hon. C. King, President of Liberia, Mr. Garcia stated the purposes of his mission, and specifically stated that,

it is the intention of the U.N.I.A. to establish trade routes through a line of steamships etc., to encourage emigration to build up the country, to transfer its Headquarters to Liberia, to bring with it medical and scientific units, etc. Therefore the Organization asks for a written assurance that every facility will be given it to procure lands for business, agriculture and industrial purposes. In return the Organization with its vast membership will lend financial and moral support to the Government to help her out of her present economic plight.

After many interviews, inspection of sites, and collection of statistics, the Government and people signified their happiness in having the U.N.I.A. operate in Liberia. The following is one of the official letters, quoted in full because of what transpired later on:

> Department of State,
> Monrovia, Liberia.
> June 14th, 1920.

Sir,   Ref. 248—L.

The President directs me to say in reply to your letter of June 8th setting forth the objects and purposes of the Universal Negro Improvement Association that the Government of Liberia, appreciating as they do the aims of your Organization as outlined by you, have no hesitancy in assuring you that they will afford the Association every facility legally possible in effectuating in Liberia its industrial, agricultural and business projects.

> I have the honor to be,
> Sir,
> Your Obedient Servant,
> Edwin Barclay,
> Secretary of State.

The convention delegates were jubilant on receipt of the news, but Garcia also sent a long confidential report to Garvey, describing among other things, the character of the officials of the government, and the existing feudal system. Gabriel Johnson, Mayor of Monrovia, and delegate to the convention, was elected Potentate. On returning home, at a banquet, Mr. Cassell, President of Liberia College, proposed a toast to "Potentate Johnson—the first Negro in the World." President King, in anger and jealousy, lifted his glass and said, "I drink to the health of the Mayor of Monrovia." Although they were related by marriage the enmity started because of the feeling that the international organization would overshadow the Liberian government.

After many detailed arrangements between the government and the Potentate for the organization, a group of six men were sent to Liberia. They consisted of: Marke, Deputy Potentate; Critchlow, Secretary; McLeod, surveyor; Henry, agricultural officer; Lawrence, pharmacist, and Jemmott, builder. Machinery and supplies were shipped with them, and subsequent shipments followed. Many Garveyites later joined the men.

In order to get the Potentate out of Liberia, he was offered the Consul Generalship at Fernando Po—the most lucrative post. He accepted, and resigned as Potentate. The indictment and closing down of the Black Star Line in the U.S. slowed down the work in Liberia.

In December 1923, the organization sent another delegation to Liberia consisting of: Henrietta Davis, Assistant President-General; Attorney Van Lowe, and Robert Poston, Secretary-General, to make arrangements for families, and a full scale colonization program. On arrival the delegation was given a reception and cordially treated. They had interviews with President King and other officials in which additional agreements were reached. A local advisory committee was appointed by the President. They were: Arthur Barclay, ex-President; D. E. Howard, ex-President; James Dossen, Chief Justice; Wilmot Dennis; Dongba Caranda 2nd; and Dixon Brown, Comptroller of Customs, Secretary to the Committee. This committee reserved the right to increase its numbers if required and sent a document dated February 16, 1924, by the delegates, setting out their recommendations to enable them to carry out their work.

On the return of the delegation to headquarters, the organization through its officers sent a long letter to President King, in which among other matters they approved of the local committee's recommendations, but in the matter of sites, asked for additional lands in other areas. The spirit of friendliness of the committee's chairman—Chief Justice Dossen—is shown in a letter dated Feb. 28, 1924, to Garvey:

It was a pleasure to the friends of emigration to note the general enthusiasm shown by our people in the program to send to Liberia Colonists of the Race in other lands, to help build up this nation, as well as to give an opportunity to Negroes abroad to enjoy the pure atmosphere of manly freedom. It is sincerely hoped that you will not fail to put over your great program. . . .

You will see that we have recommended that the first settlement be established on the Cavalla River. This locality offers many advantages to Traders, Miners, Farmers and other men of industry. Besides the climate is healthy. Please convey to my good friend John E. Bruce my kindest regards, also Rev. Ellegor. Wishing you and your Movement all success.

The local Liberian Committee sent a letter in May acknowledging receipt of communications, and setting out their plans to receive a batch of colonists in September.

From December 1923, when the delegates reported by letters the Liberian government's approval of the colonization plans, Garvey went ahead with the formation of another steamship line, called The Black Cross Navigation and Trading Company, and the purchase of one large ship to ply between Liberia and America, in keeping with the recommendations from Liberia. Later on they were to get a smaller coastal ship to trade on the West Coast of Africa, as there was a great need for this. The ship would act as a feeder for the larger vessel. This new company bought the S.S. *General Goethals,* paid $60,000 down and spent an additional $20,000 fitting it up for passengers and freight. All stocks were held by the U.N.I.A., which borrowed moneys from the members on terms of five to ten years for repayment. The ship was rechristened the *Booker T. Washington.*

March 17, 1924, Garvey held two monster mass meetings in Madison Square Garden, to launch the drive for this new venture, and also to herald the return of the delegates sent to Liberia. A petition was drawn up and sent to the President of the U.S., the League of Nations, and to all recognized governments, asking for consideration of the plan to found a nation in Africa for Negroes. In his speech, Garvey said that if America helped to establish this nation, they would, in the future, have a partner in the cause of real democracy on the continent of Africa, and at the same time end the existing resentment and bitterness of a suppressed and frustrated colored population. One of the speakers was Surrogate Judge John O'Brien, who said that many white people endorsed the plan and admired the courage of Garvey and his followers in trying to bring it to fruition.

In June 1924 the U.N.I.A. sent out a team of experts to prepare camps for the colonists. They were: O'Meally, commissioner; William Strange, mining and civil engineer; Roberts, electrical engineer; Walcott, shipwright and builder; Hurley, carpenter and builder; Nicholas, mechanical engineer, and Rupert Christian, Secretary. With these men went thousands of dollars of material for ready use on landing. Additional shipments on a later ship were contracted to be sent for, when there were storage facilities.

During this time, Dr. DuBois, in the role of Garvey's principal enemy, attended the second inaugural of President King in Liberia. He seemed to have so played on the ego of the President that when the experts landed they were promptly deported, and the shipment of materials seized. Chief Justice Dossen had died just a few weeks before, and regardless of the protests of the members of the local committee, President King acted as he did, contrary to and in utter disregard of all previous arrangements. He threatened members of his own government that he would take reprisals against them if they acted contrary to his new instructions. Large sums of money had to be collected immediately to send to the ousted men, whose families the organization also had to support; these men had given up good positions in order to serve the organization. They had to take any ship out of Liberia, then transship. Two of them were British subjects, and on their return to America were not allowed to land, but were sent back to Holland. From there, the organization had to pay their expenses, and ship them to their respective homes in the West Indies, and arrange for the care of their families, and their transportation to join them.

The delegates at the August 1924 convention despatched a letter to the Senate and House of Representatives of Liberia, setting out the entire arrangements made from the start, with copies of letters and documents attached, and asking them to right a wrong affecting the lives of so many people, and restore the tremendous financial loss and suffering incurred by them, through the actions of President King.

In the meantime the Associated Press in Washington, D.C. gave out this press release, August 26th: "The Government of Liberia, in a formal communication delivered by Ernest Lyon, Consul General, has advised the Washington Government that it is 'irrevocably opposed both in principle and in fact to the incendiary policy of the Universal Negro Improvement Association, headed by Marcus Garvey.' The note was signed by Edwin Barclay, Secretary of State for Liberia [the same man who wrote the letter of acceptance to the organization's plan]." At no time did President King or Secretary Barclay notify Garvey or his organization that they had changed their attitude and intended to cancel previous arrangements. Their actions were timed to throw panic in the minds of the convention delegates particularly, and generally to cause the members to lose heart; but the members took the blows bravely.

Following up his pronouncement, Ernest Lyon as Liberian Consul General required of every person desiring a visé to "make an affidavit before a Notary declaring that you are not connected with the Garvey Movement." President King had all the machinery and materials shipped by the organization sold, and kept the money; some of the supplies were spoilt, as they were not properly housed. He censored mails of those friendly to Garvey.

The organization's full page advertisement in the *New*

York World, June 25, 1924, setting out the whole project—sites and opportunities for colonists—brought the most unexpected turn of events, for white businessmen became interested in the minerals and rubber of Liberia. The front-runner was Firestone Rubber Company which negotiated and obtained a lease for ninety-nine years of concessions that were previously given to our organization. The terms of this lease reflect the selfishness, greed and utter disregard for the general welfare of the people of the country. Edwin Barclay bore this out. When on a visit to the U.S. in August 1925, the *New York Times* reported him as having stated:

> The Firestone Rubber Company has a concession of one million acres, and can have as much more land as it desires. . . . Labor is very cheap in Liberia, and strong, healthy men work for 25 cents a day. . . .
>
> Neither Garvey nor any of those who have been identified with him will be received in Liberia.

The honorable King and Barclay had not only satisfied themselves but America by putting her in the rubber-producing field, enabling her to supply her factories. England and France as empire neighbors were also happier to have Firestone (although a competitor) on their borders than colonies of Garveyites. President King was awarded an honor by France, and an English battleship took him on a trip to Sierra Leone. What he did not care to understand and appreciate was that the substance of freedom for any people is economic security. Even political control is reduced to a shadow government, when the ownership and control of industry, commerce and scientific development are in the hands of aliens.

In view of the fact that the United States of America had established Liberia for all colored people in the Western world, the U.N.I.A. drew up a petition to the President requesting him to negotiate with President King for an open door into that Republic. Article 5, section 13 of the constitution of that country reads: "The object of forming these

Colonies being to provide a home for the dispersed and oppressed children of Africa, and to regenerate and enlighten this benighted continent. None but persons of color shall be admitted to citizenship in this Republic." This latter paragraph was amended later to read, "Negroes or persons of Negro descent."

Millions of persons signed the petition, adding their addresses and occupations; but it was not until September 3, 1924, that a delegation was able to have audience with President Coolidge, and present same. The *New York Times* of the 4th reported as follows:

> Washington, D.C.—A Petition on behalf of 4,000,000 alleged to be members of the Universal Negro Improvement Association, of which Marcus Garvey is President-General, and concerning whose activities the Authorities of Liberia recently filed a protest, was presented to President Coolidge today.
>
> The Petition was presented by G. Emonie Carter, Secretary General of the Organization, heading a Delegation of six. It asked President Coolidge to submit to Congress at the next session a "Message embodying the sentiment of this petition," and asked the President to assist in creating "through the Republic of Liberia, which was founded through the efforts of liberal white Americans, an open door" for the reception of Negroes from the United States.
>
> The leader of this Movement, the Hon. Marcus Garvey, the petition asserted, "has been wickedly persecuted by agencies under the control of your government; and leave was asked to draw to your Excellency's attention the unfriendly act of two of your Excellency's recent Representatives in Liberia—Solomon Porter Hood and W. E. B. DuBois, in working against the interest of the Universal Negro Improvement Association in that country, being members of a rival Organization, and who used their Official positions to create prejudice against our Cause, because of jealousy and rivalry."
>
> The Memorial declares that with the growth in numbers and efficiency of the Negro Race in the United States, race conflicts seem certain to arise, and it urges the President to

use his good influence to repatriate American Negroes to Africa, and in the development of such independent Negro nations as are now existing.

The following comments on the "raw deal" Garvey got were made by the editor of the *New York Evening Bulletin*, August 29, 1924, when he investigated the matter at a high level. He stated:

> The gang now controlling Liberia oppose Garvey's entrance and they want no one in his organization, fearing, of course, that their own game will be spiked.
>
> Here are a few facts for you to consider:
>
> 1. Liberia protests against Garvey to President Coolidge.
> 2. Harvey Firestone, rubber tire King, goes to Plymouth with Edison and Henry Ford and plays a part in the "Old Sap Bucket" drama, enjoying the President's hospitality on the "Colonel's" farm.
> 3. Liberia grants Harvey Firestone a concession, which gives him absolute control of 1,000,000 acres of land where crude rubber is procurable.
>
> This land is the most valuable rubber-growing territory available in the world; the British Empire controls practically all the rest. . . . When Garvey says there is something rotten in the state of Liberia you should not dismiss his allegations. Perhaps he knows what he is talking about.
>
> He thinks Liberia's rubber supply should belong to his race, not to Firestone. Is there anything dangerous or menacing in that belief?

Some of the evils of President King's administration were brought to the attention of the world by the International Slavery Commission from the League of Nations in 1930. Dr. Christie who headed the investigating committee in Liberia, writing in the British Royal Geographical Society's *Journal*, stated that "the U.N.I.A. would have tremendously improved conditions in Liberia, and helped the country to progress on modern lines."

The presence of the committee in Liberia caused some of the detailed reports to come through the mails, which the

Negro World published. Very briefly conditions were: At periods the chief of each tribe was told that he must provide as many as two hundred able-bodied men according to his population. These men were shipped to Fernando Po as laborers. Most of them never returned. High government officials were paid for each worker supplied. If a chief, because of sympathy for the men's families, refused to let some of the men leave, he had to pay ten pounds ($50) in lieu of each man, and sometimes was flogged before his followers for "disobeying the President's orders."

Under the protection of the investigating committee on slavery, mass meetings were held all over the Republic, culminating in a huge demonstration in Monrovia, at which the people, through their chosen representatives, drew up a petition calling for the resignation of President King and Vice-President Yancy. The detailed charges against them involved: "Forced labour, slavery, gross maltreatment of the indigenous populations, and official misconduct while in office of bribery, extortion, dishonesty and other crimes." This document was signed on the first of October, 1930 by: D. E. Howard, Chairman of Committee, Dongba Caranda, R. Van Richards, W. H. Blaine, J. E. Padmore, J. I. Weeks, and N. H. Sie-Brownell, Secretary to Committee. Copies of this document were sent to the United States and other governments and the League of Nations.

At a League meeting, England's Lord Cecil—who had in mind a greater West Africa for his country—advocated a League Mandate for Liberia by "a country that can be trusted." Messrs. King and Yancy resigned, and Edwin Barclay became President; but the threat the League posed made him more cautious in his administration.

Even if the Liberian government had honored its agreements with the U.N.I.A. and the colonization plans had developed, Garvey never intended to live permanently in Liberia. He would have dropped the title of Provisional President of Africa, which was created to draw off watchfulness from the activities of the Potentate in Africa: "The more you look, the less you see." Nor did he propose to be the administrator of the colony, as he would always be suspected by Liberian officials of having political ambitions in their one-party government. His intention was to retain his substantive position of President-General of the U.N.I.A., which, through conventions, could empower him to act in any capacity, or create any office—without portfolio—to enable him to travel everywhere and seek support for the colony. For, said he, the world is my province until Africa is free.

He was a restless person and did not like to be pinned down to detailed work. His thoughts were so rapid as to agitate his mind. He was an opportunist in that he could sense an opening where the average person could not, and exploit it to its exhaustion.

His answer to the question, "What form of government do you propose for Africa?" was "the type of government that the people need, to speed up their development along all lines." He argued that all the theories when put into practice fell short of expectations, for the temperament of a people and their enervating surroundings tend to alter the very intent of their principles. Even capitalism, in a developed country of Anglo-Saxon temperament, deteriorates under an exact class system; this tends to create a class without enough spending power, and thus overproduction. A rigid socialist system among primitive people in an undeveloped country would not attract capital—the lever of development.

As our people in Africa emerge from colonialism, they must evolve their own systems, taking into consideration the mental standard and temperament of the people of each locale; and not be hide-bound to white peoples' systems; for races interpret even the Christian religion to suit themselves and practice it according to their own lights.

When opportunity is accepted as a charitable gift, it is usually used as a child's Christmas present—pleasurably and seldom usefully, with the belief that next Christmas another will be forthcoming. If opportunity is to be used wisely and effectively, it must be the tool one fashions in the crucible of one's mind.

CHAPTER TWENTY-FIVE

The attitude of the colored press toward Garvey is clearly brought out in a letter of a reader to the editor of the *Amsterdam News*:

I have been a reader of the Amsterdam News for years, and have read the many attacks made on Marcus Garvey and his organization.

The Amsterdam News has never seen any good in Garvey and I have always passed up these attacks, because I understand the situation fairly well. But when the writer of your column "Colorful News Movies" made such a sweeping misrepresentation of this man it really seems the limit. This writer, whoever he is, knows that he not only misrepresented, but told a deliberate falsehood, when he said: "His (Garvey's) estimate of them (the Negro) was that they were inferior people, unfit to mingle with men as men and unable to comprehend the fulness of American freedom. It was his aim that they should be forever segregated from the society of the world, and until themselves develop a land of which for generations back the Negro people of America knew nothing."

It is true that Garvey has not tried to flatter the Negro of the progress he has made, as other leaders have, and as white folks like the Negro to believe. Would the Negro development of a land of his own mean to segregate him or would it bring him in contact with all other nations and races and raise his status to that of a real man? But, suppose for argument's sake he did not come in social contact with the white race. Why should one rather eat the crumbs from somebody else's table than eat a square meal from his own?

Garvey has never advocated inferiority, but has tried to impress upon the Negro the reason why he is accorded such treatment. Garvey has never advocated segregation, but has tried to make the Negro understand the reason why he is segregated. If that is advocating segregation, and inferiority, then our ministers are advocates of hell, when they try to show us the reason why we will go there unless we live certain lives. No man, no organization has done more to counteract the inferiority germ than Garvey and his organization. They have taken the Negro away back to the ancient glories of Ethiopia to make him feel he is not inferior; their attitude and propaganda have forced newspapers like the Evening Journal to admit editorially that the Negro gave civilization to the world. They have challenged white audiences from Columbia University and other places. When Negro newspapers would abolish the term "Negro" and substitute "colored," it was Garvey who came forward, took the name Negro from the rut and said: "They have given it to us, we will make it a name to be respected." And it was through Garvey that certain daily newspapers print the word Negro with a capital "N."

I am sorry that Mr. Garvey's idea of the Negro building up his own social system does not meet with the approval of my friends.

Yours truly,
Ulric Marshall

New York City, Feb. 21, 1925.

The white editor of the *New York Evening Bulletin,* August 2, 1924, chided those who ridicule Garvey, and challenged colored men to equal his achievement:

It has been the favorite sport of some New York newspapers to make fun of Marcus Garvey, the Negro leader, because he is prone to adapt long and high-sounding titles and voice extravagant claims, and because some of his enterprises have come to grief. Despite all this, has any other man of his race in the past century succeeded in assembling a more representative gathering of his people? Men and women from many countries and from almost every state have met in New York at Garvey's call; they are willing to follow his leadership. And even the worst enemy of Garvey must admit that there was logic and truth in the statements he made to the conven-

tion. Here are a few of his sentences which merit consideration:

"There is no value in flattery. I wouldn't flatter you to save
my life. And unfortunately we are the most careless and indifferent people in the world. Must I flatter you when England, France, Italy, Belgium and Spain are all concentrating
on robbing every square inch of African territory, the land of
our fathers?

"Must I flatter you when the cry is being loudly raised for a
white America, Canada, Australia and Europe, and a yellow
and brown Asia? I find all other peoples preparing themselves
for the struggle to survive, and you, still smiling, eating, drinking, dancing and sleeping away your lives, as if yesterday were
the beginning of the age of pleasure."

When one follows closely the activities of world powers,
and learns the policies motivating their actions, only then
can he understand and value the intensity of Garvey's
struggles, and the urgency of his appeals. The following
quotation from one of my articles to the *Negro World*,
March 28, 1925, proves the point:

H. H. Powers, a rather outspoken exponent of Imperialism,
writing in the Atlantic Monthly magazine, February 1925,
seeks to justify the actions of the Oppressor Race, when he
stated:

"Exploitation is the primary and legitimate aim of imperialism. . . . The weak, the ignorant, and the slothful races cannot
expect to remain undisturbed in their habitat. It is much that
they are allowed to remain at all, a concession rather to the
humanity of their betters than to their own right. Interference,
guidance and control are the indispensable conditions of this
tolerance. . . . We cannot leave them to their indolent siesta, if
they hold in accidental and unconscious keeping the energies
needed for advancing civilization."

The writer goes on to show that weak and oppressed peoples all over the world are clamoring for self-determination;
then he asks the question: "What would be the result of this
much-invoked race-forbearance, save to give the child of the
future a Hottentot for a father instead of a white man?" This

is the crux of the whole situation. If white nations were to honestly and sympathetically help and train Negroes along the road to self-government, when they reached the highest possible perfection they would become the masters of the world. Their physical strength, prowess in battle, virility as a race, and adaptability to strange surroundings, would tend in a few years to produce a splendid type of black humanity, whose very self-sufficiency would cause him to say, "I call no man master." Instead of the child of the future being a Hottentot, the man of the future would be a Negro.

The Imperialist writer closes his article with the arresting thought: "Will the world wait for child-peoples to grow to the measure of these requirements when it can displace them with better stock?"

The white man is determined to have all the world and its resources if possible, for himself and his posterity. The yellow man has sensed his selfish purpose, and is marshalling all the physical, mental and scientific forces at his command, and marching abreast of the white man to glory and to power. The yellow man's challenge to the white man is, "What is good for you, is also good for me, and I am going to take mine." The brown man within the last few years has opened his eyes to the fact that he too, should organize his forces, at least to hold his native habitat, and protect it for all times. Lastly comes the black man, late though he be, and says, "We are also in the fight for the survival of the fittest. God Almighty made us a separate and distinct race, and apportioned to us the great continent of Africa with the command, "Occupy until I come". . . .

If we must live, we must be strong. Power is the keynote of this age. When all races have acquired that, and reached a common plane of world achievements, each will grasp the hand of the other and say, BROTHER; until then, the struggle continues.

CHAPTER TWENTY-SIX

In January 1925, Garvey was informed by counsel that his appeal was listed on the calendar to come up in March. As he had to pay thousands of dollars for legal expenses, he planned a speaking tour, and gave his lawyer a copy of his itinerary, which noted dates, addresses and telephone numbers. He took me on this trip.

The case was pushed up on the calendar, and when we reached Detroit he received a telegram that the appeal was not allowed, and he must return and surrender. He wired back, "Coming on first train out." He also telephoned his New York office, and asked that they phone the lawyer's home, in case his office was closed.

On receiving the messages the lawyer contacted the District Attorney, and gave his personal undertaking that he would bring Garvey in the following morning, as he was on his way back to New York City; to this he agreed. The hours on the train were tense, although he anticipated a few day's stay in the Tombs prison, and to appeal to the Supreme Court for a review of his case. As the train was pulling in to the station at 125th Street, New York City, two United States marshals—whom he later understood boarded the train at a siding—came into our coach, and said to him, "Your name Marcus Garvey?" "Yes," he replied. "Well, you are under arrest." They immediately proceeded to handcuff him. Amos joined them, and mimicked Garvey as he was hustled off the train. "Good Lord, that's a bandit!" shouted a white woman, looking back at me in contempt.

When I telephoned the lawyer and the officers of the organization what had happened they were astounded. That night at Liberty Hall I had difficulty in preventing some of the members from demonstrating on the streets. I calmed them with the assurance—which I doubted—that justice eventually would prevail.

The next morning he was escorted into court handcuffed to guards. His lawyer asked for a stay of two days to allow him to adjust the organization's business; this was promptly denied. He was committed to Atlanta federal prison, in the South. His lawyer asked that he be sent to Leavenworth, Kansas, instead, as conditions in a Southern prison were hard on a black man; this was refused. We were told that the order for deportation was ready, and would be sent to Atlanta, so that it would be executed at any time he was released. To our amazement the District Attorney announced that he had forfeited the $15,000 bail bond. We had to engage counsel to fight in the courts for months until the amount was released, every cent of which we returned to the lenders.

He was taken to the Tombs prison to await a train for Atlanta. Some of the opposition newspapers carried the picture of him handcuffed, with captions such as "Good-bye Garvey, the Tiger bagged at last." The hour for him to be taken to the train was kept a secret, so members kept vigil outside the prison; the head nurse of the New York local moved into our flat. Legions took turns to watch the place. I packed an overnight case, and gave it to a member to take to Pennsylvania Station, and followed later. Another member bought a ticket for me. Others alerted all their porter (red cap) friends to let them know what train he was going on, and to help me on.

We waited hour after hour, afraid even to go and eat. Sandwiches were passed around. At last word came through; they had him in a baggage room downstairs. Just as the guard was calling out, "All aboard for Washington," we got the signal. Bag, ticket and money were pressed into my hands, down the stairs I ran, as a kindly porter helped me into a smoking car of the moving train. When he turned round and saw me, a triumphant flash of his eyes seemed to say, "I am glad you outwitted them."

A white conductor who punched my ticket informed me that I must go into another car. I did not budge, and showed no signs that I knew what he was talking about, so he concluded I was either deaf or did not understand English very well, and left me alone. Through the kindness of others in the coach he let me know that when we reached Washington, I should get a drawing-room compartment in the Pullman to Atlanta. Fortunately the members had given me enough money at the station, as one has to pay for three tickets in order to get this completely private room with toilet attached. There we were for the remainder of the trip. I had note books and took instructions for the officers, and "messages" for publication in the *Negro World*.

When the train arrived at Atlanta the following morning, in my anxiety, I rushed through the white waiting room, hailed a white, taxi, but was courteously reminded that, "Down here, white men can't drive colored people." I got an old cab at the colored section, and when close behind him tooted the horn a few times to let him know. On arrival at the prison, I went to the office, and was told that I could not see him for two weeks, but was given all instructions as to how I could send him money, letters, telegrams, gifts, and clothes. I spoke at the Atlanta division of the organization, and returned by express train to New York City. On arrival I telegraphed him.

The blank check which he had given me to close his personal account at the Chelsea Bank I gave to the chancellor, Mr. Bourne, to take to the manager, who knew all that had happened, to have balance filled in and cashed for me, as the rent was overdue, as were other household bills. To my amazement he brought back eight dollars, and a slip from the ledger clerk verifying this balance. I had to summon all my courage to face the situation: raise money for his defense fund, pay balance due lawyer and counsel, and have his case reviewed by the Supreme Court.

A few days after my return home, I was summoned to the District Attorney's office, and told to bring all bonds and securities. He was trying to collect the $1,000 fine and costs of the case. I went, and handed him the bonds and stock certificates from all the companies Garvey operated. Some were for cash, others for accrued salaries, for which I had attached yearly signed statements from the treasurer and chancellor, countersigned by the auditor. He looked through them carefully, handed them to a clerk, who made some notes and returned them to me; the hurt in my eyes were so eloquent, that he quickly dismissed me, saying, "You may go."

I had to do everything possible to get money for his defense fund, which was not only to pay legal expenses, but to keep him in that Southern prison in a manner that made his confinement tolerable. In order to prevent this money from being confiscated, I had to hide some of it in a bank in a nearby state, and a small amount in another bank in the old section of New York. In going to these banks to make deposits, I had to rise early in the mornings, and go by devious routes, remaining at railroad and subway stations until the banks opened. Many a morning I spent anxious moments wondering if any loiterer around was a detective or a thief. Sometimes the cold numbed my feet and hands, but concealed on my person was that precious money.

In my speeches and newspaper articles, I had to interpret national and international events as they affected our people, with forcefulness and a leader's acuteness. I treated his enemies to subtle, pitying sarcasm, that made them realize that they got "the law" to do for them what they failed to do—"get rid of Garvey." Ironically Garveyism was strengthened by their vicious attacks, so it was time for them to examine its program, to see what made it indestructible; then they would come to the conclusion that Garvey was neither the fool nor the rogue they had thought him. I won sympathizers and friends for him in hard-core opposition circles, who now felt that he was misunderstood because of his demeanor.

Every three weeks or so I went to Atlanta to see him; he planned speaking itineraries for me, to raise money for his fund; and I sent out collecting lists besides. His letters were

censored, yet many people wrote him. Wherever I traveled I
sent him telegrams of cheer and greetings from the members. At times he telegraphed for more money, or special
gifts which I was allowed to have sent direct from big
department stores such as Macy's or Gimbels. When he
wanted me to come at once, the suspense and anxiety until
the express reached there was awful. If there were any maneuvers going on that made him suspicious and dull, then I
had to spread joy, and plenty of it.

One of my most memorable experiences happened on a
southern trip. When I arrived in Baton Rouge the people
were tense and nervous; there had been a lynching there the
previous night, the horrors of which were related to me in
detail. They advised that I not speak and take the next train
out of town, as they did not want anything to happen to me.
True enough; but I could not run out on them like that;
they needed comfort and cheer. So we agreed to have an
early service. After the prayers and singing of hymns, I
preached the sermon. My text was from Isaiah 40, verses
1-6. "Comfort ye my people." By the moans from the "Amen
Corner," and expressions such as, "Tell it Sister, tell it!
Hallelujah!" I felt that they were indeed comforted.

After the service a doctor from a nearby town escorted
me to his car. Before driving off he placed his shotgun in a
contraption he had erected through the open windshield,
took out a big pistol and placed that beside him; turning to
me, he said, "Sister, get yours handy." I took out my "Colt."
Now, said he, "We are ready to travel; remember if we have
to go, we must take one with us." Silently we sped on,
peering into the darkness, and listening for possible pursuers. At last we made it. His father-in-law said he would
guard the house, just in case anyone prowled around looking for trouble. Early next morning on our way to the
station, the doctor said, "All of us can't leave the South, but
those who stay must be prepared to fight and die too, for
our rights."

The journeys to Atlanta were long and tiring, although I

used to take a businessmen's special extra-fare express, leaving New York City at 11 p.m., which gave me time to do a full day's work and perhaps speak at a meeting, leaving afterwards in a taxi to Pennsylvania Station. Next morning we changed engines in Washington, D.C. and continued on through Virginia, North Carolina, South Carolina, then Georgia, arriving there the following morning. One never knows what horrible incidents may occur on these trips, as colored people have been dragged out of Pullman coaches.

At the prison a guard is stationed in the room during interviews; we felt that a Dictaphone was there too, so we were careful in speaking. Federal prisoners are those who have broken federal laws. In prison at that time were a former warden of the prison, bankers, etc. One day I saw a thin, pale white man heavily manacled to guards, walking through the corridor to the main door. On inquiry I was told, "That's Dillinger, the celebrated mail-train robber; he escaped from here already; now he has to be taken in an armored car to the hospital to have his lungs X-rayed."

A few months after Garvey entered prison he got a pass as head cleaner which enabled him to go around the buildings for inspection of the work. He wore his own clothes, attended movies and ball games. He had a fine collection of books, which I ordered from time to time for him. Other prisoners did the chores for him and treated him as nicely as he did them. His appeal to the Supreme Court was denied; his only hope now of release was executive clemency.

Three months later he asked me to get together enough of his speeches, writings and extracts of the trial, and edit them for a book of about 400 pages; he wanted this done in a hurry, for if anything happened to him there was no record, other than the *Negro World*, of his speeches and frontpage messages, as newspapers more or less carried garbled reports to induce ridicule and contempt for him. I had already compiled a collection, which was published as a first volume, and the additional matter he revised. The difficulty was to get a publisher, as most of them did not want to handle "that stuff"; eventually I had to get the *Negro World*'s printer to do the printing and binding, but I had to do all the proofreading.

I thought I had done almost the impossible, when I was able to rush a first copy of Vol. II to him, but he callously said, "Now I want you to send free copies to Senators, Congressmen and prominent men who might become interested in my case, as I want to make another application for a pardon." When I completed this task I weighed 98 lbs., had low blood pressure and one eye was badly strained. Two doctors advised complete rest. I stayed with southern friends in Montclair, New Jersey; but it was only part-time rest, as I telephoned the flat daily, and went on weekends to clear up accumulated work. After two weeks he telegraphed me to come and bring all acknowledgments of books sent; then he informed me that as soon as I was stronger, I should make a list of the favorable ones, and go to the capital to lobby on his behalf.

Of the many acknowledgements of the books received, I cherish most the one from M. K. Gandhi, the Mahatma of India, dated May 12, 1926, from "The Ashram, Sabarmati, India." He addressed me as "Dear Friend."

In Japan, K. Mitsukawa published a book, *The Negro Problem*, referring to Garveyism as the "African Freedom Movement." On one page was the Red, Black and Green flag in colors. Dr. Nkrumah, Prime Minister of Ghana (formerly Gold Coast), in his book *Ghana* made the following admission: "I think that of all the literature I studied the book that did more than any other to fire my enthusiasm was the *Philosophy of Marcus Garvey* published by his wife."

While in this prison he wrote what he called his "Poetic Meditations." He never learned versification; they were a collection of poems revealing some of his thoughts at that time. Three of which were:

First, "The Black Woman," written February 28, 1927, of which the opening verse reads:

Black Queen of beauty, thou has given colour to the world,
Among other women thou art royal and the fairest,
Like the brightest of jewels in the regal diadem
Shin'st thou Goddess of Africa—Nature's purest emblem!

Second, a poem dedicated to me; strangely, he recites the many vicissitudes and bitter experiences in his life, but finds satisfaction in this verse:

But you have been a light to me,
A fond and dear and true Amie;
So what care I for falsest friend
When on your love I can depend.

What did he ever give in return? The value of a wife to him was like a gold coin—expendable, to get what he wanted, and hard enough to withstand rough usage in the process.

Third, a prediction for Africa. The opening verse conveys the theme:

Hail United States of Africa!
Hail Motherland most glorious, bright!
States in perfect Sisterhood united,
Born of Truth, mighty shalt thou ever be.

CHAPTER TWENTY-SEVEN

The question has often been asked: Why did he allow the convention to vote such a high salary scale for officers? In fact this has been regarded as "his biggest mistake." They had to be paid according to American wages, and their salaries besides had to offset the temptations of persistent approaches for them to become inside informers. Garvey felt that if a man was well paid, he would only succumb to those temptations if he were base at heart. It was extremely difficult to get trained men with the spirit of altruism. If an applicant were given an hour-long interview outlining the ideals and activities of the organization, the substance of his reply would be, "That's all very well, but I can't live on sentiment," or "What is in it for me? I have got to live good." They had imbibed the sordid materialism of the new country, America, and as a segregated people they were remote from the tempering effects of the various European cultures imported here as well.

Each officer, on being sworn in, had to subscribe to an oath of fidelity to the cause of African redemption thus: "Should I fail this Cause, may the Almighty Architect fail me in the purpose of life." They were voted into office by Delegates in Convention to serve four years, and could only be removed before expiry of this term by impeachment at a convention; although the President-General as administrator could suspend an officer from duties, yet his salary had to be paid.

Realizing the awful financial weight some of these lazy men were causing, it was discussed and resolved at the 1921 convention that officers should be paid salaries at the minimum—half of the maximum—and the maximum could only be reached by ability and fitness. The Secretary, whose duty it was to edit and insert amendments to the constitutions before reprinting, omitted this vital clause. It was not until ex-officers sued for "back salaries" that this was discovered. Up to 1926 (during Garvey's imprisonment) all the officers—except Miss Davis and Bishop McGuire—had sued in this manner, obtained judgments against the organization, and seized its assets in satisfaction of their unfair claims. The "almighty dollar" must have assuaged their guilty consciences.

While the assets of the organization were being frittered away, some of the officers and members of branches sent to ask him if they could, at the calling of an emergency convention, vote me into office as Assistant President-General, which would empower me to use the courts to help save the assets. "No," said Garvey to me. "You would then be responsible for the acts of every rascal. It is a well-laid trap of my enemies to use the predicament of the people—into which they have maneuvered them—to 'get you,' as they have me. With you in prison, I would be left to rot in here."

On another occasion the British Honduras branches wanted him to send me down there to "restore the government's confidence in the U.N.I.A." for, said they, "Since the series of lawsuits over Mr. Morter's estate (left 'for Parent Body U.N.I.A. for African Redemption')—in official circles and otherwise, it was being felt that African Redemption would be more dangerous if it had at its disposal such a rich legacy; so we are under a cloud." Said he, "I would love for you to go down there and clear the air, but what would happen to me if you were out of the country, even for three weeks?"

The Communist Party of America, regardless of their antagonism to Garvey (as he refused to endorse Communism and prevented them from using his mass movement for indoctrination), now realized the repercussions this wanton rape of the U.N.I.A. assets was having on the morale of Negro workers and sent out a signed press release in April 1925, through its Central Executive Committee of the Workers (Communist Party) of America, under the heading "Importance of Organization of Negroes." It declared:

> The Workers (Communist) Party takes this occasion to point out to white workers as well as Negro workers the importance of organization of the Negro masses of this country. The Negro population is composed almost entirely of wage workers, agricultural workers, and the most severe exploited class of farmers, often landless. In addition to the ordinary forms of exploitation and persecution under which the white workers and farmers suffer, the Negroes have to endure the terrible burden of race persecution by which the capitalist class intensifies its class exploitation of the Negroes and also succeeds in dividing and weakening the exploited classes.

In America and internationally, in the world-struggle against capitalist-imperialism, the Negro movement is destined to play a tremendous part. The epoch of the world revolution which opened with the Russian revolution, is also the epoch of the rise of the darker races, and the two form one inseparable whole. A movement among the Negro workers and farmers of the United States must be considered, not only in the light of the class struggle within this country, but also in connection with the anti-imperialist struggles of the millions of West Indian Negroes and the 150,000,000 natives of Africa, and the awakening of the 400,000,000 of China and the 320,-000,000 of India.

The widespread awakening of interest among American Negroes in international questions, as shown in the desire to take part in the strengthening of the African Negro Republic of Liberia, and the winning of independence for the natives of Africa generally, is a guarantee of this historical trend.

This newly awakened interest of American Negroes in international affairs, which found confused but earnest expression among the rank and file of the Universal Negro Improvement Association, was one of the causes of the government's brutal attack upon the Negro organization. The diplomatic Ministers of the United States, Great Britain and France brought about the outlawing of the Universal Negro Improvement Association from African soil. The President of the Liberian republic has publicly admitted that "obligations to the great powers" had something to do with the exclusion of the Negro association from all activities in Liberia. A concession for rubber lands, claimed by the Negro association, was withdrawn and given to a big American corporation (the Firestone Tire Co.), thru the machinations of an American diplomatic minister at the same moment that the United States government made its final assault to break up the Negro association. Here we see the sharp fangs of American imperialism determined to enter and ravage the African continent just as it ravages Haiti, Porto Rico, the Virgin Islands, etc.

The Workers (Communist) Party composed of Negro workers as well as white workers, and standing for the solidarity and emancipation of the working class on terms of equality of all races, cannot stand idly by while the capitalist dictatorship attempts to destroy a mass organization of the exploited Negro people. We cannot consent that the Negro should be denied the right of organization.

The Workers (Communist) Party calls upon the workers, both Negro and white, to protest against the persecution of the Universal Negro Improvement Association.

We demand the immediate and unconditional release of Marcus Garvey.

We demand that Marcus Garvey shall not be deported.

We demand an end to the looting of the treasury of the Universal Negro Improvement Association by the courts of law.

We demand that Liberty Hall shall not be taken away from the Negro association.

We demand that the bloody hand of American imperialism shall not strangle the African peoples.

We demand that the full and free intercourse of American Negroes with their brothers of the African continent shall not be interfered with.

We call upon the Negro workers and the white workers to hold mass meetings and demonstrations together to voice their protest against the persecution of Negro workers.

We call for a united front of white workers and Negro workers as a guarantee and a promise of the solidarity of the working class, both black and white, which will bring the emancipation of the exploited classes and races of the world.

Central Executive Committee
Workers (Communist) Party of America.

Apart from local schools supported by Garveyites, the parent body took over the Smallwood-Carey Institute of Claremont, Virginia in 1925, and conducted this institution as a practical high school. They had hoped to develop it into a university, so they called it "Universal Liberty University." Despite Garvey's imprisonment and the financial straits of the organization, they bravely carried on until 1930.

The Negro Factories Corporation, which owned a steam laundry, hat shop, restaurant and lodging house, were put out of business because of some lazy unscrupulous employees and the general undermining activities of his enemies. The most irreparable loss was suffered when the S.S. *General Goethals* of the Black Cross Navigation Company, after making a trip to the West Indies, was sold for debts willfully and designingly incurred. This distressed and grieved Garvey, as the people had subscribed the money for this ship to vindicate their confidence in him. Sadly he said, "Negroes are their own worst enemies; it is a hellish task to get some of them to build, and a hellish sight to see others of them spitefully and enviously destroy the work of years."

After his incarceration some of the comments of the colored press showed a change of perception. However a Baltimore paper voiced the opinion of the old Garvey ejector brigade. It stated: "He got what was coming to him. It is better for the Race that this violent agitator is safely put away."

The *California Voice*, February 20, 1925, opined that, "Even the bitterest enemy of Garvey must realize that a New Era in the life of the Race has been brought about by this man, who alone of all his fellows stood, and fell fighting for a Cause that was not popular, even with those of his own group."

The *Pacific Defender*, at the same time, called for "optimism even in failure," and warned:

> The advent of failure is no signal for weeping. It is a call for renewed confidence and the resolution to continue to press forward. If every time a train was wrecked or a boat was sunk, the people ceased their intercourse via travel and transportation routes, what would become of the world's business? When failures come, new units of business must spring up, and must be supported by intelligent people who show some knowledge of world history and racial endeavor.

The editor of the *Cotton Farmer*, in true southern style, under the head, "President Coolidge and the Gospel Truth," in its issue of February 21, 1925, portrays the enemies of Garvey and his program as they really are:

It is passing strange, however, with as many men we have who have robbed we "niggers" out of our lodges' money, grand lodge money, bank deposits, insurance and even the poor treasury of the church, and lost it playing craps down at Sister Mamie Crawford's, and now strutting around with stove pipe hats, diamonds and silk shirts, that Marcus should be singled out for using the mails to defraud "niggers."

Who is it so solicitous about "niggers" not being robbed, and what are their real motives? There is a rat in the meal tub, and the cat will soon catch him. One thing about Garvey and his gang, they are not fussing with white folks in an effort to associate with them. They are not with hat in hand begging the white folks for money for them to have a "talking meeting" to save the race, and they are not fussing with white folks about the white man's ships; but were trying to have a ship of their own even if he failed. If President Coolidge would do the right thing, he would pardon or parole Garvey. It would be best to pardon him for they would frame him we fear.

Now, whether President Coolidge has the courage to pardon Garvey—in the face of the opposition of that element of northern boiled shirt white collared colored curb statesmen who never have done a thing but have talking meetings at the expense of some white philanthropist, and yearn for the day to come when they could entirely divorce themselves from their own race and associate with white folks—is very doubtful to the mind of this cotton plantation paper. Garvey and his ilk today are better friends to the United States than his enemy pursuers, and time will prove it.

CHAPTER TWENTY-EIGHT

Garvey has been widely criticized for stating that the southern white man—who is usually brutally frank to the Negro on questions of the separation of the races—is incidentally more of a friend of the Negro than the northern white who, because of courtesy and diplomacy either remains silent on the issue or says that in time absorption of the minority will be the solution. But, said Garvey, "I would rather be awakened to face a danger by a slap in the face than lulled to sleep by being told that I am secure from harm."

In October 1921, President Warren G. Harding spoke in Birmingham, Alabama. On the question of race relations he declared: "There shall be recognition of the absolute divergence in things social and racial . . . men of both races may well stand uncompromisingly against every suggestion of social equality . . . racial amalgamation there cannot be."

Garvey sent him a telegram of congratulations on his outspoken statement on the issues, and in an analysis of him after his death, July 1923, stated in the *Negro World*:

> If President Harding did not openly do any good for the Negro it was because he was but a slave to system and environment, which took extraordinary courage to rebuff and surmount, with the intention of doing that which was right and justifiable. Not only Harding, but any President or leader who prefers to please his immediate acquaintances and human circle rather than the voice of God, speaking through the oppressed, is bound to do as he did in all things affecting human rights, liberty, and justice, without realizing his mistake.
>
> Mr. Harding was not a Roosevelt, who would do what he thought was morally right irrespective of what his associates thought. He would not have dined a Booker T. Washington, if he believed it would have hurt him in the opinion of his friends and large numbers of people. . . . President Harding was no Reformer. . . . To do good, and that which must be permanent, we have to offend public opinion. No better example of the price one has to pay in doing good can be found than that given us by the man Jesus, who, in a life of public activity, taught us that to do good is to offend, and to suffer therefor.

In October 1925 the Negro press carried headlines such as: "Garvey in prison forms new alliance"; "Prisoner Garvey links with Race's enemies"; "Garvey and Anglo-Saxon Clubs—Alliance." How did this come about? Mr. John Powell of the Anglo-Saxon Clubs of America related in a speech at the New York City Liberty Hall that Major Ernest Cox had written a book, *White America*. It was violently criticized by northern colored newspapers. The author was surprised, however, to receive a letter from a Garveyite in St. Louis stating that, while he did not approve of all he had read in the book, nevertheless the feeling for race purity coincided with Garveyism, as did its principles of integrity and self-respect. He requested that Major Cox send a letter to be read at a U.N.I.A. meeting, in which he was to give the white man's answer to Garvey's "Appeal to the soul of white America." Major Cox's letter was so well received, that he was requested to enlarge on it, and publish same in pamphlet form; which he did, and entitled it, "Let my people go," and dedicated it "to Marcus Garvey—the Negro Leader."

Mr. Powell further related how, having to address the Georgia Legislature, he went to the federal prison in Atlanta to meet, and talk with Garvey. "When I saw him," said Mr. Powell,

> I saw a man with head erect, with eyes open and clear, unashamed and unafraid, free from all bitterness, free from all rancor; not one word of complaint escaped his lips, not one word of bemoaning; his one thought was for you—his people, and his loyal followers. . . . There was nothing that Marcus Garvey could not say frankly and freely to me without danger of misunderstanding, nor I to him, and I realized that I was in the presence of a man of the highest idealism, the noblest courage and profoundest wisdom. A man dedicated to a noble and sacred Cause—the Cause of the independence and integrity of his race.

On his return to Richmond, Virginia, Mr. Powell reported to his Club the interview he had with Garvey. The

Richmond Times-Dispatch (white) published an account of his talk. The Norfolk *Journal and Guide* (colored), under headlines spread across the page, claimed to remind their readers that Garvey, whose membership in the Ku Klux Klan had been cut short only by his imprisonment, was even now in prison taking occasion to ally himself with other enemies of the race—the Anglo-Saxon Clubs. That article was copied in the Negro press all over the country, which caused a great deal of ill feeling against Garvey; but his followers knew that his enemies were just up to their old tricks.

In the course of his speech, Mr. Powell made the following admission and statements of fact: "No decent white man in the South can hate the Negro Race, no sane man who can have naught in his heart but feelings of kindliness and gratitude toward the Negro Race." Then he related the heroic part played by the slaves in helping to build up the new country—in protecting the women and children on the plantations and raising the crops to feed the army that was fighting to enslave them. Said he, "There never was a people who under hardship and oppression showed the spirit of kindliness and forgiveness which your people have shown."

He admitted that in the South there were lynching, burnings and peonage systems, etc.; but he pointed out that in Chicago, Springfield, East St. Louis and Johnstown, Negro homes were looted and burned, and Negroes were shot down or run out of town and told to go back South where they belonged. At interracial conferences they were being cajoled, while their birth rate decreased and their death rate increased. This could only lead to race suicide. "Don't deceive yourselves," said he. "People cannot help their instincts; some of the wisest and best people are often the people who are most filled with prejudice and bigotry; we cannot take it out of them; what we can do is to realize as President Coolidge said recently that, 'We are all in the same boat.'"

CHAPTER TWENTY-NINE

There were many and varied efforts made to secure executive clemency for Garvey. In June 1925 a committee, myself included, were able to secure an appointment with the Attorney General in Washington, D.C., to whom we submitted a memorandum asking for executive clemency for Garvey; each of us spoke on a different aspect of the urgency of our plea. He advised us to tell Garvey to make his own application direct from the prison. This Garvey did in a lengthy document, parts of which have a bearing on the Black Star Line. It also embodies a petition to the President for African colonization:

> The Black Star Line was but one of the efforts towards carrying out a general plan that was joined in and endorsed by all the stockholders. As a commercial venture it may have suffered, but the end is not yet reached, and therefore it is not fair to assume permanent failure. As a demonstration to the Negro people that it was possible to attempt and carry out an organized concerted plan to overcome certain of their difficulties, it was unquestionably a success; as an investigation among business activities of the Negro race will show, that since the promotion of the Black Star Line and its earlier successes, thousands of new enterprises among Negroes sprang up all over the country and the world, tending to the economic and industrial development of the race. . . .
>
> Experience in such organization has a great value apart from the mere value of dollars and cents, and from this point of view, as well as from others, the Black Star Line was not a failure. Mere failure commercially to make a success is not evidence of fraud. The dominant question should be as a test of honesty and sincerity, how much of the large amount subscribed for stock did I receive as salary? At what time did I receive a salary for services? Did I not accept a small salary, and for only a short period, and was I not the largest stockholder in the Corporation? Is it not a fact that the people with

whom I dealt, and whose money was invested in the Black Star Line still have faith in me, and have of themselves subscribed for my defence and protection? Who can possibly suggest a better test of the honesty and sincerity of one, than to appeal to the people whose money was invested in the Black Star Line, for they are in the best possible position to understand and sympathize with the plan, and to realize that the Black Star Line was only a part of a programme, and that the feature of financial profits was unimportant.

The enterprise was at best handicapped, due to the obstacles that the unreasonable, unthinking and prejudiced of the white race naturally placed in the way of operation of such a steamship line; and to the advantage taken of those of the race of frail character and manhood, who had to represent the company before skilled and experienced white men who prey upon the unwary and unsuspicious.

After many paragraphs of arguments, he added the prayer for a pardon. Among the many reasons were:

Because I am not guilty and one can only be truly convicted by his own conscience and Christian soul.

Because I have been "framed up" for the indictment and conviction.

Because I have been convicted on prejudice.

Because it is my belief that the President who represents the highest spirit and sense of American justice, as the Chief Executive of the nation, will give such careful and impartial consideration to the plea for justice in America's name, as not to allow the sacred traditions of the nation for justice and liberty to be violated, by even the greatest influence; that justice may be given to one who is consciously innocent of the committal of crime, and whose desire always has been that of being obedient to the laws of the country and respectful of the rights of society.

Because it is my belief that the President will, by clemency remedy a wrong inflicted upon one because of his colour and place of birth, and effort to help his race in the desire for freedom and liberty in their ancestral home, a land originally theirs, and in keeping with the splendid efforts and example of Washington, Jefferson and Lincoln.

Because the act of pardon will tend to convince millions that a black man aspiring for the highest and best for his race can get justice under a Republican form of Government presided over by a Republican President.

Because the millions of blacks in America affiliated with the organization of which I am elected head, and the millions of like affiliations in Central America, South America, and the West Indies, Africa, Europe and Asia, may have no other feeling nor desire than to continue to support the professions of established Christian appeal to Government, and to feel that justice is not only for white men and a privileged class, but for one and all, irrespective of race or creed.

To prevent enemies of established order making capital out of the act of injustice, persecution and prejudice to inflame in the future, and at the time of need, the minds of millions of blacks throughout the world against "bureaucracy, oligarchy, imperialism and capitalism," which may have a strong appeal, in the light of history, for the unfortunate and oppressed whom I am endeavouring to lead by a peaceful and friendly agitation for the reasonable return of their African heritage. To uphold the sacred principles of American justice for which the noble fathers of the Republic have bled and died. To uphold the undying and sacred words and declaration of Lincoln. That this nation, armed with grand and marvellous achievements for human liberty and justice in the last couple of centuries, will not allow itself to be inveigled into doing a grave wrong to one whose only crime is an honest effort to liberate his race by the creation of a new nationalism, and because of his attempt to lead the members of his oppressed race in this direction.

That the Declaration of Independence may not be regarded in the future, by Negroes, as a selfish expression of a clannish group, but that its sentiments were intended to bless all humanity, including the future hope of the black race.

That I may be able to continue to serve the people of my race, who believe in me and who are watching with eyes of eagerness and keenness, and minds of eternal record, the white man's sense of justice as practised upon an unfortunate Negro who happens to be born and reared in an environment of American Continental civilization, being the relic of slavery imposed upon his forbears, without any argument of choice of location on their part, but by the sole desire of their masters to profit by their labour.

That my being born on the American continent as a descendant of British Colonial slaves, does not bar me from the right of working for the release of my people in America and elsewhere to nationhood, but entitles me to a respectful hearing with equal force of right—as any Negro, who was only by accident born in the United States and not in the other Colonies, as my fathers were.

Because of my desire not to be in opposition to the wish of the Government, I am willing to leave the country if a reasonable time is given me to properly arrange my many business affairs in the interest of the organization of which I am head, and to properly arrange how the investments of the people of my race in the Black Star Line can be easily and reasonably returned to them.

I further request this pardon on all those grounds that may be just, proper and legal, which are not known to my layman mind.

Because it would be a national crime to allow the Honourable Courts of the United States and the law officers of the Government to be used by one group of enemies to wreak vengeance upon another, as in my case.

That it may please Your Excellency to see the fact that millions of Negroes have consistently and continuously, through their local organizations, contributed and donated to the promulgation of the ideals for which I stand, and this has been done in the face of forced and extra efforts to hold me up to the said people, as a criminal, and in every way to discredit me by the disadvantages of arrests, prosecutions and malicious newspaper propaganda and organized under-currents. This determination and wonderful, exceptional loyalty to a Negro leader reveals beyond the shadow of a doubt that there is some longing in the souls, hearts and breasts of these people, for the realization of the ideals of their repatriation to Africa, and the founding and establishing for them there of a nation of their own.

That if a plebiscite or referendum were to be taken among the masses of the people, it would show an overwhelming majority in favour of the plan, as evidenced by the millions of signatures attached to petitions in this same matter. Arrangements could be made whereby the somewhat settled national equilibrium industrially and generally, would not be disturbed, but by a gradual system of release, and replacement, at the same time, by assimilatable duplicates, continue the migration until, in the course of probably half a century, the problem adjusts itself by the friendly and peaceful removal and replacement of stock assimilatable to the majority race.

That with the commandeering of hundreds of unused ships now owned by the Shipping Board, and which are a source of worry to the Government, the race could be easily and conveniently repatriated.

The several billion dollars due this country by Great Britain and France, Belgium and Italy, but principally by Great Britain and France could be partly underwritten by their turning over to America, for the purpose of the Negroes, who desire to return to Africa, such territories in Africa where the returned Negroes could easily assimilate with the natives and cooperate as one race for the promotion of the national ideals. When it is remembered that the slave trade and slavery in the Western world were made profitable for centuries to Great Britain, France and America, and that our generations are the relic of such slavery, the force of justice remains indisputable and leaves no other alternative than a righteous and Christian consideration of the poor Negro for his rights.

That my efforts in this direction were with the purpose of blessing the American nation and removing from its body politic an irritating problem that may otherwise end disastrously for both races. That a strong, decisive, determined attitude and action of any President of the United States, in this direction would herald to the world another Lincoln, Washington and Jefferson—the Fathers and benefactors, not only of their country, but the true advocates and dispensers of human justice and liberty.

And for all such consideration as Your Excellency may grant by way of pardon, I do humbly pray,

We the undersigned, respectfully indorse the application for Executive clemency of Marcus Garvey. Our approval is based upon the following grounds:

Our complete belief in the honesty and integrity of the Applicant, and our desire to see justice done to one who has honestly and faithfully labored in the interest of his race.

(There followed signatures by a banker, an editor, a New York City lawyer, a New York City judge, a Cleveland physician and a Los Angeles real estate broker.)

On August tenth a reply reached Garvey stating that the reports on his application were "adverse," and therefore could not be submitted to the President for consideration. The reply cited rule eight which stipulated that the trial judge and District Attorney must report on all applications for clemency.

CHAPTER THIRTY

When Mr. Sargent, the Attorney General, gave us such a patient hearing, and asked many questions pertinent to the issues involved in Garvey's case, our delegation had hopes that Garvey's application for executive clemency would have been given special consideration, in view of its implications. Our strong hopes, conveyed to Garvey, were among the reasons that he wrote so exhaustively in his plea to the President, covering all grounds that might have been involved in a conditional pardon and adding a plea for African colonization. When this application was pigeonholed in the Attorney General's department, we were fearful of the effect it would have on Garvey; but he showed remarkable self-control, and said, "This is another test to see if I will crack up."

During his imprisonment Garveyites held protest meetings all over the world, and sent cables, telegrams and letters to President Coolidge asking for pardon for Garvey.

On May 16, 1925, Garvey sent a long letter to the Attorney General explaining to him in detail that fake claims and judgments by default were piling up against the corporations and businesses of which he was head; that the ships and real estate were being attached for these fictitious claims. Could he release him, under guard, to enable him to try to save even some of the assets? The reply was that his case would not be reopened as the recommendations opposed this.

In 1926, he made another application, after the *Philosophy and Opinions* was well distributed, but received the same reply.

At the end of August 1927, the editor of the Negro newspaper, the *Pittsburgh Courier*, asked me to write an article on the circumstances surrounding the trial and imprisonment of Garvey. The title to my article was: "Who caused the imprisonment of Garvey?" This was used as a streamer across the page, and the article published in serial form, with illustrations. A few sentences were deleted, so I gave the full article to the *Negro World* for publication.

In the article I traced a well-concerted plan going as far back as 1919 against Garvey and his movement. Then in 1920, "The National Information Bureau," whose directors were Barry Smith and John Shillady of the N.A.A.C.P., wrote to the Russell Sage Foundation that "We are informed Garvey was arrested and convicted in Chicago in connection with race riots two years ago." Garvey was nowhere near Chicago at the time of the riots, nor had he been arrested and convicted there. I further related other malicious statements and acts against Garvey, the attitude of the officers of the court at the trial and after, quoting newspaper and magazine comments, and closed with this question: Was justice defeated?

I had extra copies printed by the *Negro World*, paid for them out of the Defense Fund, and had them well distributed in Washington, D.C., and by the branches to reach their state politicians and big local men. In less than three months (the eighteenth of November, 1927), President Coolidge signed a declaration commuting Garvey's sentence to end immediately; he had served two years and nine months.

Secrecy prevailed; and when the document reached Atlanta, the deportation order was served simultaneously; then the news was released. We conjectured that the only southern port from which a ship was likely to leave for Jamaica was New Orleans; so we rushed his attorney from New York City down there, to try and get a stay of execution of the deportation order, and allow him to return to New York to attend to urgent organization business. This application for a stay was promptly and curtly denied.

At the New Orleans pier, he was given a wonderful ovation by the throng which had rushed there. He spoke from the deck of the S.S. *Salamanca*. He poured out his heartfelt thanks to the millions in America who had confidence in him despite the treachery and machinations of his enemies and detractors to present him in a false light. He assured them that service to his race was an undying passion with him; the greater the persecution, the greater the desire to serve. "Be not dismayed," said he. "Africa's sun is steadily and surely rising, and soon shall shed its rays around the world. I live and shall die for Africa redeemed. Steady yourselves and go forward!"

As the ship slowly pulled out, there was hardly a dry eye in that crowd, which sang prayerfully:

Father of all creation,
Allah Omnipotent,
Supreme o'er every nation,
God bless our President.

Guide him thro' life victorious,
Save him from accident,
Grant him his aims most glorious,
God bless our President.

The tyrant's wiles shall never,
Our homes asunder rent,
The Red, Black and Green forever,
God bless our President.

One God! our firm endeavour,
One Aim! most glorious bent,
One Destiny! forever,
God bless our President.

Thus Garvey was forced to leave the shores of America, but Garveyism remained.

It is difficult to portray the various emotions of an awakened emerging people, but the love and devotion of Garveyites in the U.S. dominated their lives. They felt that what was happening to Garvey daily was aimed at them—their hopes and ambitions—and responded with a healing balm of loving attention. The divisions and chapters inaugurated "Garvey Day" on his birthday, August 17th, and sent him presents. I who served him was also dear to them. When the history of Africa's redemption is written, let it record in full measure all the sacrifices they made from 1916 on to the cause, and in keeping the searchlight of public opinion focused on the "dark" deeds being done in Africa to Africans. Garveyites have never ceased to project their dedicatory avowal:

Oh Africa, awaken!
The morning is at hand,
No more art thou forsaken,
Oh bounteous Motherland.
From far thy sons and daughters
Are hast'ning back to thee,
Their cry rings o'er the waters
That Africa shall be free.

From New Orleans the ship plowed its way through the Gulf and the Caribbean to Cristobal, Panama. He was not allowed ashore, but Garveyites secured permission to send a delegation on board, where they presented him with flowers, a purse and an address pledging loyalty to him, and support for the cause. He replied suitably, and for two hours they discussed the internal affairs of the association.

He was transferred to the S.S. *Santa Marta*, and cabled Jamaica the date of his arrival. From early that morning people started to crowd the streets from the pier to Liberty Hall. The country people who had come to market their produce helped to swell the city crowds. They wanted to be able to say to their home folks, "I saw the man," the idol of millions in America, the hope of millions in Africa, and the fear of European powers. Garvey received a welcome and ovation never yet accorded any one in Jamaica. It was spontaneous, tumultuous, inspiring and thrilling to the hearts of Jamaicans. Wharf laborers joined the milling throng, so all formalities had to be abandoned as the people lifted him to a waiting car, and then pushed it along the streets to Liberty Hall. Thousands had gathered inside and outside the building; it was impossible for him to go in, so he had to acknowledge their welcome standing on the running-board of the car. He announced that he would speak at the Ward Theatre the following night. With great difficulty his car was able to feel its way through the crowd, and then off to the home of a member at Half-way Tree. From there he prepared and sent a statement to the press.

The Ward Theatre meeting was crowded to overflowing; the Chairman was Hon. H. A. L. Simpson, Mayor of the Corporate Area. Garvey thanked the people again for the orderly welcome on his arrival, related some of his experiences in America, and asked them to support the local activities. He announced his intention of going to Central America and later to England and Europe, in the furtherance of the work of the organization.

In New York, meanwhile, I was trying to raise some more money to pay off the expenses incurred by the last legal effort on his behalf, and to finalize all other matters preparatory to joining him in Jamaica. Mr. Armin Kohn, on his return from New Orleans, being pressed by reporters to comment on the case as Garvey's attorney, gave this statement to the Associated Press: "In my twenty-three years of practice at the New York Bar, I have never handled a case in which the Defendant has been treated with such manifest unfairness, and with such a palpable attempt at persecution as this one."

CHAPTER THIRTY-ONE

Garvey sent a message that I should bring everything in the flat. I phoned several packers; only two came to look at the furniture and estimate the cost. They would not take the job, they said, as there were too many breakables to risk on a ship going on high seas. It was then I realized the immensity and costliness of the task. Here were all the books, pictures, ceramics and antiques of all sorts which it was his hobby to collect. He had no recreation, as it was dangerous to go to theatres, so his idea of relaxation was to go around to antique shops and buy these old pieces. When he brought them home he would spend time and patience placing them in the right setting, color scheme and the most effective lighting. Sometimes other objects had to be removed and new positions found for them. He enjoyed sitting in an easy chair and contemplating the beauty of the setting he had created, or the exquisite workmanship of a Satsuma from Japan, a Delph vase from Holland, or the delicacy of an eggshell goblet. Now he wanted all these things to be with him. I engaged a firm of art packers. The work took time, as the men had to pack all the small articles in cases, check and list them; then they were taken along with the large pieces of furniture to the packer's warehouse and crated. They could not be taken to the pier until a ship for Jamaica was ready to sail.

In the meantime Garvey had located a house, sent to me for the money to pay for it and to get himself settled. He wrote again stating that I must hurry; if I could not get a booking from New York I should go to New Orleans or Boston, and get a ship there. If I did not reach Jamaica by the seventeenth of January he would be gone on a Central American tour. I could not leave until the furniture was on a freighter and the bill of lading handed me by the packers, as anything could have happened to "Garvey's things," even at the last moment. But he had no thought of this, or remembrance of the promised vacation together alone. If the last three strenuous years did not warrant it, then what more would?

On arriving in Jamaica I gave him the balance of the defense fund, and my books to be checked. He gave me back fifty pounds ($200) and told me to keep it in case of any emergency at home. A few days later a secretary was sent down from the New York office, at his request. None of the consuls for the Central American countries would visé his passport for entry, so he had to plan for the European trip. After fixing up headquarters at the local premises, the Liberty Hall building, he sent for Miss Henrietta Davis, Assistant President-General, and left her in charge during his absence.

The home he had bought was a three bedroom, one bathroom house, with the necessary outbuildings. He bought it from a lady whom contractors had deceived in the construction and cost. There was no tilework, and the finish was poor; yet the American press described it as: "a lovely mansion, next door to the Governor—Garvey's Black House, with liveried servants." When the furniture arrived he arranged it just where he wanted it. I was allowed to sort and classify the books, for which shelves were built. A nameplate, "Somali Court," was inserted in the gate columns.

In April we sailed on the S.S. *Greenbrier* for England. His secretary accompanied us. His attitude towards his eleven years of struggle in America, particularly his imprisonments and all the suffering they caused us, were brushed aside as past history. For, said he, "I never look back; there is no time for that; besides it would make me cautious. How could I dare for the future, when the past is written with so many warnings?" He turned the pages of his past life as an avid reader turns the pages of an adventure story, and loses interest in the early chapters after reading them. Those who get hurt in the tense moments of the adventure are only regarded as necessary props to the build-up of the hero. He was quite as impersonal in this regard as any reader.

In England, because of the prejudices against colored people, it was difficult to secure lodgings. After driving around for hours we went to the Hotel Cecil in desperation, and strangely we were accommodated there. "The Cecil" was a swanky London Hotel where gaitered flunkeys bowed us in. We could only afford to stay there two days. However, he secured rooms in a lodginghouse, and two weeks after that he rented a private house in Castletown Road, West Kensington, and we remained there until September.

He bought another typewriter, employed a white stenographer and set up an office. He busied himself contacting African students and seamen. For the entire period of our stay he did splendid work in organizing and financing the underground movement to all parts of Africa. Meetings had to be held privately, as seamen would lose their jobs and students would be flunked in their examinations, or anonymous letters would be sent to their parents or sponsors to the effect that they were "keeping bad company."

He organized colored people living in London, spoke in Hyde Park, sent circular letters to Members of Parliament and some church and liberal-minded secular leaders explaining his program, and pointing out to them the urgency of taking an interest in what was causing smoldering unrest in the colonies and protectorates. After all this preliminary work, he decided to hold a big meeting, so as to crystallize individual interest for action. He used names and addresses in the telephone book to send out invitations, and nothing was left undone to acquaint the general public of the meeting at the Royal Albert Hall on June 6, 1928. The fifty pounds of the defense fund which he had given me to keep were commandeered.

Garvey did not figure on the unconcerned attitude of the

average English person to what goes on in the far-flung Empire. They were too phlegmatic even to be curious. In their opinion it was the "higher-ups" who benefited from the wealth of Asia and Africa, therefore unrest and riots in these places were not their concern. The only way to rouse their interest was to make them feel it, as Gandhi had when he influenced Indians to stop buying and wearing foreign-manufactured cloth and clothes; they even used hand looms to weave their own cloth. This pacifist campaign brought the textile industries of Lancashire and Yorkshire almost to a standstill. When thousands of workers were unemployed, they became aware of the suffering of the Indians, because they felt the repercussion right down to their empty stomachs. They were impelled to form grievance committees, to "have something done about it."

Because of this traditionally indifferent attitude, only a few people to attend the meeting, although a high-class musical program was advertised. He brought over Miss Ethel Clarke, soprano, and E. B. Knox, a speaker from America. At the organ was Edgar Pito; Reginald Forsythe accompanied Miss Clarke, Meny's Band rendered selections, and Dr. Charles Garnett, M.A., was Chairman. Garvey did not seem discouraged by the poor turnout; he felt that he had made the mistake of overrating their humanity. But it gave him greater concern about the outcome of his work and the need for greater silent, penetrating forces if he was to be effective. He had the program and speeches printed in pamphlet form, and sold to the members abroad.

Only persons of African descent could become registered members of the organization and take part in its internal discussions. But most of the wives of the male members of the London branch were, though English, very helpful in the work, so an Auxiliary was formed for them, as they were sincere in their work to enhance the standing of the men whom they had chosen to marry.

In August we went to Europe; crossing the English Channel we landed at Dieppe, and entrained for Paris.

There we were taken around by officers and members of the local "Comité de Défense de La Race Nègre," and our knowledge brought up to date on happenings in the French colonies. They and Garvey planned future joint action. I recall an amusing little episode while there: A Frenchman who had visited Montreal, Boston and New York joined our table one evening. With his broken English, and my schoolgirl French, we seemed to have carried on the conversation as a team, exchanging information about Provincial France and America's Southland. When the Frenchman rose to go, he asked Monsieur, if he would be so kind as to permit him to return to converse with Mademoiselle another time. The embarrassed Frenchman was told in these short curt words, "She is my wife." Later on a peeved spouse said, "Why don't you put on some weight? You are so frail." But how could I?

He and his secretary returned to London for the weekend to attend to incoming correspondence. On their return they went to Geneva, to lobby at the League of Nations. He had not sufficient money to take me. From Paris, we went through Belgium, on to Berlin for two days, then to Hamburg, where the Liberian Consul General, Mr. Massoquoi, was kind and helpful. I was left there for a few days to enable them to return to London and send money for my passage. Left alone in Paris and Hamburg, I was better able to walk around the streets, and get a close-up of the people as they lived. I viewed them and their countries as tourists usually do; yet I was aware that their lives to us had a deeper significance, because they were the people who made up the colonial powers, who had joined others in partitioning Africa to buttress their economy.

In Paris, we visited the Louvre, Pantheon, Notre Dame Cathedral on the Seine; we went to historic Versailles, Belleau Woods, which was a gaunt reminder of the havoc wrought by the German invaders. In Belgium we saw a replica of the Battle of Waterloo, Flanders Fields of poppies red. One question kept running through our minds: Was all this slaughter and destruction in vain?

Germany was the defeated nation, her colonies had been taken from her; yet Germany had made a greater recovery than France, because her people were disciplined, regimented and scientifically trained, while the French—though loving and lovable—lacked the virility and stamina of their neighbors; hence their birth rate was much lower. They depended on colonials as cannon fodder in wartime.

American goodwill aid had rebuilt many historical places in France, and American tourists provided a great revenue in Paris and southern France. The Germans had not only staged a comeback, but were looking forward to another war of conquest; the spirit and minds of the people were geared for it, as were their industries. Glider schools experimented with the most advanced designs in the air; even the toy factories produced small-scale models of the most revolutionary types of ships, trains and guns. Germany was smirking covertly at the Allies, who had disarmed her but not the scientific minds of her people. France discovered years later that it takes more than the will of a people to rebuild broken fortresses in a modern, progressive world.

In September Garvey conducted several meetings in England, the last one being held at Century Theatre, Westbourne Grove, London. They were well attended, as the members made house-to-house contact with circulars; the musical items were of a high standard.

End of September, we left England on the S.S. *Empress of Scotland*. Among the passengers was the Hon. Mackenzie King, who was courteous on the promenade deck. On landing at Montreal each of us received from the immigration official a visitor's landing card. As Garvey could not go to the U.S. to speak, he sent me as his deputy. The itinerary allowed no rest, except on midnight trains. After I left he was arrested for "illegal entry," even though he showed the arresting officer his landing card duly signed and stamped. The branch officers had to get a lawyer; they sent a telegram to Canada's Prime Minister, but Garvey was not released until the next day. The only explanation he got was that a mistake had been made. But rumor had it that as the Presidential election campaign was coming to a close the Republicans did not want him to speak for fear his speech would influence the voting Garveyites in the U.S. The newspapers had a big scoop with headlines such as: "Canadian government bags Garvey," "Garvey caught entering Canada," and "Garvey in jail again."

He wired me at two different points for money. I sent him through Western Union a total of $800, practically every cent I had raised at paid meetings, after paying all expenses, and giving the branches a percentage. He mailed me a second-class ticket for Bermuda, stating that was the only accommodation available for that date. He sent a similar ticket to his secretary who was on vacation with relatives in Buffalo. On board ship his secretary had enough money with her to pay extra for first-class accommodation. When I met him and remarked on it, he said, "Well, if it was the other way about, I would get some more nasty headlines in American newspapers."

The voyage down from Montreal was a rough and stormy one. He was glad when the ship docked at Hamilton, until he was confronted by soldiers and policemen guarding the entrances to the pier, who told him that he could not land. I had to speak for him that night. The authorities did not want him to see and speak on the awful repressive measures under which Negroes lived; it was just like the South, although a British colony. The island is made up of islets of coral formation; the top soil has not much depth, so the people grow surface plants such as lilies and onions. They depend on the tourist trade for existence; that is why they cater to all the prejudices of southerners. I wrote two articles for the *Negro World* on conditions there. We went on to the Bahamas, a group of small islands and cays. The chief town is Nassau, where similar conditions to Bermuda prevail. He was allowed to land and courteously treated by officials. This was our last stop before returning to Jamaica.

When his life insurance premium became due, he could not pay it, as the exchange on the dollar was so high. He sent to cancel the policy, but did not let me know until the bank in Jamaica refused to release the amount of the surrender value without my personal attendance to sign for same. I asked him to allow me to put aside a portion of the money, but he refused, saying he needed enough "to buy a printing press, and secure a place on Cross Roads for office and meetings." In March 1929 he started publication of the weekly, *The Blackman*, which continued until 1931.

He never had a car while in the United States, because our flat was not far from the office, and he said, "As a boy I was accustomed to long walks. It keeps me fit." In early 1929 the American Garveyites sent him a secondhand Buick; when this car's engine became worn, they sent him a used Hudson. He never learned to drive, as he was always too preoccupied with his thoughts to watch the road. At the time of his arrest on the income tax charge, he asked permission to phone me at home. He took up the receiver and completely forgot our home number. The guards and reporters guffawed at him (some reporters were always tipped off to be on hand when the law enmeshed him)—to them it was so funny.

He sent for another secretary from the New York office, got a house near us, furnished it, and housed both. His sister was installed to look after them; her husband had died. He paid them American scale wages; they even had the car at their disposal. After a year's employment, he sent them on vacation to America. In 1931 when we at home were suffering great deprivations, and he was being pressed to meet organization bills, I suggested to him that some retrenchment should be made where they were concerned. He calmly and deliberately said, "These girls are Americans. It is from America that I get most of the money for my work. They are strangers here. I have got to make them happy, or they won't stay. That is why I give them presents, and take them for outings. This encourages them to work cheerfully, and to be loyal to me.

"Suppose one or both of those girls wrote home that they were neglected and unhappy. Such a letter might be taken to a newspaper office and hot off the press would come news made up in evil fertile brains to the effect that Garvey had these girls in his 'Monkey Island' under appalling conditions, that the Garveyites should stop sending him money, and get the girls back to 'God's country.' You know these newspaper men would never publish a denial from the girls. Sometimes I like what I do, other times I hate like hell to do the things I have to; but in my work, I must get the best use out of every human being with whom I come in contact. I thought you realized this long ago."

Perfume helped his concentration, and it was for this purpose alone that he used it. His favorite scent was "Quelque fleurs," possibly because it reminded him of a tropical garden. He usually carried an extra kerchief wet with this perfume. In case he had to speak, he cupped it in his hand and inhaled it; with half closed eyes he remained until called on to speak; then he was ready.

My hair, let down, thrilled him. It was long and naturally wavy; he asked me never to cut it. The first time he saw it down, curiously he felt some strands and said, "Why, it is soft." As I tossed my head, he exclaimed, "Oh, but it is so live!"

When he was angry with me, usually over some almost impossible task he set me to do in a hurry, he would sulk; soon however, some new worries at the office or elsewhere, would send him back home like a hurt child to be humored and comforted.

The sea had a stimulating effect on him. From the deck of a ship, by the shore, or in retrospect, he loved it. They both demonstrated similar natures—quiet if undisturbed; but—even as the placid sea becomes tempestuous with the interfering winds—so did Garvey with his opponents.

CHAPTER THIRTY-TWO

A pen picture of happenings in Africa at this period appeared in the *Gold Coast Times*. The article was reproduced in the *Negro World*, December 17, 1927. In closing, the editor warned that "Sahib" administration and misrule ultimately causes the fall of empires. He wrote:

> The black race has never wronged the white race in the long contact between these two branches of the human family, while the former can bring an indictment against the latter with such counts as the slave trade, land expropriation, punitive expeditions involving the massacre in cold blood of defenceless tribes, and the liquor traffic which will weigh heavily against Europeans in the balances of eternal justice. The black man has borne with fortitude the trial and burdens which the white man crossed the seas to impose upon him; but the worm is turning, and there is a mental revolt against the alien yoke, which calls for repentance and reformation on the part of the white man, if a serious clash of color is to be avoided in the future. . . .

> Lord Meston in the London Sunday Times, deals with the matter from a different angle. The writer believes that the white man in Africa has reached the second and the most difficult stage in his relations with the backward races. In his view the Britisher shone in the earlier stage when order had to be restored. . . . But in the second stage, after order has been restored and such influences as commercial exploitation have replaced paternal rule, the native is forced to make "the acquaintance of a different type of Englishman, whom he neither likes nor respects." This second stage he describes as difficult enough in any circumstances; but when on top of this the white man begins to dispossess the native of his land, to demolish his ancestral customs, and to drive him to want and distress, it is but natural that resentment and racial bitterness should be the result. Dealing with a different aspect of the same subject, General Smuts of South Africa, remarked the other day that "native opinion is largely in revolt and the natives are seething with discontent all over Africa."

There has been change in the character of colonial administration since the early period. . . . The idea of developing the Dependencies inhabited by the darker races for the purpose of bringing wealth to the British people and of relieving unemployment in England now dominates Colonial policy to such a degree as to obscure the vision of administrators and to make them overlook the happiness and contentment of the native populations. . . .

The right to a fair hearing and to a full measure of justice is now practically denied to the natives when they have occasion to appeal from what they conceive to be injustice at the hands of Colonial Administrators to the Crown as represented by the Colonial Minister. A few years ago a native deputation from South Africa with a real grievance was turned away, for the simple reason that the aggressive party was the South African government, over whose policies the Imperial authorities seem to have lost all control. In West Africa the new policy is to trust the man on the spot implicitly for the sake of maintaining official prestige, even if it involves the denial of justice. . . .

History supplies several instances showing that the disruption of Empires has often followed the delegation of wide powers to satraps in outlying possessions to run the show in their own way. It is morally certain that if the ultimate authorities in Germany had before the war taken steps to restrain the excesses of their Colonial Administrators and to provide for better government of the natives, the sympathy of the natives would not have been alienated to such an extent as to induce them to desert the Germans on the approach of the Allied troops. The lesson which the Germans derived from their experience during the war ought not to be lost upon other Colonial powers.

The reflections of the colored press after Garvey's deportation from America conceded victory for Garveyism. The magazine *Opportunity* in its January 1928 issue opined:

Garvey was sent to prison on the technical charge of using the mails to defraud, a circumstance with but slight relationship to the important facts of his activities, and by a legal conviction which did not destroy that influence which seems to be uncommonly irritating to the authorities of several governments, including his own. No one dismisses his name now three years after his conviction as that of a mere criminal and exploiter of ignorant Negroes. It would be worth the inquiry to learn why this lone black figure, bumptious and flamboyant as he is, can call forth in such concert the interests of those governments with black subjects, in protecting them from his doctrine. . . .

Garvey, we fear, is more the symbol of a peculiar mood in Negroes than inspirer of it. He has succeeded in articulating some of the long crushed and unformed desires of the black masses, and he has done it with the usual glamor and arrogance of mass leaders. Only by considering these desires and their possible embarrassment to those governments with interests into which they cannot comfortably fit, does Garvey and what he represents become dangerous. It was as right as it was legal to send him to prison; but this neither touched the movement which bears his name, nor the mood of the least advantaged of his suppressed peoples the world over, of which this movement is an expression.

The *Chicago Whip* admitted that Garvey demonstrated to the world that colored peoples could follow their own leadership:

Marcus Garvey demonstrated to the whole world that the colored people of America and the black people of the world can organize. Under the mighty banner of the red and green and black, almost three million people joined his ranks, captured by a program which appealed both to their heads and their hearts. This vast army with one aim and one idea proved to the Nordic people that the colored people were not to be forever split up and incapable of following one leadership.

R. A. Martin of Cuba, in a letter to the *Negro World*, October 25, 1930, viewed Garvey's work in history's perspective, when he stated:

History supplies us with many instances where all great Movements and reforms require great length of time to be made an accomplished fact. Yet we find Negroes, and what is worst, not the ignorant Negroes either, expect Marcus Garvey to have driven England, Spain, France, Belgium and other powerful nations out of Africa overnight, and established an independent government, where these so-called big Negroes could go and sit in their big offices as Presidents, Senators, Congressmen, Governors of states and other exalted positions; and because such did not, and could not happen within such period, they all to a man . . . began to steal and exploit the very people that they had sworn to lead and protect. Not one of these men, away from Marcus Garvey, has even given one year of loyal and honest service to the cause that they had sworn so much to protect, even to the extent of their very lives.

Negroes must remember that there is no short cut to fame, success and independence; they will have to go the whole way as all the other sub-races of the human family went in achieving power and honor.

Rev. R. R. Porter, writing in the *Negro World*, November 22, 1930, described true Garveyism as symptomatic of a religion. He stated:

I do not know whether or not Marcus Garvey is aware of the fact that he has given the world a new religion; nevertheless he has. . . . Just as Jesus and Guatama have been misunderstood, the same holds true of the founder of Garveyism. The early Buddhists misrepresented things to win converts; the early Christians did so for the sake of sensation; the Mohammedans did likewise to outwin Judaism, Mazdaism and Christianity; and many of the present day followers of Garveyism are misrepresenting true Garveyism, simply because they do not know of its sublimity; and those who openly oppose it for no other reason than that they do not hold its founder to be a sublime person, should remember this: It is not always through sublime persons that great things come into life. . . .

To me true Garveyism is a religion, which is sane, practical, inspiring and satisfying; it is of God, hence a devout Garveyite cannot deny the existence of God, but sees God in you, I and the world. He knows God because he is a part of God, and is assisting in the making of the Kingdom of God on earth. He respects all religious beliefs, yet he holds fast to that which he believes is best—Garveyism. He regards the rights of others and obeys the laws of the land where he resides, being mindful of the fact that once he is true to himself, others, and his religion—through the right understanding of the One God, One Aim, One Destiny—he, too, shall enjoy life, and live abundantly in the Kingdom of Heaven on earth, and that Africa shall once more become the land of the Good, Strong and Wise.

In May 1928, students at Howard University in a debate differentiated between "The Man" and "The Movement," and unanimously agreed, as expressed in the following:

> Washington, D.C.—In a debate that was filled with eloquence and intelligent discussion of the Negro Problem, students of political science at Howard University, unanimously agreed that Garveyism was the solution of the international problem of the Negro. . . . The Debaters on the affirmative cited historical facts to show that RACE has been a decisive factor in the political life of man; that the Negro had been ridiculed and made an object of contempt, due to his not building a state of his own. Garvey's philosophy was distinguished from the man Garvey; one of the debaters adding that Garvey was temporal, but Garveyism was eternal.

CHAPTER THIRTY-THREE

The Sixth Convention was held in Jamaica, B.W.I., August 1929. Everything from the parade to the sessions was a replica of the pageantry and serious discussions of the American conclaves. The Fifth had been convened during his imprisonment, only to transact urgent organization business. From January on, extensive world-wide advertising was done: "All Negro Institutions, Organizations, Churches, Societies, Lodges, and peaceful law-abiding, legitimate and constitutional Movements" in the world were asked to send Delegates to this world Convention.

The following are most of the items on the agenda which were deliberated on:

1. The political and social freedom of the entire Negro Race.
2. The presentation of evidence to the League of Nations for an adjustment of the international problems.
3. The founding of three Negro Universities, with Technical Colleges attached, in America, the West Indies and West Africa.
4. The creating of general economic opportunities in agriculture, industry and commerce for the Race, whereby a brisk and proper trade relationship may develop between the three Units.
5. The acquiring and controlling of agricultural lands for the scientific development of agriculture, and also the establishment of factories and industrial institutions in various Negro Communities to guarantee permanent employment to the people of the three areas.
6. The launching of a new line of steamships to facilitate trade and commerce throughout the world.
7. To establish Embassies in the Capitals of the world, to represent the interests of the Race, and to watch and protect their rights.
8. To establish newspapers in the Capital cities of the world, in order to shape sentiment in favour of the Race.

Whatever Garvey planned was in terms of the future: a goal for others to work toward, and expansive enough to require many leaders. He consistently gave them the ultimate in planning. These proposed goals sweeping changes were part of a ten-year plan, which, even if partially executed, would have far-reaching effects on the status of our people, and upset the established order that limited their ambitions. For this, and other reasons, we find those same controlling forces attempting to repeat in Jamaica the work of destruction they carried out in the U.S.

Among the former officers of the organization who had

connived among themselves and secured default judgments during Garvey's imprisonment was G. O. Marke, the first Deputy Potentate. All these men had the same lawyer, introduced to them by Amos, the Special Investigator of the Department of Justice. By arrangements the plaintiffs only received a part of the moneys so obtained.

In 1929 Marke, who sued the U.N.I.A. Inc. later than the others, through his New York attorney retained Mr. J. H. Cargill, solicitor, of Jamaica, who applied to the Supreme Court to enforce the New York judgment of £7,527 ($30,-000) against the Jamaica U.N.I.A., its properties and assets. The matter came up before the Chief Justice, Sir Fiennes Barrett Leonard, who had previously served in the judiciary in Africa. Garvey obtained affidavits from officers of the parent body in New York, and explained to the court the position of the various units called U.N.I.A. The original incorporated body from 1926 was not under his control. Since then there was an incorporated parent body, the Kingston division, which owned Liberty Hall, 76 King Street, a chapter in Rollington Town, which had paid down on an unfinished building, the St. Andrew division. These were under the unincorporated parent body, whose trustee and trustees had contracted to purchase "Edelweis Park," and also held in trust movable assets such as: restaurant and soda fountain equipment, a frigidaire, six typewriters, office furniture, printing machinery, etc. The Kingston division's hall was bought by the poor members years before Garvey returned to Jamaica. They had accumulated this money by contributions and entertainments, and this was common knowledge. Now the vicious and rapacious hand had stretched across the Atlantic Ocean to seize from them what they had taken years to acquire.

Garvey retained solicitors and barristers for each unit, and did all he could in the court to protect the people's assets. He was tried for contempt for not producing in court books of the Saint Andrew division, yet he was not an officer of that or any other local branch and so did not handle or have in his possession or keeping their books. He was fined twenty-five pounds on the thirtieth of July, 1929. The Chief Justice ruled that in his opinion, there was no difference between the incorporated New York body, the unincorporated parent body, and the Jamaica divisions; therefore he ordered the sale of all properties and assets held by these units or their trustee or trustees.

The Chief Justice refused to stay the sales pending the appeal—a crippling financial blow to the organization, especially in respect to the legal expenses for each unit to have their appeal argued in court. Mr. Lewis Ashenheim, of the firm of Milholland, Ashenheim and Stone, solicitor appearing on behalf of Garvey, wrote a letter to the Administrator General and the Court's Bailiff, informing and warning them that the matters involving the sale of Liberty Hall and other assets of the U.N.I.A. were on appeal. For this he was tried for contempt of court and fined three hundred pounds by the Chief Justice.

In December 1930, before their Honors, Justices H. I. C. Brown, Clarke and Law, the appeals were upheld and costs awarded. But in the meantime Marke had died. The executrix of his estate claimed he had no assets to settle the orders made by this court against him and his estate. Who got the curse money? Through the Properties Insurance Fund, the government of Jamaica eventually had to settle with the Kingston division for their Liberty Hall.

In Jamaica in 1929, there were no political parties. The elected members of the Legislative Council were Independents—independent in views and in pocket—who were not paid to serve, and were elected by the votes of persons who had either property or salary qualifications. The poorest in the island, therefore, were unrepresented as far as their real personal needs were concerned, and suffered under class representation. It was the general opinion of the "higher-ups" that the poor man, having "nothing at stake," had nothing to protect. Black men who had risen to positions of prominence and affluence, had done so by individual efforts, in spite of economic handicaps. They were the privileged few, and would not jeopardize their positions by any joint attempt to lift up "dead weight," meaning the masses.

The birth rate increased with unemployment, as idleness encourages child production. Despite infant mortality the population pressure, not finding outlet abroad, would at some time let off steam. The grocery trade, wholesale and retail, was in the hands of the Chinese, whose ancestors came to the island as indentured laborers. Now their offspring were the traders. The Syrians and Lebanese practically monopolized the clothing and shoe trades. Thus money that had to be spent to buy the barest necessities of life went into the pockets of alien traders.

The educational system of the island, and for that matter all the other British West Indian colonies, was not geared to the ambitions of the young generation, and the needs of the times; hence there was only one technical school, no polytechnic, and no university in the entire area. The high schools were mostly concentrated in the corporate area—Kingston and St. Andrew Parishes. These schools prepared students for junior, senior and higher schools examinations, on question papers sent by Cambridge University, which in turn received the students' answers for correction and rating. Therefore in most of the parishes of the poor, the intelligent children who could not afford to be boarded at or near the high schools, were denied higher education. However, elementary school teachers, lay readers and ministers, who were dedicated to the advancement of the children, gave private lessons in high school subjects.

Twenty years after this time, when the Colonial Office found it expedient to relieve the overcrowding at their universities, by establishing one in the West Indies, many "better class" people opposed it. Some said, "It will cheapen university education," which they still considered the privilege of their class.

All these, and other adverse conditions created the urgency

for reforms; although it was not Garvey's intention on his arrival to go into local politics, now he felt impelled, and added this to his already burdensome duties. He and his colleagues formed the Peoples' Political Party, with a program of reforms toward changing the bad conditions under which the masses labored. In a Municipal by-election their candidate, J. Coleman Beecher, was successful. Later Messrs. Sherwood and Wilks were elected to the Kingston and St. Andrew Corporation. The next candidate they sponsored was Rev. Dr. Veitch, who won a seat in the Legislative Council.

An election to fill vacancies in the Legislative Council was coming up in January 1930, so the party officers and himself drew up a manifesto. The following are the fourteen planks of his platform:

1. To secure representation in the Imperial Parliament for a larger modicum of self-government for Jamaica.
2. Protection of Native labour.
3. A minimum wage for the labouring and working classes of the island.
4. The expansion and improvement of Town and urban areas, without the encumbrances or restraint of private proprietorship.
5. Land reform, and All-Island Water Board, to secure domestic irrigation and industrial supplies.
6. The compulsory improvement of Urban areas from which large profits are made by Trusts, Corporations, Combines and Companies.
7. A law to facilitate the promotion of Native industries.
8. A Jamaica University and Polytechnic.
9. A National Opera House.
10. A law to impeach and imprison Judges who, with disregard for British justice, and Constitutional rights, dealt unfairly.
11. The creation, by law, of a Legal Aid Department to render advice and protection to such persons who may not be able to have themselves properly represented and protected in Courts of Law.

12. A law for the imprisonment of any person, who by duress or undue influence would force another person to vote in any public election against his will or good judgment.

13. The granting to the Township of Montego Bay and Port Antonio the Corporate rights of Cities.

14. The beautifying and creation of the Kingston Race Course into a National Park, similar to Hyde Park in London.

As leader of the party he spoke at Cross Roads Square on the tenth of September, 1929, to open the campaign, and presented their manifesto; he elaborated on all proposed reforms. After this meeting he was arraigned in court on a second contempt charge, the basis of which was the tenth plank of the manifesto, regarding the impeachment of judges. Garvey felt that judges are placed on the bench to administer by due process of law the systems prevailing in their particular country; but they are human beings, not robots.

He was tried before three judges of the Supreme Court, the same Chief Justice presiding as in the Marke case. In the course of the trial Garvey endeavored to explain to the court that the "tenth plank" was only proposed legislation. To the surprise of many lawyers, the Chief Justice interrupted him, and stated as follows:

> The matter has been considered and dealt with in the Empire since the days of King William III of England. This is an Act seldom used, possibly never used, in the life of anybody now alive, where Governors or Judges, or high Officers, who are unjust to other persons may be imprisoned. You will find that law in the books, though you will see no illustration of its use, at any rate of many years.

Garvey had to plead in his own defense, as the funds of the organization were exhausted with the Marke case. The Chief Justice ordered him imprisoned for three months, and imposed a fine of one hundred pounds ($400). Justice Law concurred, but Justice Clarke said he was unable to agree, in regard to the penalty, and in his written judgment he stated:

It is immaterial whether the words were used as the result of spleen on the part of an unsuccessful litigant; whether they were used as a mere device to further a political candidature, or with any other purpose or intent. A man who, like the respondent, claims to be leader of any section of His Majesty's subjects should understand the broad principles of public welfare which are involved.

The Courts are the King's Courts, administering the King's justice, and an insult to the Courts is an insult to the Crown itself. . . .

Now, in cases of this sort, the Court takes action, not to revenge any offence to its dignity, but rather to protect its usefulness as a public safeguard; and if Mr. Garvey let it be known that he sincerely and fully retracts what he said, the principal aim of this kind of procedure has been achieved.

Had Mr. Garvey not taken this step, I should myself have had not the slightest hesitation in concurring in the imposition of a sentence of imprisonment of 12 months.

In the circumstances, although punishment is clearly essential, I do not think that a definite sentence of imprisonment is necessary. The Courts possess such stability and such great power, that they can well afford to be generous to offenders of this class. I am sure that there is, in fact, never any vindictiveness in their sentence, but it is essential not only that they should actually do justice, but that they should also appear to do so with all possible mercy.

CHAPTER THIRTY-FOUR

For a "First Class Misdemeanant" at Spanish Town prison the only punishment was confinement. I arranged with the proprietress of a lodging house nearby to look after Garvey's laundry, and send in all his meals. At one of my regular visits to him, he said that the mortgagee threatened to foreclose on "Edelweis Park," and further stated: "I am powerless to help, being here; you are the only person who can save the situation, by mortgaging the home, and giving a bill of sale on the furniture. I have arranged with the Trustees for you to take over 'Edelweis Park' in your name, in order to protect your interest. Papers will be drawn up to the effect that whenever they are able to pay you off, you will transfer the property to them. In the meantime they are to pay future expenses on the place." I acceded to his wish. The interest on the transaction was at the high rate of eight per cent, for we were desperate.

On his release from prison, Garvey had only a few weeks in which to campaign; his opponents had taken full advantage of his imprisonment. The white candiate, Seymour, who opposed him, got a black man who had a drug store at Cross Roads as his manager; he was so personally vindictive and hateful that many persons thought he was the candidate. Voters were intimidated and told that if they voted for "Garvey's Party," their names would be "taken by Government." However, Garvey felt that his party's manifesto of reforms for the people's benefit would sell itself to the voters, as against independents who had no programs; so he left his St. Andrew Parish, and spent the last week helping the other candidates of his party.

It is strange how gullible people can be, especially when their emotions are at the highest pitch, which was the case during this election campaign. We had a wooden statue of an African woman holding a light in her upturned hand, which was kept on our open verandah, and lit at night; when he came home he turned off the light. One night a black sedan drove in and took it away. A new gardener, who was sitting on the road bank with his cronies, saw the car enter the driveway, and thought it was the doctor, as I was in my early pregnancy, and ordered to bed for six weeks. But he got suspicious when the car backed out and speeded up the road.

It was said that the reason for the kidnaping of the "African Lady" was that they regarded it as a fetish, which if destroyed would deprive Garvey of his "African power-Obeah." A few weeks later the head was found in a grass common, and the torso in a cemetery, showing evidence of a post mortem. The pieces were never brought home on account of my condition. The sedan that drove the thieves did not belong to a poor ignorant man; but superstition, although derided and ridiculed by the intelligent people, was resorted to by them in desperation to "break Garvey."

The following is the gist of Garvey's campaign speeches:

We of the Peoples' Political Party are here to ring in the changes. Fourteen men are wanted at this time in the Legislative Council to pledge to work solidly in the interests of all the people. Which is the duty of every statesman so elected. We find such a policy in countries like Cuba, Guatemala, Spanish Honduras and other small countries, where a great feeling of national consciousness exists. Only in Jamaica there is not that feeling, because very few of our statesmen have any love for the populace.

The problem of unemployment must be taken up and dealt with and my Party will see that the Government take steps to raise a loan of three million pounds to develop the Crown lands in the parishes, thus giving employment to thousands who are in distress and want. If the United Fruit Company can make millions out of bananas here, I do not see why the Government could not make millions out of a Crown Land development scheme, which would also improve the condition of the people.

I am not prejudiced against any class in Jamaica. I love all Jamaicans—white and black—and all those who have made Jamaica the country of their adoption, but all classes should co-operate for the common good. We want Jamaica to stand out as a beacon of Race tolerance and goodwill.

My Party will agitate for the building of modern homes by the Corporation on the easy payment system, as is done in other countries. So that the working people will be relieved of the high rates of interest now being charged them on mortgages. This will also encourage others to own homes.

Workers should be insured against sickness and accident whilst employed. What right has the Corporation to employ men to blast rocks, to use dynamite or dig marl without some sort of protection, so that if they become incapacitated their families would be provided for? This is one of the first things we will see about if you exercise your franchise in our favour.

The earning capacity of workers must be increased, which will benefit all classes of society. In this way workers will be able to spend more, having earned more. No encouragement is being given to the Natives to foster and promote industries. The result is that Jamaica has grown up to be a country of consumers. Out of our by-products of agriculture we produce nothing. We import shoes, clothes, hats etc., when most of these things could be manufactured right here. Canning and tanning factories would be a great encouragement to the farmers in the country parishes, whose surplus fruits go to waste and the skins of their animals bring little or nothing.

My opponents say, I am against white and fair-skinned people. This is not so. I am against the class system here, which keeps the poor man down; and the poor are mostly black people. It is only natural therefore, that their interest should be nearest and dearest to my heart.

If I were a white man I would have the interest of white people at heart; if I were a Chinese, it would be but natural that I would make as much money as I could and send some of it to my people in China. If I were a Syrian, I would sell my cloth and goods at as high a price as I could get for it, and help my people in Syria and Lebanon. But as a man who fears the wrath of Almighty God, and loves all humanity, I say, let us all join together as fellow Jamaicans and ring in the changes for a New Jamaica.

Wint, the opposing candidate in St. Ann, Garvey's home parish, was particularly bitter and abusive; he led the fight, and used his influence as an elementary school teacher to turn the schools into campaign centers, and had the children sing his songs. The burden of his opposition to Garvey was:

Garvey said that the labouring man should get four shillings per day, with an eight hour day. Could the smaller people who had to employ labour send such an impossible man to the Council? If Garvey wanted to go to Africa, let him go there by all means, but it was an insult to every Jamaican to tell him that his aim in life was to go back to African savagery—to darkest Africa, Garvey's Mecca. . . . Garveyism is a poisonous cult. Intelligent Jamaicans must join in stamping out this menace to the happiness and prosperity of our Island home.

When the election returns were announced for the twenty-ninth of January, 1930, Garvey was a shocked and grieved man. He had lost. Wint's reason for his own success was, he said, due to the fact that "I did not ask a single individual to assist me, but the gentry of the parish, and the respectable intelligent of the masses took up the fight themselves, at their own expense, with the result now known."

Garvey held meetings and thanked those who had voted for him and his party. He explained to them the many low and hateful tactics of his opponents and their backers. Said he,

> My speeches and utterances were being recorded with the hope that they could have been used to send me back to prison. You were told, "Don't put him in the Legislative Council, you will make him more powerful." Under the Party system a man is as powerful in a Legislature as his Party, which derives its power from the voters; and intelligent voters cast their votes, not merely because they like him, but because he is bound by the Party's plan for their betterment. . . .
>
> Theophilus Wint—a black man—has spoken of Africans as "savages" in a "dark land." But little does he know that Garveyism has given light and hope to millions there, who are determined to restore it to its ancient glory. A day will come when Wint and his children will be glad to go to Africa. The thousands who attended and cheered at the Party's meetings, indicate that if you, the poor people had a vote, our Party would have been sent to the Legislature. The voters have turned back the clock for another ten years, but Party system is well established in your minds, and it will come, it is bound to come.

In a letter dated February 1, 1930, to the *Daily Gleaner*, and reproduced in the *Negro World*, A. Wesley Atherton commented on the campaign thus:

> The answer to your grossly unfounded charges, as also a most able defence of the sound political principles for which he stood, and which you tackled in your editorial, was contained in Mr. Garvey's letter, published in your Saturday's issue. I am not pretending, therefore to be able to handle the situation any better than he can; but just as in the interest of a privileged group you so rashly denounced his political stand, I consider it a public duty to write in defence of this man of sorrow who, because he has failed in a gallant attempt to further help his people, must again be slandered, maligned and scarred by the fire-whips of avenging foes.
>
> Truth crushed to earth will rise again is a dictum which, in the present case, will eventually manifest itself in a political upheaval far greater than the one we have just experienced. The full importance of possibly the most remarkable political program ever evolved in this country must, in time, penetrate the consciousness of a people hemmed in by every economic barrier. Marcus Garvey preached no strange political doctrine. He enunciated no far-fetched theory that could not be reconciled with the basic formula in the science of government. He propounded no baseless faith that taxed the imagination and placed him in a category of a fool. On the face of his manifesto, there is absolutely no doubt that his election to the Legislative Council would herald the opening of a new era in this country which would benefit by statesmanlike enactments, the like of which we have never known here before. He stood for a minimum wage, a working man's compensation act, protection of native industries, higher free school education, the compulsory employment of a higher percentage of native labor, land reform, an eight hour day, and other commendable reforms of legislation. Thus he became a marked man; the entire plutocracy of the Island rallied against him. He has suffered political defeat, but his principles are established; they will find a voice, even in the Legislative Council within the next five years.

Rum and human depravity blocked the path of Marcus

Garvey. The terrible reverse which he received at the polls was due in no sense whatever to lack of organization. With the limited means at his command, his campaign could not have been better organized. He has lost in what was almost a rum war, a money scramble. With the bait dangling before their gaze—the red linen of filthy lucre—Negro sons of African slaves, in this enlightened age voted away their birthright, and suffered themselves to be indentured for another five years under conditions that have sucked their vitals to the very bone. They traded on the future happiness of their children, and trampled their manhood into the dust. With the whip of the slave master still cracking in their ears, they followed the stream of molten gold down the hills of St. Andrew to vote against Marcus Garvey.

They stabbed him fiercely in the back, and while now, recovering from that brutal wound, he stands before the bar of public opinion, facing the charges of his traducers, those of us who can, must help, and those of us who cannot, must weep.

But the mournful dirge of the Peoples' Political Party, not of Garveyism, will not be sung in this generation, nor in the next. It shall synchronize only with the passage of time into eternity. Both causes are immortal, and must survive all human, material barriers and impositions. Marcus Garvey has secured a wider niche in the hall of fame.

It would not have been difficult for Garvey to get the U.N.I.A. branches in the French and British territories of the West Indies and Haiti to organize the Peoples' Political Party in all these units. Had he succeeded in Jamaica, this was his aim.

The ground work of the political emergence of a people must be preceded by clearing away the brambles of uncertainty and doubt in their minds as workers, as to their origin and status; therefore race pride is necessary to strengthen and give impetus to voluntary and involuntary speeding up of the construction of political freedom. In the long run those who now decry us as racists will become proud of the Negro blood in their veins—when the foundation of racial

uplift produces the superstructure of political freedom.
When that time comes, they will say to the world, "Look
what we have done."

CHAPTER THIRTY-FIVE

In October 1929, Garvey was elected as a councillor to
the Kingston and St. Andrew Corporation. Owing to his
three months imprisonment, he was prevented from taking
the oath of office and functioning as a councillor. From the
prison he applied for leave of absence, but was refused it by
a majority vote of one of his colleagues. The solicitor for
the corporation advised that it was discretionary. On his
release from prison, he was allowed to subscribe to the oath
of office, and took his seat. He attended three meetings of
the council; to his surprise his seat was declared vacant for
an alleged nonattendance at three consecutive meetings. A
by-election was ordered. He petitioned the Governor, asking
for the Attorney General's ruling on the matter. He got no
action. During the early campaign, February 1930, others
opposed him, but on nomination day he was returned unop-
posed.

Arising out of the underhanded tactics used to keep him
out of the Council, an article was printed in *The Blackman*,
which stated in part:

> The Corporation is entirely opposed to the welfare of the
> country. . . . The Government is also bereft of common de-
> cency, not to say, dignity, and common sense. It is true our
> faith in the local administration of affairs is being sorely tried;
> perhaps we should not be, but our confidence in British fair
> play is not upheld by the manifestations we behold from day
> to day.

Garvey, T. Aikman and Coleman Beecher were brought
before the court for criminal libel against His Majesty's

Government in Jamaica. In his defence he explained to the court that Beecher was circulating manager of the newspaper, and had nothing to do with writing articles. Aikman as literary editor wrote the editorials and articles, including the one in question, which he, Garvey, did not see before it appeared in the newspaper, as he did not read over Aikman's editorials and articles.

The judge acquitted Beecher. At the end of the trial he referred to Aikman as "more or less the tool of Garvey," and sentenced him to three months' imprisonment. Garvey, he said, was criminally responsible and he sentenced him to six months. Notice of appeal was given; they were granted bail. When the appeal came up for hearing, it was allowed. Barrister W. Foster Sutton, instructed by H. A. L. Simpson, solicitor, argued for Garvey, and Barrister E. Campbell, M.Sc., LL.B., instructed by D. Evans, was solicitor for Aikman. Later on a Special Commission was set up to probe the affairs of the City Council; on the grounds of its findings, the body was dissolved.

This year, 1930, the condition of the poorest class seemed to have worsened. Unemployed men and women roamed the streets begging. In the parishes they had no money to plant out their little holdings; hundreds of children could not go to schools on one meal a day, and walk miles on emptiness. Thousands of others left the elementary schools with no knowledge of earning a living, and nowhere to go to acquire technical training. Frustration among them had created young petty thieves and loafers. There was no outlet abroad for able-bodied workers; malnutrition was taking its toll, but the fecundity of the people was undiminished.

Unable to do anything for the parishes, as he was not in the Legislative Council, and being hampered in the Corporation Council in getting his resolutions through and put into effect, he formed in June "The Workers and Labourers Association," to see what organized effort could do on behalf of the poor. He led a deputation to the Governor, asking him to investigate the distressing conditions of the masses of the island, and to use his influence towards remedial measures. Nonchalantly the Governor replied that in his opinion, there was "no unusual suffering."

His next move was to draw up a petition to the King, through the Colonial Office, and to send copies to Labour Members of Parliament, and other liberal-minded men and newspaper editors in England. The result was the appointment of a Royal Commission to investigate the political and economic conditions in the West Indies. At the end of September he held a monster meeting in Kingston at Coke Chapel steps (the outdoor forum) to tell the people the good news. Mr. J. Denniston, treasurer of the Workers and Labourers Association, introduced him. He complimented the people on their good behavior during the times of provocation, strain and misery, and outlined the matters to be brought to the attention of the members of the commission.

One day during the latter months of my pregnancy, he brought home an acceptance for me to sign, so that he could get some money to pay pressing bills of the U.N.I.A. I told him I could not sign it, as the house and furniture were mortgaged; besides I had already backed other notes for him. I was in no condition to be further harassed. He left and returned in the evening. He repeated his request, adding the great urgency of the need. I was lying down, too worn out and disgusted for words; I shook my head in refusal. He put some clothes in a grip, and went over to the house where his sister and two secretaries lived. Two days after, I felt as if I was losing my baby, so I sent for the doctor and my mother. At the end of the week, I sent the gardener and maid over to him for their pay. He told them he had no money; they told me they would stay on a week more. When he came a few days later, my mother opened the door for him. She did not scold him, only asked what happened to him. This was the opening for him to pour out his financial woes to her. Finally he said, "So you see mother, when she turned me down, I couldn't take it; she is all I have to depend on. I just had to go away. Tell her for me." He returned at night with his grip, but we never discussed the incident.

On the seventeenth of September, 1930, our first son was born at home. The maternity nurse in attendance telephoned him the news. He came to see what the baby looked like, beamed all over his face, and returned to the office, like most proud fathers, to say, "I have a son." He inserted an announcement in the newspapers of the birth of Marcus, Junior.

He arranged for and attended the christening at St. Luke's Anglican Church. After that we received a letter from a branch in Liddes, Evaton, South Africa, wishing the child God's blessing, and stating that he should have an African name: "Call him 'Tsepo Musi.'" Musi means ruler; Tsepo, hope to be free. Out of the presents of money I received for the baby, I bought a Holstein cow heavy in calf. When I told him, he said, "Why did you? A cow is hard to handle." But, said I, "You can't borrow a cow." Afterwards I discovered, by tracing a registered letter addressed to me, that he had instructed the postmistress to hand to his secretary all my registered letters. How much of Junior's gift money he got and used for the organization's work, I never knew.

When the cow calved, and was going dry, I sold her, and bought a Jersey cow heavy in calf, but it was the rainy season, and not wise to bring her down from the hills. In deep distress, one day Garvey came home and borrowed that money. I had to sell the calf, and all my ducks and fowls to pay for the cow, as he was unable to return the amount.

On three occasions in Jamaica he was approached and urged to retire from organization work. Once by an Englishman, who was attorney for absentee owners of an estate. The other two occasions were by an English-born Irishman, who was a merchant. The contacts were at home; the last time the merchant came, Garvey was ill and going to England for an operation. I phoned Edelweis Park for Garvey; in the meantime the gentleman asked me to remain while he talked to him, as my presence might help him to make a wise decision. I listened as he pointed out to him the hopeless financial position he was in, and pleaded with him to retire—say from ill health. Said he, "You can't escape from the net around you, and we can't help you; see what happened to Ashenheim, although he was only acting in his capacity as a lawyer. If he hadn't been, the consequences would have been greater. If you retire there are many influential people here who will back you to start life on your own. For your family's sake, give it up."

Garvey with head down listened intently, then he lifted it up and said, with feeling, "You will never know how much I appreciate the kindness that prompted you to speak as you have. Sometimes I long for peace and security, but where could I find it? Everywhere I went the sufferings of my people would haunt me, and the accusing hand of God would disturb my waking and sleeping hours. No! I just can't stop."

Between 1932–33 he continued to serve the Municipality. One of his most far-reaching resolutions was:

Be it resolved that this Council for the purpose of carrying out civic improvements, particularly involving better water supply, better lighting, installing of proper sewerage system, improvement to slum areas, building a Town Hall, erecting new Fire Brigade quarters, laying out recreation grounds and all such other works of magnitude that may be necessary as improvements within the Corporate Area, approach Government for the purpose of securing the necessary authority to float a local loan of five hundred thousand pounds to undertake the carrying out of these improvements immediately, particularly as a means of relieving the present and continuing state of unemployment and hardships among the people. Be it further resolved that the City Engineer be requested to prepare plans and estimates involving the general cost of all these improvements for the guidance of the Council in laying before the Government the manner in which the amount asked for will be spent.

In speaking on the motion, he said that depression was being felt in the big cities of Europe, England and the U.S.A. Their statesmen did not ignore it. In fact they dare not. So with initiative and planning they put into effect measures to alleviate same—the dole, relief works, feeding of school children, old age pensions, etc. The Legislative Council, instead of tackling our problems at this level, ignored it, and continued their individual, narrow policy of getting a bridge built, a stretch of road repaired, or a water tank erected. Let us set them an example in sensible planning and make the people of Kingston and St. Andrew happy.

> Some of you will ask where is the money to come from? It is right here in Jamaica. Just recently I read in the newspapers that a man died and left 650,000 pounds. There are many planters, merchants, and business men, who have made their money here, and are wealthy; but alive or dead, they do nothing to benefit the people of their communities; they have no national spirit. But they could be asked to subscribe to a loan for development, for which they would be paid interest; this act would also ease their consciences.

The opposing arguments were that such socialist planning had lost the Labour Party in England an election; they did not intend to assume big responsibilities, as they could hardly manage what they had in hand. Put to the vote, the motion was lost. It was grievous to him that legislators in both councils refused to legislate for a better Jamaica from the grass roots up; but he warned them, one day these docile people will rise in the power of their wrath, and tear down the walls that keep them ("the lower classes") low. In July 1932, he started a daily evening paper, the *New Jamaican*.

While his efforts were being opposed, the question was being strongly argued in Washington, D.C. that the U.S. government should take over the West Indian islands, as part payment for England's war debts. But American politicians are also businessmen, who knew that in accepting the islands, being so poor, their country would only be "buying trouble." A Senator, in opposing the proposal said: "Why should we relieve England of those alms houses by paying for them? Then more good American dollars would have to be dumped down there to make them working units. It is better to have our 'bad debts.' "

When England's elder statesman, in referring to the colonies said, "What we have, we hold," Garvey's opinion in this regard was, "What you have for years been squeezing in your grasping hand will one day get so warm and vigorous, that you will be forced to hand it to a younger Empire-holder. But when he gets it, he will realize that it is too dangerous for his grasp, and with traditional English diplomacy, he will ease it down beside him, and say, 'Let us walk together as partners.' "

The night of the fifteenth, and until dawn of the sixteenth of August, 1933, Jamaica experienced a cloudburst—torrential rains, accompanied by high winds and fork lightning. Homes were washed away, lives lost, fields flooded; fallen fruits blanketed the ground underneath battered limbless trees, water mains burst, and devastation was everywhere. Angry Nature had added to the misery of the poor, and to the inconvenience of the "better-off" people. Into this scene of confusion and distress our second son arrived that afternoon. His father named him Julius, after Caesar, and Winston, after Churchill. He was round faced and dark, resembling him. Junior called the baby "Chubby." He also was christened at St. Luke's Anglican Church.

About a month after his birth, a bailiff served me with a summons for over a year's taxes due on the home. I had to attend court, in order to make arrangements to pay it. My name was not called until the afternoon session, during which time I had to suffer the indignity of waiting in the court's corridor, and the discomfort of a nursing mother. When the baby was about three months old I had to take him to a doctor for vaccination. On the main street of the city I met an old schoolmate, whose greeting was, "I haven't seen you in ages. What are you doing with this little black baby?" The old concept of skin-color distinction, and the idea of "raising one's color" by marriage dies hard with our people.

CHAPTER THIRTY-SIX

In considering the staggering war debts of European nations to America, politicians and economists looked to Africa for lands in barter payments, where they could establish colonies for colored people, to live and develop, under governmental and expert technical guidance, by tapping the mineral resources of the lands. Here is a partial reference to the plan by Stephen Leacock in the *Washington Tribune*, and reproduced in the *Negro World*, February 27, 1932:

> Farsighted political economists, in attempting to solve the problems of debts due America from European nations, are putting forward the suggestion that America accept payment in African lands instead of in money. . . .
>
> Europe could get a new start by giving up territory that it cannot develop, since, at the same time, it loses its staggering war debts. America would gain an outlet for stagnant industry and unemployment. . . .
>
> Compared with Belgian rule in the Congo, America's attitude toward the Negro is heavenly. . . . The American Negro —outside of the satisfaction of seeing his fellow man lifted from the miseries of slavery, disease and ignorance—gets an opportunity to reach the top in the world of industry. He is intelligent, but his educated men and women find the high places of American industry closed to them. The development of an American colony in Africa would offer the Negro, because of his ability to withstand the African climate, the opportunity he does not get in America.

The proposed plan did not materialize, as the economists had to leave it to the politicians, to whom the vote was more important than planting a stake on the rich continent. The isolationist spirit, the willingness to leave Europe to stew in her own juice, predominated. The colored politician echoed it, with traditional loyalty to American soil, and not caring to leave "good white folks," to live and work among "savages."

The editor of *The Mercury* points out three main handicaps to our progress. He stated: "The Negro has three chief burdens—poverty, and apparent insouciance when it comes to supporting his real worthwhile men, and his blind faith in his church, and its leaders." Hand-picked leaders were but the mouthpiece of complacency and subservience; this is borne out from a speech made by Dr. Moton, Principal of Tuskegee Institute, at St. Paul's Church in Virginia, November 1930. The Governor of the state, introducing him, said: "By his sane leadership [he] has endeared himself to, and won the confidence of all Races." Dr. Moton made the following leading pronouncements:

> I take my hat off to the white man for the simple reason that he respects the women of his Race; the Negro as a whole does not have the proper respect for his Race. . . .
>
> The white people do not want the Negroes to go back to Africa, especially those in the South. We love white people, we love to have their approval. You will not find any Race in the world that will be as loyal to white people as the Negro. I would not leave America; I would not leave the South; I am not discouraged; there is no reason to be.

Dean Kelly Miller, in a signed article reproduced in the *Negro World*, May 21, 1932, confessed his disillusionment, and came to the conclusion that the Negro must save himself. He stated:

> There is still a lingering hope in the minds of an unthinking leadership that salvation will come from political parties. Negro religious and educational leadership has relied upon the philanthropy of the North to redeem the race from the besetting weight of ills. But the flagging spirit and waning interest of this vicarious philanthropy clearly indicates that little fur-

ther dependence can be placed upon salvation from that direction. I myself, at one time, believed that the race could confidently look to the Christian religion, under the Protestant form, for salvation. But my views have been greatly modified by the sad experience of the past forty years.

The Catholic Church with its powerful organization could bring no greater glory to its name than to vindicate its divine claim by solving a problem which other agencies have given up as being insoluble. But as a Catholic statesman once said to me, the Church is able and willing to cope with every feature of the race problem except that of social equality. Ah, here's the rub.

Capital and labor all over the world are on the verge of fundamental conflict. The Negro stands hesitant between the two as to which side he may best look to for salvation. Whether he subordinates himself to capitalism or communism, he does so with the hope of vicarious salvation. In his weakness he feels that he must "fly to the rock that is higher than I."

Of all the various brands of race leadership since emancipation, that of Marcus Garvey alone sought to make the Negro his own self-savior. The debacle of his statesmanship was due to the woeful inadequacy of the means at his disposal for the accomplishment of the colossal task he assumed.

The race today is without any effective leadership that leads to any definite objective. But all thinking leaders are now convinced that there can be no vicarious salvation. The Negro must save himself or be forever lost. The spasmodic independent efforts that are being put forth in business, politics, and social procedure show plainly that the Negro is now beginning to look within instead of without. Outside influences will assist and encourage him to more efficient self-effort. It is demonstrated folly to think or say any longer—"lo, here or lo there, is the kingdom." The kingdom of heaven is within you.

S. A. Haynes, writing in the *Negro World*, May 6, 1933, under the head, "Through black spectacles," summarizes the work of Garvey, and says he should be given credit for all he achieved:

Marcus Garvey, whose philosophy of racial solidarity and Negro autonomy in Africa astounded the imperialists and scared the easy-going, patient, conservative Negro, can now drink deep of the cup of victory for which he paid dearly. Far, far away from the streets of Harlem and thoroughfares of American Negro life and culture, some of the very people foremost in fostering his persecution and sealing his exile from the country, now find it safe to clothe Garveyism in a new name and dispense it fearlessly to a race dying because of the ineptitude of its leaders; stranded in the wilderness of American civilization because of the treachery and hypocrisy of its men of light and learning.

Garvey led the way in mass organization of Negroes; he blazed the trail in militancy; he sacrificed his freedom in one mighty effort to give to the Negro a higher emancipation. His absence from the American scene has not profited the Negro as was anticipated and heralded. The Bectons, the Father Divines, the Bishop Graces, the Moorish-Americans make no impress on the governments of the world; theirs is a program of consolation through emotional and spiritual complacency.

Garvey gave something to the Negro which neither time nor place can retrieve. Most of his enemies, particularly those of the Negro Intelligentsia, now agree that Garvey was essentially right in the fundamentals of his program. They agree now that there can be no real freedom and independence for black men anywhere without mass action and uncompromising leadership.

Garvey erred, but his errors faded into insignificance before the concrete contributions he has made to Negro thought and culture. He gave to Negrodom a Black Philosophy, profound in depth, startling in its repercussions, inspiring in sentiment and in fact.

He brought the Negro people of the world into one family through the propagation of a program which gave birth to an international comity between them. The universality of this program bridged the chasm between Negroes everywhere.

Garvey demonstrated two things: (1) That Negroes can be organized; (2) That Negroes are eager to repose confidence in and support sincere Negro leadership.

By his uncompromising utterances, Garvey brought the Negro problem forcibly before the world.

Garvey deified black and gave Negroes a racial consciousness not before attained. When he invaded the United States he found "black" a symbol of regret, excuses, and pity; the trademark of inferiority. Garvey changed the order of things. He made "black" the symbol of honor and responsibility.

Garvey's clarion cry of "Africa for the Africans," those at home and those abroad, gave more publicity to Africa and the Negro than any similar effort since the Negro's emancipation.

Garvey sold the Negro to himself with the same zeal and enthusiasm that white Americans, Englishmen, Frenchmen, Italians and Japanese use preserving their racial identities.

His philosophy of a black culture has done much to bring the Negro into greater intimate fellowship and communion with the Motherland Africa, and with Negroes in distant lands.

Garvey, through his noble experiments, with the Black Star Line and the Black Cross Navigation and Trading Company, demonstrated the possibilities of the Race in the fields of commerce and industry. For years his organization provided honorable employment for Negro men and women. At one time there were more than 1,000 on the organization's payroll in the United States alone.

Garvey encouraged the Negro to scale the highest peak in human endeavor. He sent three delegations of black men to the League of Nations, two to the republic of Liberia. He appointed Commissioners and sent them to represent the Race in foreign lands. The gesture buoyed the Negro's self-respect and gave him a new hope, and a new vision.

Lest we forget, Garvey has not failed. Slowly, but surely the mists of prejudice, jealousy, ignorance are being rolled away from the racial horizon. The American Negro's bitter experiences with the purposes of rugged Americanism, plus the sufferings he has absorbed during the depression have served to convince him that Garvey was not, indeed, a charlatan, a devil, or a naive, but a FRIEND and COUNSELLOR, who came to serve him and his generation.

Lest we forget, Garveyism is now sweeping the lanes of Negro life everywhere; it is obscured by fictitious names and hedged in by renegades, but it is Garveyism just the same. Common gratitude, fairplay, and a sense of justice demand that we give Garvey due credit for his vision and his courage to follow it through without counting the price.

CHAPTER THIRTY-SEVEN

Garvey's frontpage articles to the *Negro World* weekly were as forceful and foretelling as his speeches. The following is a typical one. In February 1932, under the head, "Europe's doom—Africa's opportunity," he declared:

Fellow men of the Negro Race,
    Greetings:
    The war clouds on the international horizon are once more gathering, and it is most likely that at any time a Continental conflict will break out, through the militaristic tendencies and designs of Europe, which will ultimately engulf the world in another holocaust.
    It is for such a time that the four hundred million Negroes of the world are preparing themselves, when the opportunity will be presented to strike the blow in Africa for our liberation. It is hoped that Negroes everywhere will prepare themselves for the time when they will be called upon to stand together as one mighty whole to blast a way toward those changes that are desired by us universally. Critics have speculated as touching the programme of the Universal Negro Improvement Association, claiming how impossible it will be for us to accomplish the things which we have set out to do, but all reasonable minds can see and readily admit, that the changes which will bring about better conditions among Negroes will not so much be instigated through war by the Negro himself as by the very people who have robbed, exploited and killed us for hundreds of years. The great Colonial governments of Europe will, of themselves, strike the blow by

which the four hundred million Negroes of the world will be made free, and Europe is just lining up for such a contingency, as is evident to all.

Let us get ready, let us organize now more than ever for the putting over of the programme of the Universal Negro Improvement Association. We want victory, and we must have it. We want a government of our own, and we must have it. We want freedom, true liberty, real democracy. We must have all these things. It is not a question of whether the other fellow is going to give it to us under his government or not; it is a question that we must go out and possess ourselves of that which we desire.

The only way we can have freedom is when we, by our own effort, have laid out the foundation of a great government that we ourselves will control. For such an opportunity, I repeat, we wait, and may God hasten the day. Let Mussolini rave, let Germany clamor for African soil, and then in a short while we will see Europe so ablaze, that it will take more than human effort to smother the flames. Europe is fast gravitating to her doom. The nations of Europe have seen their day and time. Like Rome, they will crumble and fall to pieces, and as in the fall of Rome came the resurrection of other empires and mighty nations, with the fall of the present monarchistic, capitalistic and despotic empires of Europe will come the resurrection of a great African state upon which the sun will never set.

There is one thing about us: we are determined. If it takes eternity, we shall win our cause.

I have the honor to be,
Your obedient Servant,

By July 1934, the depression in America of the last two years had fully affected him, as Garveyites had been unable to support the organization. Colored Americans suffered even more than white ones, for the former depended mainly on employment for a living; in turn their small banks, insurance companies and businesses collapsed faster. White women now had to do their own housework—the colored woman's last resort for work; homes and farms went under the hammer, with few buyers at give-away prices; the Wall

Street crash caused rich men to commit suicide rather than face the haunting fear of daily wants. This crash sent panic throughout the commercial, industrial and business areas; and so it went on down the line, as bulk buying came to a standstill and money became frozen.

Overproduction at that time was the root cause of the slump in business. Under a strictly capitalistic system, feeding the machinery of war is good business for industries; but at the end of a war, it takes time to change over to peacetime production, and years to find foreign markets in countries impoverished and ravished by war, whose currencies are so far below par as to make trading with a dollar country almost impossible. Such recovery is slow. These, and other factors caused a recession in trade, and, as from a creeping paralysis, slow business bogged down in depression. Relief measures and President Roosevelt's New Deal were bringing America back on her feet.

In Jamaica, Garvey's mail was being tampered with. It is said that there was some censorship, and Americans complained that some letters had been returned marked "addressee unknown," or "fictitious address." In September 1933, most of the machinery at the printing plant was seized for debts, and he was forced to cease publication of the *New Jamaican*. He called a convention for August, so that the delegates could decide what should be done, and started to publish *The Blackman*, as "a monthly Magazine of Negro thought and opinion."

The Seventh International Convention opened on the first of August, 1934; despite the terrible financial strain he held the usual parade and public mass meetings. Now, more than ever, people wondered at the courage of this man. At the first business session, he gave a survey of all the past activities of the organization to make the race economically independent, from their own sources of unit operations, and an account of the treachery and hateful jealousy that caused colored men to destroy every effort, until now they were even reduced to the pitiful spectacle of lining up at soup kitchens and receiving financial relief. What a different scene it would have been had the Liberian colonization been allowed to develop, and the ships to trade freely. The delegates discussed conditions at length, and decided to remove headquarters to London, and on a five-year plan to build enterprises as the earning capacity of the members permitted in the future.

In December the mortgagee foreclosed on Edelweis Park, and put it up for sale at public auction, at which a relative of his bought the place for even less than the accumulated principal, interest, taxes, etc. An agreement was made by which the U.N.I.A. remained as tenants, as the new owner had no immediate use for the property.

Anticipating his leaving the island, Garvey agreed to an auction sale of all our furniture, by the man who held the bill of sale on them, who collected every penny in reduction of the mortgage. The day after the auctioneer had ceased to cry going! going! gone! we stood in an empty house, except for a bedroom suite, the books, and two large pictures and vases left unsold. This did not affect him as I thought it would. He looked forward to living in England despite his asthma and the damp climate; he would be at the hub of world affairs. He never felt crushed by crises; future events could overcome them; his view was not shortsighted.

Two days later he left us for England, with instructions for me to rent out the home, get two rooms somewhere, as my mother's home was being remodeled, and in time he would send for us. He had sorted out some of the books which I was to ship to him, the balance, as well as records, papers, etc., were to be stored at Edelweis Park. As soon as the newspapers reported his departure, the doctor brought me a bill for payment, which was incurred during and after my pregnancy with Junior. I was also served a judgment summons for an unpaid balance on an acceptance. I had no idea that these amounts were still outstanding, and had to make arrangements for their payments by monthly installments, out of the small irregular amounts he sent us.

He leased a part of a house at 2 Beaumont Crescent, West Kensington, London, and in August the same year (1935) sent for Miss Daisy Whyte, his secretary in Jamaica, after financial reverses had forced him to send home the other two. He also employed an English stenographer. As *The Blackman* gained subscribers, he had to get more help, so he sent for another clerk, who formerly worked at the headquarters. When she was leaving he instructed me to crate and ship "collect from consignee" the two large paintings. One was an oil painting of himself. I did so. About four months later, I received a letter from the shipping clerk stating that I had placed him in an embarrassing position, as he had done me a favor in shipping the pictures "collect." Mr. Garvey had not taken delivery of them; warehouse charges, etc., plus freight, must be paid by me promptly. I had to borrow the money and pay it. I wrote Garvey about it; he replied that there were more urgent matters there that had to be met.

CHAPTER THIRTY-EIGHT

In the summer of 1935, we find him speaking in Hyde Park on Sundays during fair weather. His subjects were the colonies and their peoples, and the topical subject of the Italo-Abyssinian War. He secured liberal-minded white people to preside at the meetings. His persuasive eloquence drew large crowds. The following is a report of an indoor meeting:

> Mr. Garvey addressed a meeting of the West Kilburn Liberal Association, London, October 10, on the subject: "The Crisis in Abyssinia." The meeting was attended by Liberals of the District, and was presided over by Mr. Ernest J. Cove. Mr. Garvey spoke for an hour, and created a great deal of interest and enthusiasm over the Abyssinia affair. Arising out of his speech, the Association started a fund to assist in providing Red Cross equipments for the soldiers of Abyssinia. After the

speech, there was an enlightening discussion of Abyssinia's condition at this time.

In his "News of the World" column in *The Blackman* during this year, there were many items that touched on the sore spots of colonialism, among them the following:

South Africa. Nov. In speaking at the 1830 Memorial Settlers Association held in Johannesburgh recently, General Smuts declared: "The only way to eliminate the fear complex which besets our white population in the face of the Native masses is an increase in the white population. Many good people would be willing to be more progressive in their outlook, if this dangerous fear complex could be removed."

It is cruel to pretend that there is no scheme to submerge the Negro. All around there are manifestations of the fear of his rising to be a real man.

St. Vincent, a little Island in the West Indies, where some unfortunate people created some disturbances recently, has now passed some severe sedition laws, to prevent the people from ever repeating what they did. The local press is to remain under permanent censorship. To publish anything critical of the Government invites a fine of one thousand pounds. To hold public meetings, and say anything of the same nature means imprisonment. Yet we have listened to public speakers in Hyde Park here, who have criticized any and everything political, religious and otherwise, and we have never seen or heard of speakers being arrested and imprisoned for free speech. Free thoughts, if not expressed in the newspapers or at meetings, cannot be imprisoned, nor can they be imprisoned in the people's minds either. So think on, St. Vincentians! Freedom of thought for freedom, is your right.

In an article in the December *Blackman*, he wrote, under the head, "The Task of the New Negro—a New Africa":

Our civilization is travelling at a rapid speed. In its motion it carries with it the hopes, desires and fates of all peoples. Sensible people, realizing their positions in this speedy movement of time and circumstances, calculatingly sober down themselves to a proper understanding of what the changes mean to them in particular, and when they have satisfactorily analyzed conditions they apply them in relationship to themselves, so as to gain such advantages as would tend to give them satisfaction, as civilization moves on to its changing epochs.

Unfortunately, the Negro group has not sobered down itself to a proper understanding of these circumstances and conditions, and many go forward blundering and blustering to realize ultimately, that we are placed at a terrible disadvantage in the comparative progress with other groups in the civilization that environs us.

Civilization should be an urge to embrace all its benefits and to improve upon its accomplishments. It is a practical result of the application of man's mind upon his material environment. It grows and expands only in keeping with the creative force of human intellect. It rises and falls with the ambition or retrogression of the particular people who are willing to lead or to stagnate. The civilizations that we know were the practical results of the application of the various groups to the development of certain phases of life in their particular periods. Our civilization today is the positive result of the creative thought of those who are actually mastering our politics, science and industry. The Negro laments his position in the midst of these changes, whether they be upward or downward, but has failed within modern times to apply himself to the willingness of doing, of creating for himself, thereby establishing his own place in civilization.

Must we conclude that the Negro has no feeling, no passion, no desire for anything? Naturally not. The Negro is human like any other creature. His hopes, his ambitions, his desires should be no less; hence it is our duty to stir him from the four corners of the world to the willingness of doing— doing that which is praiseworthy, which is noble, which is humanly grand.

He must build his civilization. At least he must fashion the civilization in which he lives to suit his particular purpose and needs.

No useful purpose is served by complaining against the incidents and accidents of an environment that is man made. It is for man in his supreme urge—in his willingness to do—to sacrifice in doing, to so plant around him the atmosphere of things, as to make himself satisfied, indeed joyous and happy in the pride of knowing that what he wants he has made.

1935 has brought changes to the world, and among them is a universal thought of what Africa is to be in the future. No sober or sensible thinker will deny the arresting truth that Africa is today a new country—new from outlook, new from consciousness, new from environments and conditions. Out of this newness will arise, in the next century or so, a new political order that will lift the old continent to a new position or place in the firmament of national glory. Like old Europe, Africa will change into many native nationalisms, and men and women who were once slaves, serfs and discounted creatures will become living forces in the material progress of a new civilization. This, at least, is the hope of hundreds of millions of people today, who probably a year ago never thought in that direction. Mussolini's Fascist madness and brutality has paved the way toward the hastening of a new national life, which otherwise might have been stifled for another century.

Africa has registered the indication of approaching time. It will be beyond the power of man to turn back that time, for God Himself has spoken.

CHAPTER THIRTY-NINE

The American Garveyites, on hearing that he had pneumonia during the winter of 1936, felt that he needed home care. So their officers wrote him stating that they would be willing to book our tickets for New York, where I could, by speaking, raise enough money to pay our way on to England, and settle us on arrival there. He did not agree to this, fearing that the children might be kidnaped by his enemies and held for ransom, which he knew the members would endeavour to pay, perhaps only to find the dead bodies of his sons. There is an African saying: "If you can't ketch Quakoo, you ketch his shirt."

The moneys he was receiving were not enough to finance the volume of work for the organization and publish the magazine; so our going was deferred for these priorities, until June 1937. He arranged for us to sail the first week, together with a maid. In the preparation to leave without adequate funds, I missed the thoughtfulness and unsolicited service of the Garveyites in America, who were partly made up of naturalized West Indians, but whom the American atmosphere had mellowed with the spirit of giving and doing—unlike most Jamaicans at home, who had nothing to give but their services, and even this they withheld. Yet they asked so much of others. Truly they go to bed with the "gimmes," and wake up with the "wants."

Just before leaving I wanted to get a doctor's advice about our younger child, so I took both of them down to a doctor whom Garvey had made a job for in the New York office during summertime, to enable him to pay his way through Howard University Medical School. He was now a successful doctor and had no children. He gave the child a once-over, and said, "He is a fine healthy boy, image of his father. Don't let him have liquids in the evenings." He turned to Junior and said, "So you are Marcus? Well, I wonder which of you will follow in his footsteps?" In passing the dispenser's window she asked me for the fee. I told her the doctor had not prescribed any medicine, so I did not think he would charge me. "Yes," she said, "he just phoned me to collect it." I gave her an amount, and she informed me that all doctors' scale of fees had risen since January; I paid the amount asked for, took the hands of my children, and walked the sunny streets until we reached a friend's office, where I borrowed a shilling for tram car fares to take us back home.

We landed at Avonmouth. He came to meet us. In appearance he had not changed much, though his hair was thinning out in front. He was pleased to see the children. They had on the warm suits he had sent them, and walked about the waiting room. As his eyes followed them, they dwelt particularly on Julius, who walks like him. When he realized I was looking at him, he laughed; in sheer delight he said, "I must have been just like him as a boy," then, in a subdued tone, "I wonder what the world of tomorrow will do to him." On the boat train to London he asked about conditions in Jamaica, if there were any perceivable changes.

He wanted to send the children to private schools, but the fees were high. When the London County Council free schools opened for the fall term, I chose a nice one at Kensington Gardens, and took them there. Then, I recalled a scene at our home in Jamaica in 1934, when Junior was almost four years old. The head Black Cross nurse, a delegate to the convention, came to see the children. Junior sat in an armchair in the library, showing her pictures in a brochure of New York City. His information was so accurate, that she said, "Darling, how is it you know so much about New York?" He thought for a while, then looked straight at her, and pointing his finger at himself for emphasis, he said, "You see, Nurse, I was in New York before I was born." In amazement she related this to his father, and added, "We will have to raise a lot of money to educate this boy."

Every summer the Canadian government permitted Garvey to visit there in the interest of the organization. He left me in charge of the office, with written instructions, and took his secretary. In Toronto, he conducted a Regional Conference, not only of representatives from the U.N.I.A., but other fraternities. A group of Garveyites attended from the state of Michigan, for a special meeting. In introducing Garvey, State Senator Diggs said: "I regard this not only as a great privilege, but I do not think I have enjoyed anything more since I left the cotton fields of Mississippi than to see, hear and present this great Negro to you."

At another meeting the Mayor of Toronto attended. Garvey referred to the Industrial Exhibition which he had seen, and the thrill it gave him to see the rapid scientific progress Canada was making. He thanked the Mayor for all courtesies extended to him and to Garveyites. In closing he said, "Just as French Canadians, in deference to France, still speak French, as English Canadians feel proud to be a Dominion of the British Commonwealth, even so, the New Negroes have an undying love for our Old Country; although some of us may never go back there, we are going to help those at home to make it a free and progressive country in our generation." At Sydney, Nova Scotia, Mayor Mather welcomed him.

At the end of the conference he left on a trip, which he described in *The Blackman* as follows:

I sailed away from England on the 12th August, and returned on the 20th November, 1937. My trip was for inspecting the activities of the Branches of the Universal Negro Improvement Association, holding a Conference at Toronto, Canada, of the American and Canadian Branches, running a Summer School at Toronto, for the month of September, and visiting each Island of the Leeward and Windward group of the British West Indies, which were all done within an arranged period with great satisfaction. Closing the Conference on the 31st August, I conducted the School of African Philosophy, which by the end of the month had graduated several persons for U.N.I.A. leadership in America and Canada. In October I started a trip to Nova Scotia and New Brunswick in Canada. I had the most splendid receptions in the Maritime Provinces, and was overwhelmingly received at Sydney and Glace Bay.

By the 7th October I had journeyed down to Halifax from which Port I boarded the "S.S. Lady Nelson" on the trip to the British West Indies and South America. I spoke at all the Ports from St. Kitts to Demerara, and at each and every place met a tremendous concourse of people who had assembled to do me honour on my first visit to the respective places, with the exception of Barbados and Trinidad, which I visited before. I spent two days at Barbados, Trinidad and Demerara respectively, and those two days will long be remembered in the history of those countries.

At other places of the West Indies my stay ran into hours,

but even though the time was short, the enthusiasm ran so high in each and every place as to have made the trip more than satisfactory. The Universal Negro Improvement Association in the Islands have before it a wonderful work for development. Considering the programme of the Conference in which the American and Canadian delegates accepted that of the last Convention, which involves the development of the Negro of the entire world in the new Five Year Plan, it is expected that these Islands, as soon as they start to shape themselves, will become beneficiaries of a grand and noble effort of Race redemption.

I desire to express my deepest thanks to all the good friends in all the islands, who did their utmost to make my trip the success it was. The friends I met in St. Kitts, Nevis, Antigua, Montserrat, Dominica, St. Lucia, St. Vincent, Grenada, Barbados, Trinidad and Demerara will never be forgotten.

My trip to the West Indies has proven a boon,
I hope to come this way again soon,
I met there men, and women too,
Whose hearts rang out with joys anew,
I ne'er shall such joys forget,
As coming from those friends I met.

He gave a typical West Indian speech at St. Kitts, which was published in the *Union Messenger*, a local newspaper, and later reprinted in *The Blackman*. The following are extracts:

Mr. Chairman, Citizens of St. Kitts: It is with an abundance of pleasure that I am with you this morning to meet you, and talk to you. The Chairman struck the keynote when he said that the purpose of my visit was to help. That is not only the purpose of my visit, but the purpose of my life—to help my fellow men. I am doubly glad to see the make-up of the audience. At a glance I can see it represents all classes of the community. But there is a special class that I am specially interested in, and that is the more unfortunate class. . . .

It is God's purpose in the creative plan, that he shall be happy. I don't like to see misery; it is hellish, devilish and ungodly. God never made misery; it is the result of the mistakes of man. But if you can get men to go right, they will lessen their own misery. . . .

When God equalized men's soul, he gave them a free will and free expression. When we suffer in this life it is because we are not using this free will and expression. . . .

I like people who look like me. Everywhere you turn you find them. They seem to live in spite of the hell that surrounds them. But it is not always going to be so, for we are approaching the scientific age when oranges that were once sour are now made sweet, and sour oranges have no market. So it is that "sour" people will die out to accommodate superior people whom God intends to have and keep and bless. . . .

It is useless for man to approach God as though it were possible to change Him. God, in making the earth, made it with rigid laws. . . . The stars, sun, moon, etc. never change. Everything remains the same irrespective of our desires, for God is a fixed God. He does not change. He is eternal. When He made man he said, "By the sweat of your brow you shall eat." From that time man has been on his own responsibility —on his own legs. If he does not think out his own way of life, he will fail, and who do you think is going to shed a tear for him, when by his ignorance he has reduced himself to disgrace? Have you ever seen the stars stop twinkling because of your sorrow? Or the sun stop shining because you are sad? This may be a strange philosophy for a small town, but it is true. . . . The earth on which you live is God's, but the material accomplishments of the earth are man's work. I am introducing to you a new philosophy of life, although I may only be able to touch the fringe.

Here God has given us probationary life, and some of us stay around and run amuck, most of the time in rags, stealing and making ourselves a nuisance. If God were like man he would say to us, we don't want you up here to mess up heaven. Our souls, our intelligence should be like unto God. When we cringe and commit crimes, we bring down God to nothingness. We must live up to the dignity and honour of His intelligence by possessing our souls and using our minds. It is no excuse to say you are too poor and down trodden. I put myself before you as an example. I refuse to be in rags. I am determined to be a man among men. I was born 50 years ago in a West Indian country town in Jamaica, where black men have no special advantages, but disadvantages; where you are slated to be a cow-hand or labourer, a blacksmith or shoemaker. I looked at the system that man fixed for me, and I said this does not suit me. If you have not the ability to fix yourself up, the other man is going to fix you up—and some of you are darned well fixed up right now.

A lot of people today are suffering from their own faults. If you know the world you would know that the greatest men had humble beginnings. But before they started life they found out what use they could be. Men like Ford, Rockefeller, Carnegie, Lipton, started from the lowliest walks of life, and gradually growing. When they died they left the world thinking. Wealth is not all; it is the intelligence of man that counts. An intelligent man can always find a way out. But I have never seen a successful fool. Somebody always takes what he has away from him. It is a fool who is always in rags; a fool is always complaining, always telling you somebody is against him; always going to the Obeah man to give him luck. But let me tell you that there is nothing outside of you as strong as what is inside of you. That power inside you is the stronger. If you don't understand this, then you are only a bit of flesh and other men will trample on you. Why come here like a flying fish, or a sprat, that nobody remembers after it is fried and eaten? We must not allow any theory or system that is not for our good and welfare to swallow us up. It is purely a question of mind over matter. Men can do things to my body, but never to my mind; I shall leave the influence of my mind after I am dead. You can read the minds of men in books, like Shakespeare's *Othello* or the Gospel of St. John. You must postulate a philosophy of your own way of life, if you are to find a way out. God blesses those who help themselves.

The average West Indian child spends his school days in the Elementary Schools; after that he is finished with books. He coins his own language—bad words, and that completes his education. Why should a man confine himself to his backyard, where his bad words are law? The energy that most of you put behind your bad expressions if used in the proper channel would make you Alexander Hamiltons and other great men.

My friend, you have to buck up, and make your own civilization what it ought to be. Read! read! read! and never stop until you discover the knowledge of the Universe. If you don't understand the compass of your own world, how can you navigate properly? Christ Himself paid tribute to intelligence, when he made it clear in the parable of the talents. Spend a little less on food and a little more on books and newspapers, for today it is a struggle of wit against wits, brain against brains. . . .

This is a small place and things of importance do not happen here very often. So anyone coming in from outside is regarded with suspicion. You need not be afraid. I have not come here to steal anything. But what I would like to steal away is ignorance, so that when I cross the Caribbean I can dump it into the deep Atlantic Ocean.

I like the country very much, and the people too. You are very hospitable here. Everywhere I went I was received with open arms. . . . Try to make your little country the best spot in the world. Get hold of the land, and don't let it get away from you. The men who own the land make the laws. Own your own house and land; then you will be a respectable citizen, and God will approve of you. May the blessing of Almighty God be upon you.

In the early issues of *The Blackman* for 1937, his column, "The World as I see It," contained the following interesting items:

Germany is still teasing Europe. She has moved her cruisers into Spanish waters for the purpose of finding incidents to legalize the affair of her broadsides against the Spanish government, with the hope of igniting the powder box that will blow Europe to pieces.

Whether the blowing-up comes this way or not, all of us are looking toward the explosion. That is why the Negro Race ought to be prepared, because when the explosion comes in Europe, sparks will be flying everywhere.

Roosevelt has made his trip to South America to cement the friendship and fellowship of the American Republics. This is indeed a wise move and can well be understood under the leadership of a man as studious and philosophic as Franklin D. Roosevelt. He knows that sooner or later Europe will kick off and may try to convey some of her troubles to the Americans.

———

A company has been formed to promote white settlement in the highlands of Tanganyika, and the promoters of the scheme, under the chairmanship of Lord Chesham, have already obtained the necessary land from the Tanganyika Government, with the approval of the Colonial Office. The area for settlement—an inner circle of the high-lands round Sao Hill—is about 6,000 ft. up, fertile, sheltered, well-watered, and blest with a pleasant climate.

———

Denied the right to occupy their $20,000 mansion in the exclusive Edgemont Hill section of Westchester by decision of Supreme Court Justice Lee Parsons Davis, Monday, Captain and Mrs. Joshua Cockburn will carry their case to the U.S. Supreme Court.

The injunction was sought on the ground that there existed a clause in the deeds of the properties owned in the district which stated, "that no part of the said parcels shall ever be used or occupied by or sold, conveyed, leased, rented, or given to Negroes or any person or persons of the Negro Race or blood, except that colored servants may be maintained on the premises."

After hearing the evidence and arguments in March, Justice Davis reserved decision. At the trial the Cockburns contended that they were not Negroes. Citations from textbooks on anthropology and the history of man, and arguments as to the definition of the term "Negro," enlivened the hearing.

The Captain Cockburn referred to was the Captain of the first ship of the Black Star Line. He is black and his wife is fair-skinned.

———

No one desires to be unfair to Haile Selassie. The only sad thing is that he has been unfair to himself, to his country and his country men, by acting in a manner not consistent with ordinary political intelligence necessary to our age, in understanding the machinations, cunning and vile methods and systems of Governments and peoples.

He kept his country unprepared in a modern civilization whose policy was strictly aggressive. He resorted sentimentally to prayer and to feasting and fasting, not consistent with the policy that secures the existence of present day freedom for peoples; whilst other nations and rulers are building up armaments of the most destructive kind, as the only means of securing peace and protection, he relied on the peculiar policy of leaving everything to the Almighty Wisdom of the Universal Creator, Who in all history, has never yet taken political sides between two rival human political forces and powers. For God to maintain his equilibrium, He cannot take sides in human political differences between peoples and nations, otherwise He would cease to be the God of all. On the one side we have the Pope of the Catholic Church blessing the Crusade, and on the other side the Coptic Church fasting and praying, with confidence of victory. Surely God was not on the side of the Italians and Fascist Mussolini dropping incendiary bombs and mustard gas from the air on defenceless people in their own country?

The Emperor fled to England for help through diplomacy. The Italians have slain the Rasses or Rulers of the Provinces. Everywhere is death and desolation. When Ethiopia again stretches forth her hand to God, it will have to be a hand of progress.

CHAPTER FORTY

Colored children were rarely seen in England at this time; so he enjoyed taking the boys out, as they attracted attention. Junior went more often, as they could discuss cinema shows. He was intrigued by English remarks such as these: "Aren't they lovely? . . . such large black eyes! What beautiful white teeth! They speak English, too. Can I just touch him for luck?" Julius became so accustomed to being admired, that one morning when I was taking them to school, he stopped suddenly, and said, "Mom, is anything wrong with me?" I looked him over, and assured him that he was just right for parade inspection. "Oh," said he, "that's not for today. No girls admire me this morning."

In February 1938, Garvey rented a house at Talgarth Road, a few blocks away from the office. It had been vacant for some time, so I told him to have coal delivered in the bin before we moved in, as damp walls are injurious to health. The coal arrived after the furniture. The house was large enough to accommodate living quarters and office, but he observed, "It would be too risky to do that, only to have some old clauses revived in a court action, to get me out of the place, for using it for business purposes."

He had the furniture put where he wanted it; he assigned me a room on the top floor in the rear; his secretary had the large front one, and the maid the smaller one. On the second floor were his bedroom, bathroom and library. Two sitting rooms were on the first floor, and in the basement, the dining room and kitchen. I asked him to transfer us to the sitting room in the back, and distribute the few pieces of furniture there to the front room and the dining room. "No," said he. "Up there the children are out of the way, and not distracting to me." At times his father's disposition asserted itself in him over milder influences; so that one could trace the similarity of actions. The inheritance complex is stronger in suppressed people, so that, although a man may strive to be what he wants to be, basically he is made up of what has been, the genesis of which gives him impulses to do and become what he does not wish to be; therefore he usually denies the labels his actions merit.

After measles Junior contracted rheumatic fever by kneeling on one knee on the bare floor behind an arm chair, playing machine-gun bombardment with Julius (our room had only a small carpet and a strip for the bedside). That knee became drawn and painful; the fever lasted three weeks. I had to put a frame over his legs to keep the pressure of the blankets off them. The strain was terrific to keep the fire in the room going, nurse him, and go up and down the stairs for nourishment and hot water.

His Dad came upstairs almost daily; from the doorway he would ask how he was, or come to the bedside and talk to him for a few minutes; but he was always too busy to stay any time. There was only one bed in the room, so I had to use a bedroom chair. Julius could not go to school, as the maid had no time to take him; from not getting enough fresh air, he had bronchitis. I was at the breaking point one day when I asked Garvey to stay with the children, and give me a chance to go downstairs to his room and get a good rest. "No," he said. "I don't know how to attend to them, and don't like to see them sick; in fact I don't like to see suffering anyhow."

In the fourth week of Junior's illness, he suggested that I try to get him out of bed. I told him what the doctor said, that he must be kept warm in bed, for in his emaciated condition if he got a chill it might develop into pneumonia; although the pains did not travel from joint to joint, yet his heart was a bit weak. In describing the pains he felt in the affected knee, Junior told him, "It is like lightning striking through it, and my heart trembles." Said his father, "You must be brave. I don't want you to become a weakling. When the asthma bothers me, I try to throw it off, knowing full well that when the body becomes weak the forces of man, and even nature, seek to brush you aside."

At the end of the fourth week, the doctor called us together, and said that at this stage the case required a bone specialist and the necessary nursing care in an orthopaedic hospital ward. The joint was rigid but if he got immediate care it could be straightened out. Garvey's reply was that if the specialist could not come to the home and treat the child, he had no intention of sending him to a hospital. Downstairs, in the hallway, the doctor said to me, "You are the mother. The laws of this country protect a child's health despite the whims of the parents. . . . I will make all arrangements for him at the Princess Beatrice Hospital, where an eminent specialist will treat him."

At the hospital the waiting patients were quite willing to allow the little West Indian boy to be examined first; in fact, they were rather solicitous about him. After examination, the specialist called in the senior medical officer and the superintendent; they conferred, and told me that the child must be left in the hospital; they would notify his father of their decision, and he would have to pay one guinea ($4.25) weekly for him. When I told him that evening, he said I had no right to leave Junior there, for who to tell if it wasn't a plot to hurt him, in an indirect way, by harming the child.

However, two days after, he went to see him, and visited him often during the three months he had to remain there. He took him chocolates and a volume at a time of a set of ten of the "Children's Encyclopaedia," by Arthur Mee— editor of *The Children's Newspaper*. In this manner, although absent from school, Junior was well informed. The other little patients who could walk gathered around his bed at times to hear him tell in a dramatic manner all about the world and its people. Garvey also became a center of attraction, because he was "Marcus's father."

When I took Julius to see Junior, he also came in for a lot of admiration from the nurses, who occasionally took him to their quarters, breaking the rule of no male visitors in dormitories; they loaded him with sweets and toys. The ward sister once said to Garvey, "You have two fine boys; Marcus is a remarkable child for his age; we are doing all we can to make him walk again."

In the summer of 1938 he left us in England for his annual visit to Canada, this time to hold the Eighth Convention. He did not take his secretary. She said she was tired, so he had one from New York to meet him there. The morning just before he was to leave he handed me four pages of typewritten instructions, and told me I was again in charge of the office. Two pounds ten shillings ($10) weekly was for house money and personal needs of the family, which amount was not to be deducted until the staff were paid. His being in Canada meant that extra moneys from entertainments would be taken to him by the delegates; so balancing the budget was taxing, to say the least of it. Anyway, I earned the compliment for my sex, from one of the English typists in the office, when she said, "It takes a woman to do it."

At the end of August, Junior's leg became slightly drawn; it had been out of plaster and put in a hip-length pure wool sock. I rushed him back to hospital. The specialist examined him and said I would have to consent to ether being administered in order that the leg could be straightened out and replastered. What the boy needed was sunshine, and, said he, I will confer with the senior medical officer and the school doctor to confirm my opinion that he must be sent to an orthopaedic home in the south of England, where violet-ray treatment will be given him. At the consultation, the senior medical officer suggested that I take him back to the West Indies for sunshine until he recovered. The school doctor, a lady, asked smilingly, Where was the objector? I told her he was in Canada. "Well," said she, "you must decide. This child is intelligent and should not be allowed to grow up as a cripple."

I sold a diamond ring, booked our passages, and cabled an S.O.S. to my aunt for the balance. I told no one of my plans until the night before sailing, when I informed the maid that she must stay and take care of Mr. Garvey. I checked off with his secretary some jewelry, which I put in the safe, as well as the balance of money in hand and two letters—one containing a statement on the office transactions, the other marked personal, explaining the urgency of Junior's case, and that we would stay at my mother's home. I also handed her the keys to the safe, and one for the clothescloset, in which I left overcoats and all heavy clothing. She was upset, and said, "How am I going to tell Mr. Garvey?" Just hand him the letters, for, said I, "If Junior fretted and died in an orthopaedic home away from us, he would blame me to the world, for not using good judgment in his absence." The headmistress of the children's school, in answer to my letter, stated that she was sorry to lose them, but that I was acting wisely in taking Marcus to a warmer climate; he showed promise of being a scholarship boy.

Early September, we sailed from the Royal Albert Docks on the S.S. *Casanare* for Jamaica, via Amsterdam, where we stopped to fill her coal bunkers; we spent a day, leaving at night through the illuminated waterway to open sea. The last we saw of England were the white cliffs of Dover, which are symbolic of the austerity and aloofness of her people. The ocean was calm the entire voyage, which gave us an opportunity to rest and revive our spent bodies. Off the coast of Haiti, the news on the bulletin board made the officers and seamen realize that on their return to England, many of them would be called up for duty in the Navy.

While the ship was being docked, the stewardess took the children up on deck. Soon after she returned to complain that a crowd of "native workers" were on the pier waving to them, and the children did not respond, would I come up and greet them, which I did. The reason for the crowd dated back to the riots in "the merry month of May," when laborers all over the island gave vent to their years of pent-up resentment against their conditions by striking for better wages and working conditions. The vast army of unemployed joined them, adding another demand: "We want work." The angry neglected masses were on the march.

Black men ordered owners of motorcars out of them, and if they said haughtily, "Do you know who I am?" or "You will pay for this," the rioters smashed the car, and said, "Walk, you son of a gun, as we have walked for years on hungry stomachs." It was not a race riot or a color riot; these desperate men and women felt that they must now, with their own hands, destroy anything and everything, that represented the class barrier, which had kept them away from good food and decent homes and, in short, a happy life. The violence simmered down; a Union was being formed, but the air was still charged with demands and threats. The rumor had spread that Garvey was coming, so much so that the *Daily Gleaner* printed the following:

> The Gleaner understands that Mr. Marcus Garvey, President General of the U.N.I.A., who has been away from Jamaica for some years, will return to the Island within the next two months. He is, so far as our informant was able to state, still in Canada, and should travel to Jamaica by one of the C.N.S. liners.
>
> Mr. Garvey's visit to the Island will be for the purpose of gathering first hand data on the labour situation here, so that on his return to England he can make direct representation to the Home Authorities. It is not anticipated that if he does visit the Island . . . he will endeavour to establish any Unions, or otherwise organize labour, though it would be obviously, very interesting and eventful should he make such an effort.

The late Sir Stafford Cripps, a former Member of Parliament, in *The Tribune*, October 7, 1938, made this comment on Jamaican conditions: "On Monday last, I returned from a ten weeks' holiday in Jamaica, where I had witnessed British Imperialism at work, with all the tragedy of poverty, suffering and suppression that such a system necessarily imposes upon a subject and exploited population."

Despite the fact that it was later published that Garvey was not listed among the passengers, the crowd of laborers had gathered anyhow. Many of them had been loading a banana boat on the other side of the wharf, singing, "Come Mr. Tallyman, tally me banana. Bunch!" The reporters asked me many questions—"Do you intend to take any part in politics in Jamaica? Will you pave the way for Garvey to come later on?" When I asked the children why they did not wave to the crowd, Junior looked thoughtful and said nothing. Julius, dramatizing his words with a sweeping downward motion of his hands said, "When I saw them like that I was amazed." While working, the banana carriers wore stained and tattered garments. The boys, living abroad, even for a short time, were becoming out of tune with the norms of island life.

The day after we landed, I took Junior to the Public General Hospital in Kingston, and handed the senior medical officer the letter from the specialist; he was very considerate and courteous, and arranged for the orthopaedic surgeon to look after Junior, and gave him a private room, when he objected to staying in a ward where the children were hollering and speaking badly. The surgeon kept him in for a few days to remove his plaster, X-ray the leg and put on another plaster. After that he attended hospital fortnightly as an outpatient for nearly two years. The surgeon gave him the best care and attention, even beyond the point of duty. Because of my financial condition I was not billed by the hospital.

On arrival, I was just in time to lose the home by private sale, as the rental could not pay for the mortgage, taxes, water, insurance and repairs for damage by termites, which are prevalent in the tropics. Anyhow I figured on getting a small balance, but to my surprise a firm of lawyers had lodged a caveat against the title in the matter of an equitable charge I had given years ago to finance the purchase of two linotype machines for the printing plant. There was a balance still due, plus interest, so I only received fifty pounds ($200) from the sale of our home.

I wrote and told Garvey everything, but got no reply to two letters. So I wrote his secretary, who informed me that he was angry because I had taken the children back to Jamaica. While he had not given her any message to give me, yet he said that in Jamaica we were better off than he was, where a shelter and cold weather were concerned. I had to pay the monthly installments to the doctor and on the judgment summons. Junior had to be nourished and carefully watched. I had to push him in a wheel chair to and from school. How long could the fifty pounds last? I took charge of my share of my father's estate, and started to develop it to be revenue bearing.

Early January the following year his secretary came out to Jamaica on vacation. She brought a package with two suits for each boy, some books, two letters, each with one pound ($4) enclosed. I told her she could take back the two pounds to him, and tell him that when he is able to make it up to the past four months' support, he should mail it. She said, "I could not dare do that. He missed the boys very much, and was worried over Junior. Every Friday he puts five shillings ($1) each in their postal savings. Money was slow in coming in, and somehow he felt that with your family connections they are alright." Yet he should have known that the attitude of relatives and some friends would be, put colloquially, "If you make your bed hard, you must lay down in it." When the secretary was returning to London, we sent him a package of Jamaican delicacies. He sent two pounds ($8) about every three weeks for what he called "pocket money," but the support never came; he always complained that he had "to keep things going at the office."

The Eighth International Convention was held in Toronto, Canada, from the first to the seventeenth of August, 1938, which was his birthday, and was appropriately celebrated. The city went gay to welcome people from all parts of the world, and trains came across the border from America packed with members. Having closed his four years of administration as President-General, he resigned, and was reelected for another term of office. In one of his speeches he made this point:

> The changed aspect of the world's political situation forces upon Organizations changed attitudes, and in this the U.N.I.A. is not found wanting. . . . Within recent years its work has been carried on quite differently, to the early days of its foundation. Many of the world changes that have affected the Negro for good, have been quietly engineered by this Movement, and even at this time it is undertaking one of the most colossal programmes to be engaged in. . . . The leaders of the Association have learned to do more effective work quietly

than by continuing to make declared statements, which may lead to embarrassment and confusion.

From Johannesburg, Samuel Matsalula closes his report on the atrocities in South Africa thus:

> Africa is full of the melancholy wails, sobs and groans from every city, village and hamlet, and all these mournful noises issuing from thousands of separate hearts have conglomerated into one great sound of affliction and what a sad plight it is to behold . . . but still there is a bright optimism, because under the surface of our oppressor's tyranny, is undoubtedly gathering a latent moral force, and once it breaks through the obstruction that holds it in check, and follows the law of forces long retarded, will leap into ascendancy with such rapidity and energy, that will amaze and bewilder men; and all their intended fatal and ruthless obstacles will serve as stepping stones to the higher and nobler lives, to the enjoyment of Black Majesty, which nature will undoubtedly provide as it did to those who preceded us in civilization. Oh, that I shall live until that seemingly fallacious and impossible time comes to pass.

CHAPTER FORTY-ONE

In 1939, Garveyites and others who had lost so much, and suffered thereby during the depression, made a combined effort to petition the U.S. Congress to inaugurate and finance a colonization program for their transportation and settlement on lands contiguous to Liberia, to be acquired in settlement of war debts owed by England and France.

They worked for many months procuring the signatures, occupations and addresses of persons desirous of going, until two and a half million were received, and duly checked later on. These events are reflected in the *Congressional Record*. While they were thus engaged, the colored armchair politicians got busy. They could not allow Garvey's program to be financed and sponsored by the government; they worked on their white political bosses. So only a few senators from the South were willing to sponsor the bill, the most notable being Senator Bilbo. Unfortunately he was very unpopular with our people, as he was coarse and rude in his attitude to them; but he was a sick man; perhaps he wanted to make amends for his past conduct, or he felt that it would relieve the pressure of the colored people on the economy of the South and leave the poor whites with greater opportunities. Whatever were his motives, he took the petition, and with the aid of others framed a splendid bill, in which he did not even mention the words "colored" or "Negro," so careful was he not to offend our people this time. He referred to prospective migrants as "Citizens of the U.S.A., who may qualify for membership in Liberia," knowing that only persons of African descent are eligible for Liberian citizenship. The Bill was presented to the 76th Congress, April 24, 1939. The following are extracts from the *Congressional Record*:

Be it enacted . . .

Title I.

Section 101. This Act may be cited as the "Greater Liberia Act."

Section 102. It is hereby declared to be the intent of Congress that the benefits and provisions of this act shall apply to citizens of the United States who may qualify as eligible for citizenship in the Republic of Liberia, and who by their physical fitness and climatic adaptability may qualify as migrants to be permanently settled in the territory hereinafter provided for those who shall have voluntarily expressed a desire to become migrants under the provisions of this act.

Title II

Section 201. (a) The President of the United States is hereby authorized and directed to enter into negotiations, through the Department of State or otherwise as he may deem appropriate, with the Governments of the Republic of France and of His Majesty the King of Great Britain, respectively, for the purchase by the United States of, not to exceed 400,000 square miles of territory of either or both such countries adjoining the Republic of Liberia, or capable of annexation to the said Republic of Liberia.

Section 703. Until Congress shall have been able to estimate and determine the annual cost of the operation of this act and the available income for the same, the President is hereby authorized to utilize the following funds and credits to put this act into immediate operation and to finance the initial expenditures in connection with this act;

(a) All customs, Federal internal revenues and other Federal taxes levied and collected within the territory of Greater Liberia.

(b) All payments in gold or in cash paid by the Debtor nations to the United States by virtue of World War debts, whether the same is a so-called token payment or any other form of cash payment.

(c) Not to exceed $1,000,000,000 (one billion dollars) of any funds of the United States available and not allocated for any other purposes; Provided, that if such funds be not available, the President is hereby authorized to pledge the credit of the United States in an amount not to exceed the said $1,000,-000,000 in order to secure funds.

Colored politicians and writers did not study the provisions of the bill or the benefits two and a half million of our people would immediately derive from it—whose future the United States government would underwrite to enable them to expand, eventually as a National Unit, from doorman to President, without limitations. No, in their blind hate of Bilbo, of Garvey, and in their selfish disregard of the appalling conditions of the masses of intelligent, ambitious people, they abused Bilbo, and influenced legislators to vote against the bill. Mr. Bilbo died soon after.

This Greater Liberia Bill was the culmination of previous efforts made by some of the southern states, through their political leaders, at the request of Garveyites, to seek federal aid for African colonization; notable among those efforts was Senator McCallum's resolution to the Mississippi Legislature in 1922, which reads:

Be it resolved, by the Senate of the State of Mississippi, the House of Representatives concurring therein, that we do hereby, most solemnly memorialize the Congress of the United States of America to request the President to acquire by treaty, negotiations or otherwise from our late war allies sufficient territory on the continent of Africa to make a suitable, proper and final home for the American Negro, where under the tutelage of the American government he can develop for himself a great republic, to become in time a free and sovereign state and take its place at the council board of the nations of the world, and to use such part of our allied war debts as may be necessary in acquiring such territorial concessions, to the end that our country may become one in blood as it is in spirit, and that the dream of our forefathers may be realized in the final colonization of the American Negro on his native soil, and that the spirit of race consciousness now so manifest in the American Negro may be given an opportunity for development under the most advantageous circumstances.

In 1936, the State of Virginia had sent the following Memorial to Congress:

Whereas there is valuable land sparsely populated in the Republic of Liberia a portion of which land is reserved for American Negro colonies, and many of our Negroes evidence a desire to live in an independent nation of Negroes, and strive to achieve a high and honourable race destiny;

Therefore be it resolved by the House of Delegates, the Senate concurring, that the General Assembly of Virginia memorialize the Congress of the United States to make provisions for the colonization of persons of African descent, with their own consent, in Liberia, or at any other place or places on the African continent.

In the West Indies the proposal for African colonization by West Indians was also being discussed. Captain C. Greig, writing in the Barbados *Advocate*, and reprinted in the *Jamaica Standard*, March 13, 1939, surveyed conditions in the islands; and, citing overpopulation as the principal cause, he proposed colonization on the West Coast of Africa, where he had lived previously. In part he wrote:

There is enough land on the African Continent under our Mandated and Protectorate systems to absorb the entire surplus populations of the West Indies, and I am not talking of desert but fertile lands and high forest. . . . This would provide a constant future outlet for over-population in the West Indies. . . . I read in the Advocate of Saturday week that the Imperial Government had made a free gift of 8,000,000 pounds to Czechoslovakia and had promised a loan of another 8,000,000 pounds. Further enormous sums have been expended on refugees from foreign countries.

If this be so, is it too much to hope that some such expenditure could and would be undertaken by the British Government to help their own Nationals out here in their present plight. More especially as a good part of it could be regarded in the light of a national investment, the interest on which would be paid . . . once the Colony was firmly established, out of their revenue and indirectly by the volume of trade both ways, to and fro, with the United Kingdom, which would take place once a Colony of this size, with adequate resources, was added to the Empire. . . .

The ordinary busy man in the streets in England knows nothing of the troubles of the West Indies, and in consequence cares less. Because he does not care and is not interested, the Press tells him nothing. It declines to publish free copy now, for which, if the public interest were really aroused, they would gladly pay. On the other hand the troubles of the Jews in Germany and of the Czechs are known to countless millions the world over, for the Press is plastered with pictures and details of their plight day after day and month after month.

In short, they are "News" and we are not. The fact that they are "News" means that the Press will vie with each other to secure first details of their hardships, with the result that world wide indignation and sympathy has been aroused, while the fact that we are not "News" leaves us still struggling with a problem incapable of local solution. . . .

Germany wants colonies and has already pointed to the unrest in the West Indies as indicating our inability to manage an Empire, that has grown too large and cumbersome. This brings the situation on the fringe of European politics and at once gives it an importance which it would otherwise lack at home.

Colonization of West Africa by West Indians was just what England and France did not want; not even for individuals to go there, unless they were screened before leaving; hence the proposal was ignored by some, and squashed by others.

For the year 1939, in his column, "The World as I see It," in *The Blackman*, Garvey pinpointed important world moves on the part of the white statesmen:

> On May 12th, the British Prime Minister announced that the British Government would be prepared to facilitate the settlement of Refugees over the whole of the interior of British Guiana. This announcement was made following a report by a special commission that was sent to that Colony to investigate the conditions there. The whole scheme is aimed at settling the wandering Jew and to give him another foothold where he may establish himself for another generation or two. It is evident that British Guiana has been made the pawn against the majority race that occupies the country who are colored people.
>
> The following is a West Indian comment from Basse-Terre, St. Kitts—"The contention will always hold good that West Indians should be settled in British Guiana in preference to Jewish refugees. In view of the fact that 3,000,000 dollars has been found to settle 5,000 refugees, the ways and means of settling even a lesser number of West Indians there could also be found if the British Government was as energetic as it should be in discharging its obligations to His Majestys subjects in these parts."

———

Hitler wants Colonies! is the cry, and to give them to him would be a fatal mistake. Britain has Colonies—and to keep them in their present state is not only a fatal mistake, but an offence against humanity. Why? Kabinah Kwansah comments on some of the conditions in the colonies is an enlightening answer:

"The Colonial Office exercises complete control over the lives of 55,000,000 people. In many parts of the Colonies Sedition Ordinances rigorously curtail liberty of speech and freedom of the Press. In Trinidad an assembly of ten or more persons for a political purpose constitutes a breach of the Sedition Act.

"In Barbados, during 1937, a 23 year old unemployed labourer was sentenced to ten years imprisonment for leading what would be called a hunger strike in Great Britain.

"The Gold Coast has probably the most enlightened administration in West Africa, but only nine of the 29 members are Africans. How can this puny minority represent the people of the country? In the Protectorates even this token representation of the people does not exist; the High Commissioner rules by decrees.

"Burdensome taxation and intolerable Pass Laws ensure an abundant supply of cheap labour for the farms of white settlers in Kenya, Nyasaland and the Rhodesias.

"Nyasaland inhabitants leave behind their wives and children in the villages, and trek 600 miles to Southern Rhodesia to earn sufficient money with which to pay their Poll Tax. The result is disruption of the life of entire communities. Any show of resentment is brutally suppressed. During 1931 in Southern Rhodesia native workers of well-known copper mines demonstrated against a cut in wages, which coincided with a rise in the Poll Tax, and were mowed down by machine-gun fire.

"Prevailing conditions in the Colonies amount to this: poverty, malnutrition, disease and ignorance. It is the duty of British democrats to remove these evils immediately. It is their duty also to extend to the Colonial peoples the same rights as they claim for themselves, and to encourage the rise of free, democratic institutions. For though we must not give Colonies to Hitler, neither must we perpetuate the ill deeds of Britain."

President Roosevelt during the month of April, made an appeal to the world, in which he said: "You will realize, I am sure, that throughout the world hundreds of millions of human beings are living today in constant fear of the new war or even the scare of wars. The existence of this fear—and the possibility of such a conflict—is of definite concern to the people of the United States, for whom I speak, as it must also be the complaint of the other nations of the entire Western Hemisphere." Has the President forgotten the fact that fifteen million American Negroes have always lived in fear and dread of the future, brought about by the never ceasing prejudice of the white people of that country who outnumber them?

No President of the United States can speak of justice to the world without having the Negro question thrown in his face, and although President Roosevelt is recognized as a very able leader, and one who has done his best for the Negro in America, it must be recognized that he is still President of a nation whose hands are not clean. It will be a long day before America will be able to speak to the other nations by way of leading them into following her example.

Garvey seemed destined never to have any respite from the evil actions of members of his own. In September of 1939 the Supreme Court of British Honduras gave its final decision in the celebrated Isaiah Morter will case, which had its beginning in 1922 when Mr. Morter came from Belize for the convention and for medical attention. He was our guest, and was greatly impressed with the work being done, especially in Africa. When he died he left a will in which he bequeathed almost all his estate to the U.N.I.A. for African redemption. His properties in British Honduras included a small island, abounding in mahogany, coconuts and chicle, from which chewing gum is made. Relatives and others contested the will before it was admitted for probate. The question whether "African redemption" involved improper activities had such a bearing on the whole case, that it went from court to court for over twelve years, even after the will was probated, to prevent the parent body U.N.I.A., under Garvey's control, from getting the legacy. During this time he sent an eminent barrister to Belize and England, and retained a solicitor and a barrister in Belize to attend to this matter, all this costing about one thousand pounds. Finally the court awarded judgment in favor of a

U.N.I.A. Inc. of New York City, which was represented by one man, without members and with no program for African redemption.

CHAPTER FORTY-TWO

On the eleventh of January, 1940, Garvey became ill. His Indian doctor diagnosed it as hemorrhage in the brain, which caused his right side to be paralyzed. The doctor instructed his secretary to notify us of his condition, but said that with care he might live for two more years. He had a white housekeeper then, but his secretary, Miss Whyte, Mr. McIntyre, a Grenadian clerk in the office, and Mrs. Youssof, a native of Bechuanaland whose husband was an Ethiopian, took turns to nurse him, as he refused to go to a hospital. He gradually improved, and his speech became plainer. Miss Whyte was an Anglican, so she asked her Minister to visit him; Mrs. Youssof was a Roman Catholic, and she asked a priest to see him, and a Father Clark came regularly.

In March, when Junior was able to do without his crutches and his leg was permanently out of plaster, I had his picture taken with Julius beside him, and sent it "to Dad with love." His secretary in a letter to me said, "When he saw the picture of the boys, he looked at it steadily, then tears came down his cheeks. He insisted on keeping it under his pillow. For days he has been sad, and will hardly eat. I don't see why he is acting this way. When the first money came in through the mails, he ordered me to send them two pounds ten shillings which is ridiculous as there are bills to be paid."

Lying paralyzed on one side, and unable to get around, he now felt and understood the suffering of Junior, who might have been a permanent cripple. Did the picture of his two young sons arouse his paternal instincts?

A comment often heard in America, even after his deportation, was: "It is too bad this man was not let alone"—from persons who felt sorry for this hunted man. "Stop pursuing him," they said. "Let him settle down, and have a chance to put through his program." But it would have been contrary to human nature for his pursuers to have given up the chase until the kill was made. His program was built around three fundamentals:

1. Uniting the peoples of the West Indies, the colored population of the U.S.A. and Africans at home into one brotherhood for betterment and uplift.

2. The redemption of Africa from the exploitation of her lands and labor.

3. African nationalism—nationhood being the only organized means by peoples for self-expression and self-determination in a well-ordered world society.

Each of these points struck a blow at the various systems of maintaining "white supremacy," the proponents of which keep black men down and beneath them, as a platform on which they stand and tell the world how big and powerful they are; this gives them stature. They regarded Africa as a breadbasket for Europe, her minerals and raw materials vitally necessary to their industries and commerce, to maintain them as leading nations of an advanced white civilization. Therefore every effort Garvey made in furtherance of his program retarded their progress. If Garveyism succeeded, their superstructure would topple, as unwilling shoulders eased them down to bear their own weight and burdens. The self-protecting policies of nations override human kindness and consideration of others.

In this invisible battle of opposing wills, the mind is the deciding factor. In terms of materialism, the strong imposes his will on the weak, and feels that as long as he can rule by law, or death from the air, his position is secure. He disregards the possibilities of the awakening of the minds of the retarded and oppressed, gauging the latter's mind by his lowly material condition and position. However, awakened minds transcend material handicaps; and in time and place fashion weapons and fight their way to freedom. Who can see and stop the ideas in men's minds before they are translated into action?

There are seven important stages of Garveyism:

1. Awakening and uniting Negroes the world over.

2. Changing the thinking of the aroused to a realization of manhood potential abilities.

3. Channeling the newly released emotional energies and resentment into constructive individual and racial interests.

4. Mass sacrificial work and struggle to reach embryonic nationhood—the interim stage.

5. Through legislation and otherwise, to stress mass education along scientific and industrial lines, also character building, which are the sinews of any nation in peace or war.

6. The preparation of nationalists for the grave responsibilities of leading and directing young nations, whose people have been denied the privileges and advantages of early preparation.

7. The final efforts to unite and keep together the young nations, not only to protect themselves, but to lead those still suffering under colonial and protectorate rule.

Thus the scope and timing of the work of Garveyism is inconceivable to the average mind, and can only be rightly assessed in the context of world history, as time demonstrates it.

It was customary for colored people to be used to do the "dirty work" for white people; so naturally no better tools could be found than Garvey's own people to destroy him and his work. Besides, they were only too glad to get him out of the way, as they were being eclipsed by the rising sun of Garveyism. Gone were the days when these starlets were looked on with childish awe by the masses, who formerly regarded them somewhat in this vein:

"Twinkle, twinkle, little star!

How I wonder what you are."

In their anxiety to get on with the job they never studied Garvey to find out where his weakness lay. Had they done so at close range, they would have realized that unjust opposition brought out all the fighting qualities in him; but having a complex disposition, if he were kindly treated he could be trapped, mainly because of his belief in his fellow-man. An instance was when a man from an interracial association in America, pretending to be the victim of discrimination, he being the only black man as their sub-officer, phoned Garvey at home, and subsequently came there twice. He explained what he called his predicament—he received a small pay, for which he did more work than the others; he wanted to resign, but could not do so unless he was assured of a job in another organization. Garvey was most sympathetic, and said that while it was only at conventions that officers were elected, yet as Administrator he could call a meeting of the Executive Council, put his case before them, and perhaps they would agree to his being taken on temporarily at a better salary than he was now getting. He returned to our flat for the results, which were favorable. However, he insisted that Garvey write him a letter offering him the position, but not mentioning the fact that he had sought it. Garvey, unsuspecting, did so. The man used this letter to get a raise of pay, then to ridicule Garvey, whom he said had "asked him to join his African nonsense."

In assessing the leadership of Garvey, it must be considered that it was his faithful followers, wherever found, and numbered in millions, who by their exemplary conduct under provocation and repression, gained for him the title of an outstanding leader. To them he was their "CHIEF," the name they and his associates called him. He believed in them, and they in him; this mutual faith and love consecrated the task of leadership, and the devotion of the followers.

In computing the membership of the organization, to say that it was about six million is no exaggeration; yet it can never be accurately arrived at, as there are divisions, branches and chapters of the U.N.I.A. besides chapters of Garveyites under different names in fraternities, and "pockets" of Garveyism as a philosophy among study groups, etc. Besides, Garveyism is a COMMON FAITH. A member sent him a poem of salute while he was in Atlanta prison; one of the verses reads:

> Look up, Brave Heart! You struggle not alone,
> Nay, you have soldiers whom you've never known.
> Revive your faith; press ever firmly on,
> For lo, Almighty God is on His throne.

The man, woman or child who has heard Garvey speak, or has read his writings becomes inspired, and if converted to Garveyism is a changed person in outlook; however, most of them will not give him credit for the change.

The parent body had no record of all members in each division and branch, as the locals only sent lists of names of those who sent in their quota of subscriptions. A division in a town like Raleigh, North Carolina had a membership of ten thousand, but few of that number were paid up, especially when jobs were slow; or in northern towns where a plant closed down hundreds would drift to a more prosperous town or city. It was too dangerous in some locals to have the names of some supporters or Garveyites listed as members for fear of reprisals, in their jobs, churches, or even in their family relationships. The locals controlled their own funds; they were registered or incorporated under state laws; so it was just a malicious accusation whenever Garvey's enemies declared all revenue from local membership dues as "going into the coffers of the Parent Body." In many places in Africa and the West Indies they had to operate secretly or quietly; therefore not much financial support came from these areas. The agents for the *Negro World* took advantage of the situation, which made the newspaper a strain on the U.N.I.A.'s funds; yet the paper had to be sent out to keep the people informed of our point of view.

It was Garvey's speaking ability that brought in funds; people flocked to see and hear him. To understand his magnetism and persuasive eloquence as a speaker, the testimony of William L. Sherrill, later President-General, suffices, as he relates his conversion in Baltimore, Maryland years ago:

Here was I, a successful business man with a family, member of a church, a lodge, and fully insured to protect them. I did not have to join anything else. I subscribed to the anti-lynching campaign every time a Negro was lynched. I did not like to hear people talk about conditions of my people, as I had overcome many of them; let everybody else do likewise. I argued this way against the persuasion of friends.

One night on my way to a show, I saw a huge crowd outside a church. I went up and said, "What's going on in there?" A lady turned to me and said, "Man alive, don't you know that Marcus Garvey is in there talking? Yes, indeed, Garvey in person." "Shucks," I said, "I may as well see what he looks like." I could not get near the windows, so I had to get a ticket for standing room only. I squeezed in, until I could get a good look at him; then suddenly he turned in my direction, and in a voice like thunder from Heaven he said, "Men and women, what are you here for? To live unto yourself, until your body manures the earth, or to live God's Purpose to the fullest?" He continued to complete his thought in that compelling, yet pleading voice for nearly an hour. I stood there like one in a trance, every sentence ringing in my ears, and finding an echo in my heart. When I walked out of that church, I was a different man—I knew my sacred obligations to my Creator, and my responsibilities to my fellow men, and so help me! I am still on the Garvey train.

What weapons did this crusader use in battering down the walls of oppression? He enlightened the minds of his people so fenced in, and they, in their newly acquired strength, and spiritual urge, used it to undermine them. He looked at the world as through a telescope and saw what lay beyond, to warn and prepare his people for "the tomorrows in the lives of peoples and nations."

CHAPTER FORTY-THREE

Garveyism has been dubbed "Black Zionism," but if Jews are God's chosen people, then Africans are God's favored people.

Jews had to pledge their personal and financial participation in the Second World War in order to establish their homeland in the portion of Palestine now called Israel, surrounded by hostile Arab countries; they experience great hardships to maintain themselves on the poor soil, but the Jews of the world continue to send help to the homeland.

Africans are spread over the whole continent; the descendants of the dispersed Africans in the West Indies, Central and South America are in the majority in the islands, British Honduras and British Guiana. They are all becoming in time self-governing territories. That the colored Americans did not plant their own stake in Africa in the twenties to establish their rights in the homeland and their ability to govern themselves is regrettable. However, the tripartite global implications of Garveyism have no parallel in history.

Garveyism is neither an escapist program nor an abdication of Negroes' rights in America, as suggested by some of his northern critics to slur Garvey and ridicule the real importance of the African colonization proposals. African redemption is an outlet by which the race will develop and expand to the stature of men and women with national prestige and economic security, thus enhancing the position of those who remain in America to fight for full citizenship rights. It is common knowledge that economic pressure causes race friction. One is bound to respect people who through their own efforts cease to be beggars—of jobs, political patronage, better conditions, and social privileges. Thus the Garvey agitation helped the American equal-rights demand, for no longer were colored people depending on this as their only saving grace; white people knew that, and reacted accordingly.

True fellowship of peoples of different races must be based on mutual respect and esteem, free from condescension and tolerance. The law cannot successfully enforce "social equality" without the existence of this state of mind.

The colonists could have used their technical training gained in America to develop the natural resources of Africa and become wealthy, even as white American companies are now getting rich out of Liberian concessions.

There can be no decline of Garveyism, even though every effort was made in America to wreck every big scale colonization plan by the U.N.I.A., its affiliated organizations or by statesmen to Congress, and other legislatures. As Garvey said: "Be assured I have planted the seed of African nationalism so deep, so far and wide, [it] cannot be destroyed, even by the foul play meted out to me."

Today in Africa and the West Indies young nations are emerging, and all Negro America takes pride in these achievements, being blood brothers of those who are seated at the United Nations' meetings.

It is said of Garvey that he was extravagant and bombastic in speech. True, but would not the Englishman, with his Anglo-Saxon frigid calm say the same thing of a Panamanian or Nicaraguan mass leader, who was speaking for the freedom of his people? Garvey so believed in the potential ability of his race to control its own destiny if unfettered and unhampered that nothing he said in this regard seemed to him far-fetched, and time has proven him right.

The awakening of a dispersed race dormant for centuries and the challenge to their over-lords—so that once awakened from their racial trance they would be able, in time, to throw out the usurper—had to be accomplished by drastic utterances to arouse both races. But this accomplished, he changed his speeches and writings to exhortations on the preparations necessary for colonists and pioneers in all walks of life.

The only ground on which white people are really united is RACE; neither language, religion, nor political systems have as cohesive a force for all nations; and because of this knowledge many white leaders deplored the idea that Garvey, too, should organize his race, and the colored yes men echoed agreement, and called him "a Racist, in a world that was gradually breaking down racial barriers." But to the oppressed and submerged masses, that gradual process was too slow to affect them in their lifetime, if it was left mainly to the change of heart of the dominant race; for man behaves as his very nature dictates; it is only the veneer of his culture that hides his impulses and passions.

Studying the systems that control the various white nations, and their application and implementation toward black, yellow and brown races, one must come to the conclusion that the white race is well enough organized to try to maintain its leadership of the world. Some are diplomatic enough not to flaunt it, others maintain a conspiracy of silence on the matter; but he who has to face the barriers daily, or try to avoid the pitfalls, feels and knows that it is ever-present in a greater or lesser degree in all parts of the world; therefore it behooves the black race to so position itself for recognition and respect, and not be tethered by the will or pleasure or displeasure of the superior(?) white race, who are free.

One may well ask the question: How free can he be? Or: How free is his freedom? The answer may well be, to do as he darn well pleases to other races: He has the power. But in this reckless exercise of his freedom, he often becomes a slave to his own weaknesses and baser nature, thereby eventually causing him to retrograde. Seeing this happen under his very eyes, Garvey constantly warned his people to be prepared for freedom; for it involves grave responsibilities and restraint. Whether our freedom is obtained by political upheavals or gradually, by pressure from within or without, we must be prepared scientifically and technically to co-operate in Africa for the common good.

In 1955 a white American in writing about Garvey stated that "it was doubtful whether Garvey could find today in the United States the ready response that greeted his early proselytizing efforts." Isn't it axiomatic that it is oppressive and repressive conditions that generate mass leaders? The conditions in 1916-19 were modified by 1924 under the aggressive leadership of Garvey, and so on as the years went by. Garveyism is not static, for the different stages of its program coincide with the development and uplift of our people.

American critics treat Garveyism only as it applies to colored Americans and gleefully assert that, because they helped wreck the colonization plans and the ships they defeated Garveyism. If it were possible for Garvey to come back in the flesh, he would tune his utterances and actions to participate in the new political freedom of the West Indies and West Africa, the foundations for which he cleared the way and built. To the minority in the U.S.A. he would say, but for a few self-satisfied and self-seeking, jealous Negroes, you too could have been established in a self-governing Greater Liberia.

Integration of the minority race group into all phases of the life of the nation will be a national victory, hastened to its climax by international opinion regarding the treatment accorded Negroes as the barometer of American democracy; but in the years to come, the practical realization will be absorption. Lacking the prestige of a Greater Liberia nation of their own in the motherland, it will turn out to be a hollow victory. Garveyism planned that the units should complement each other, and demonstrate to a skeptical world the ability of colored Americans not only to fight for their rights in the land of their birth but to venture forth to

Africa and build and man their own democratic nation, and prove that they had served their apprenticeship well under the hardy stock of the Pilgrim Fathers in the building of an American democracy.

Professor Gordon Lewis, writing in the *Jamaica Gleaner*, September 9, 1957, under the head, "American debt to the West Indies," stated that the most important tasks of the Federated West Indies will be the development of foreign service, ambassadorial representation, and trade relations, as soon as they are relinquished by the British government. The cultivation of diverse relationships with every nation disposed to be friendly to the West Indian cause will greatly help—America being foremost, for, said he, "The West Indies can indeed lay claim to American friendship and affection. In their own way they have given much during their history to the American cause."

He related the enormous stimulus the West Indian trade gave to the early economic development of the American colonies; their mutual interests caused Pitt's abortive plan for their federation into a wider Imperial Parliament; the West Indies gave to the federated American colonies men like Alexander Hamilton, the first Secretary of the Treasury, Jost Van Dyke, architect of the Capitol buildings in Washington. The Emancipation of 1834 gave a tremendous spurt to the abolitionists' cause in the United States; and, added Mr. Lewis:

> In the following century Jamaica itself gave to the cause of Negro freedom the name and fame of Marcus Garvey; for although few will condone the Black Fascism and the Messianic power-ambition endemic in Garveyism, the movement he created was at least instrumental to the growth of proud self-consciousness in the American Negro, and aptly illustrated the vital importance of the dynamic agitator in the history of freedom.
>
> Mills' phrase is—"it is always the discontented that makes for progress." Garvey was that, and one day Jamaica will do his memory adequate homage.

He further stated that West Indian Federation is a challenge to the American neighbour to honour the finest element in his nature, and closed the article by stating:

> There is real room for adding American friendship to the English connection, but it must be a friendship wherein the terms are shaped by the West Indian nation on a basis of equality with the American neighbour. In this way the United States will repay the debt they owe to the West Indies in the best of the American tradition.

CHAPTER FORTY-FOUR

"Africa for the Africans, those at home and those abroad," is not merely a slogan; it is a just demand, a reasonable expectation, a righteous hope, a faith in the Creator's purpose. It is the pulsating heart of Garveyism—therefore a vibrant call for dedicated Negro lives, and a challenge to the integrity of colonial powers in that continent.

How well it has succeeded in the homeland, its trials and struggles leading to its eventual fulfilment are evidenced in the secret reports in the archives of the colonial offices of England, France, Belgium, Italy, Portugal and Spain, to which few writers will have access, since they prove what awakened black minds can achieve in defiance of lashings, imprisonment and bullets. It would hurt the prestige of colonial powers for the world to know that a lone black man caused them so much concern; that their statesmen had their ears to the ground to hear of his every movement and utterance. Thought they—If Garvey was not stirring up a mass uprising, was he playing for a convenient time? Or was it to be a sit-down strike in the mines and elsewhere? Above all what was going on in the minds of these Africans? What messages were the tom-tom drums relaying in the dead of night? Houseboys (house servants) were suspected; so were Headmen, even when they disclaimed any knowledge of Garvey, or of trouble brewing. It would be unwise even at this time to record names of those who journeyed to all parts of Africa to spread the doctrine of freedom.

There could be no full scale acceptance to the invitation of the King of Abyssinia in 1922, as the only means of transportation at that time was by ship to the Port of Djibuti, then by French railroad to Addis Ababa, the capital—a costly and tedious journey by which one could not easily transport machinery and household goods. However, many individuals went, and were well received by the government which was only too glad to utilize their professional and technical skill. The French and Italian governments became greatly perturbed, and asked Abyssinia to stop the influx of Western world Negroes, as they might form a pocket there, and trickle over the borders to stir up trouble. From then on persons desirous of going had to get the Abyssinian Consul-General to get jobs for them with the government, especially in schools, or satisfy him and his government of the immigrant's financial ability to set himself up in business. They also had to declare that they were not connected with the Garvey movement.

Although the Liberian Government required a declaration even more stringent, still the Garveyites continued to get into the country. In his lifetime Garvey had a common understanding with them, that their denunciation of him was to enable them to pursue the work of Garveyism in Africa, to help leaven the whole.

From other parts of Africa, both seamen and students have been indoctrinated in Garveyism in England, France and the U.S.A., and on their return home, quietly and secretly spread the gospel of Unity and Freedom; some have become leaders, have created dedicated followers by their teaching and inspired faith. It is not difficult to maintain loyalty in followers to the cause of liberty in a land of their own, where they are in the majority.

Seamen have done magnificent work in carrying the

Negro World and leaflets in basic English to ports of Africa and Asia. A seaman once said that when his ship docked at Vladivostok, East Russia, he said to himself, "Here is where I won't be able to make a single contact"; but he was wrong; before he left that port, he was introduced to two West Indians who had married Russian women, and made their homes there. Said he, the pride and joy in the eyes of those men were indescribable when he told them of the world movement for freedom led by Garvey and handed them the literature. Seamen set up chapters of the U.N.I.A. in out-of-the-way places like Sydney, Australia, and Honolulu, Hawaii.

During the years Garvey had representatives of the U.N.I.A. in Paris and London, there was, besides, always an African representative in London to keep in personal touch with Africans working for freedom. The expense was terrific. Some had to give up the work because of lack of funds; others worked in their spare time for a gratuity, which, quite often, Garvey had to give out of his salary, as this did not seem so important a work to his colleagues. At times Garvey could not risk the person's identity being known to them, particularly when the reward was made for valuable information sent personally to Garvey.

Under the adversity of European rule in Africa, tribal wars were suppressed so that all Africans could be available and in condition to exploit the mineral and other resources for the benefit of European companies and cartels. This also had the effect of uniting all Africans in a common cause of freedom from the white man's rule.

Garveyism brought to all Africa the heartening assurance that their descendants in the New World, and indeed everywhere, were one with them in the struggle to throw off European rule, and that it was a possibility. For, argued Garvey, in a speech in March 1923:

The germ of European malice, revenge and antagonism is so deeply rooted among certain of the contending powers that in a short while we feel sure that they will present to Negroes the opportunity for which we are organized.

Out of the very reconstruction of world affairs will come the glorious opportunity for Africa's freedom to build a national power in the Motherland. . . . The critics ask: Is this possible? and the four hundred million courageous Negroes of the world answer—Yes.

Let no man, let no power on earth turn you from this sacred Cause of liberty. I prefer to die, at this moment, rather than cease my work for the freedom of Africa.

Garvey had no intention of going to Africa for the purpose of stirring up revolt. He knew his people would be mowed down by machine gun, and he hated bloodshed. Many rumors were purposely spread to keep colonial officials worried and uncertain of themselves. After Garvey's deportation from America, it was reported that he would try to enter Africa disguised as a seaman. The same source reported that if he did he wouldn't be imprisoned, as that would make a martyr of him and fan the smoldering fire of freedom into a flame, but that he would be done to death quietly by one of his own people and his body dumped at sea. He was also barred from entry otherwise. He had to be content to remain afar and publicize the struggle for his beloved Africa; for while they could bar Garvey in the flesh, they could not contain his spirit of freedom, then permeating the very air of Africa. For, said he, "I am only the forerunner of an awakened Africa, that shall never go back to sleep."

Mohammedanism is more of a unifying religious force in Africa than the Christian religion, splintered as it is into many denominations; yet the latter have done very good work in the educational field there.

As awakened Africans started to shake themselves free of their encumbrances, Prime Minister Jan Smuts of South Africa sensed the danger, particularly to his territory, and in an effort "to strengthen white South Africa" he made overtures to all European nations, for joint European exploita-

tion of Africa, under a regional system—East, West and
South. White Americans were also invited to participate. He
said to American correspondents at an interview: "Africa is
teeming with wealth. . . . I am all in favour of white Americans coming to Africa with their capital and I suggest the
idea of consultive councils in which America, as well as
Britain, France, Belgium, Portugal, Spain and other interested countries would be represented."

This proposed European-American plan coincided with
those of the Axis partners (Hitler and Mussolini) who ex-
erted pressure—ineffectively however—on France to become a passive Axis partner in the following scheme, the
report of which was released by Arno Dosch-Fleurot, from
Marseilles in October 1940, and stated:

> The Axis Powers are now directing the attention of Conti-
> nental Europeans to the vast continent to the South. An Euro-
> pean-African autarchy is, they say, made necessary by the
> new distribution of the world power. "Europe the head, Af-
> rica the body," is one of their slogans. "Defence of European
> civilization in Africa," is another. The pre-war partition, with
> Britain and France holding most of the territory is, according
> to Axis publicists, against the general European interests.
> They propose to open Africa to general European settlement,
> with the greatest power in Africa going to the countries capa-
> ble of sending the biggest number of settlers. These countries
> are Italy, Germany, Scandinavia and the various Slavonic
> countries of Central Europe. The same countries which earlier
> provided the United States with most of its immigrants.
>
> Due note is taken by the Axis of the fact that emigrants
> previously became citizens of the countries of their adoption.
> In the new African settlements, ties of emigrants to their home
> countries are not to be cut. Under the plan of the Dictators,
> each European country with settlers in Africa, will have a
> Dominion in Africa.

The intention of both of these plans was to use Africans
to provide, procure and process for shipment, the wealth of
Africa to the marts of Europe and America, so as to enrich

and exalt white nations, Africans being regarded by them as the "lesser breed"—the beast of burden for them. However after World War II both the vanquished and exhausted victors had to change their plans, and face the stern reality of Asian and African demands.

In April 1923, Garvey, in his article to the *Negro World*, "Who and what is a Negro?" made the following statement regarding the political amalgamation of the white and colored peoples in South Africa:

> More than a year ago the natives of South Africa started to press the limited white population to the wall in the demand of "Africa for the Africans." The prejudiced Boers and others were willing then to let down the colour bar and admit to their ranks socially and otherwise the half-breed coloured people whom they once classified as impossible hybrids, to be despised by both whites and natives. Now they are endeavouring to make common cause with them, so as to strengthen their position against the threatening ascendancy of the demand for a free and redeemed Africa for the blacks of the world.

In an editorial dated March 29, 1923, the Abantu-Batho of Johannesburg states among other things:

"The Cape Coloured people have been promised absorption by politicians, particularly those of the Dutch race. . . . Indeed we are suspicious that all this talk about absorption is a political trap which has been set to capture the coloured vote in the Cape. It is the business of the politician to strengthen his position by getting as many supporters as possible. To do this, he must, of necessity, be diplomatic. That is to say, he must know how to get around the people, and the only way to do this, is to put before them a beautiful picture of what one intends to do. There can be no doubt that to the Cape Coloured people the idea of their absorption by the white race presents a beautiful ideal, for the attainment of which they are prepared to sacrifice everything. They cannot be blamed, for this. As a distinct community they have no past, no traditions, no laws, and no language which constitute the pride of every race of mankind. These sons of Hagar are in an awkward position. They despise the people of Hagar, because

Hagar's people are despised by the people of Abraham. They are suffering because of the gulf that exists between their mothers' people and those of their fathers. . . . The difference between the treatment meted out to the Coloured people and the Africans does not in any way signify that the whites have more consideration for the Coloured people. It will be remembered that when Lord Selborne left this country in 1909, he warned the white people of South Africa against putting the Cape Coloured people in the same category as Africans, because that would unite the two sections of the African peoples to fight for their common rights. Since then, the policy has been to differentiate in the treatment of the two sections so as to make combined action impossible. Thus it is not saying too much to aver that the real object is to make the Cape Coloured people a buffer between Africans and Europeans. As a buffer the Cape Coloured people can never have the same rights as whites. Now the question is: what are they to do? Will they be satisfied with a position of this kind? Or will they follow the lead of our cousins in America and classify themselves as Africans? In our opinion this is the only way to the salvation of the Cape Coloured people. They are Africans and not Europeans, and the sooner they realize it the better."

White people will seek every opportunity to fraternize with any race in the world, even the one despised yesterday, if by so doing they can strengthen their position, whether it be in Europe, Africa or elsewhere; but it is for four hundred million people who have been discriminated against throughout the world to take a decided stand, and for once we will agree with the white American, that one drop of Negro blood makes a man a Negro; so that 100 per cent Negroes, and even 1 per cent Negroes will stand together as one mighty whole to strike a universal blow for liberty and recognition in Africa.

White South Africans did use the colored people to further their own political and racial interests, but thirty-three years later, when their numbers had been equalized by European emigrants, their votes were taken from them and they were relegated to the category of "native Africans."

The answer to the question, What became of the African slaves taken to Europe, Central and South America, during the traffic in human beings? is contained in one word: absorption.

In England in 1772, a test case was made by Granville Sharpe, in which he produced an African slave in court, and argued before Judge Mansfield, that slavery was incompatible with English law. The Judge's decision freed approximately fifteen thousand slaves in England, at that time. Freed slaves and their descendants have contributed to Europe's greatness, but history written by white hands ignores any mention of them, except in a few isolated cases such as Pushkin of Russia and Dumas of France.

All of the New World, from Canada to Chile, received African slaves. Brazil received the greatest number through the Portuguese traffic, and countries like Chile and Canada the least amount. All of these slaves have been absorbed into the majority populations, of Indian-Spanish, and Anglo-French. Thus Africans have contributed to the development of the wild countries of Central and South America. Their blood has been mixed with the Indians' and has watered the sod to throw off the yoke of European oppression and bring independence to Spanish and Portuguese-speaking Americas.

He has enriched the culture of these countries with his buoyance of spirit, his faith in God, the music of his soul in song and dance, even when all seems lost; also the durability of his stock under adverse conditions has strengthened the Indian, Spanish and Portuguese stock to survive and procreate abundantly. Thus have these countries gained materially and spiritually while Africa is not given any credit for same.

The need for ships of our own is still great, although we now have an alternative mode of transportation by airplane. The West Indian Shipping Company has been in operation for years. Ghana (Gold Coast), the first African nation to emerge from colonial rule, launched its first ship of the

Black Star Line of Ghana, at the close of 1957, and showed the world what Africans can do on their own.

Under their own national registry, saboteurs can be dealt with summarily, as a deterrent to others who may succumb to bribery and corruption, and attempt to destroy their own shipping line.

Garvey's Voice, the present organ of the U.N.I.A., is being circulated in all parts of Africa. Colored newspaper men in America who used to ridicule Garvey and sneer at Africa and its people, now take pride in writing about the progress being made in "that rich continent by our blood brothers."

The great essentials of the character of a people are integrity and stamina; these determine not only their ability to shape civilization to their needs and ambitions and to maintain it, but the type of progeny they will rear to carry on the legacies they leave behind, their way of life and their relations with weaker peoples.

Since civilization is but a continuity of movement, and the lifespan of particular types is counted in centuries, the indications are that the darker races of the world will be next in ascendency. Let us therefore continue to build moral qualities in our character so as to insure peace and happiness for all.

CHAPTER FORTY-FIVE

To whom shall we liken this man? The *New York News* described him:

"As ruthless as Napoleon. As zealous as John Brown, Marcus Garvey has become the world storm center of his race's fight for equality. Who can say that after the storm, the atmosphere will not be clear?"

In an article to the *Jamaica Standard*, January 26, 1939, Randolph Williams, formerly employed by the organization, gave another comparison, thus:

Like Frankenstein, he discovered late that he had created a huge thing, that he alone could not manage, and that he could not trust others to help him with, fearing that his helpers, not understanding the intricate mechanism of this thing would destroy it. He had worked out a programme that needed a few generations for its completion, something that was no one-man's job; he attempted to accomplish it in a single generation, and chiefly by himself. He suffered from great impatience, and was constantly mortified that others could not give themselves up as completely to the Cause as he could. Because of this great impatience, when he should have put all the resources of his huge Association behind one single project, and "put it over!" he tackled half a dozen and succeeded with none.

One colored critic in London likened Garvey physically to Dessaline, one of Toussaint l'Ouverture's generals. A man who came to scoff at one of his meetings left converted and said, "That man is a God-sent leader."

The editor of the *Kansas City Call*, February 20, 1925, called him a zealot and an iconoclast. In conclusion he wondered if after all he had not evoked the admiration of white men by his smashing changes:

> His call to the Negro to be his own man, has helped us. We wonder if there is not deep down in the hearts of white men, who have seen the uniform conservatism of the Negro in America, an admiration for this one black man in recent times, who objected to the conditions and did what he could to change them. We are sure we are proud of Nat Turner, and every other black man, who in slavery days objected to that evil, and it does not lessen our pride in them, that they too were law breakers.

In a letter to the *New York Sun* August 8, 1922, a correspondent likened him to "the 'Stormy Petrel' of his Race—a plain ordinary man, well educated, but without the pride of learning which is characteristic of some of the more notable of his critics who cannot understand how he has got such a hold on the masses, whom they have for years neglected and looked upon with a sort of pitying contempt. These people know that Garvey does not despise them, and that he is honestly trying to help them, and they will follow him to the ends of the earth."

A Brooklynite writing in the *Negro World* called him "a Black Moses, who endowed from God with the gifts of faith and courage wrought miracles for his people in a shorter time than it took Moses leading the children of Israel toward the promised land; they having Jehovah's own presence with them, supplying their material and spiritual needs, fighting their battles, and conquering their enemies."

A *New York World* reporter, who had studied Garvey while reporting his conventions and trial, described him in a Sunday issue of the newspaper, June 1923, as a group psychologist and idealist planner, but not practical. He wrote:

> Marcus Garvey can lay claim to being a most successful student of group psychology. His powers to weld Negroes, —heterogeneous in thought and environment—into one solid phalanx, working for the same ideals, have been almost uncanny. A forceful and convincing speaker, nimble-minded in debate, and seldom permitting himself to be put on the defensive; it is an interesting study watching him exercise complete mastery over a gathering of from three to five thousand of his followers.
>
> A witness during the trial likened the Defendant when speaking to his audience to a Master-Musician, who had complete control of his instrument, and playing on it at will. It was a fitting description of Garvey holding his audience completely under his spell at Liberty Hall. . . .
>
> Conceiving and attempting to put over big things is his speciality. Even Harlem with more than 180,000 Negroes has only come within the range of his mental calculations merely as a spoke in the wheel. Few of his ideas ever reached the stage of fruition, but this was not because all of them were devoid of merit. There were some deserving of favourable consideration. But idealism is one thing, the application of practical methods is another. With him practicability very often had to give way to idealism and egotism.

Some writers mistakenly named him "Marcus Aurelius," until it was thought by many that Aurelius was his middle name, because this philosopher is identified with the thinking that instead of disliking or despising people unlike us, we ought to act on the premise that "the Universe has need of them."

The name Garvey was given to my great-grandfather by his slave master, in place of his African name. Said he: "I shall so work that in the years to come, this name shall be synonymous with FREEDOM."

A former associate said of Garvey: "If you are a hard worker he is easy to get along with, but when angered or antagonized he bellows defiance. Being born under the influence of Leo—the Lion—may have some effect on his disposition."

After he left us in Jamaica, he sent from England a horoscope for each child, stating that these would help me to understand their respective dispositions better, and to develop their best qualities. Julius, being born on the sixteenth of August, and his Dad on the seventeenth, come under the same planetary influences. To those who believe in Destiny and say, "it is written in the stars," or for the curious and skeptical, the horoscope reads as follows:

> You are proud of Race and readily won by kindness. You love the big things of life, and are inclined to ignore the details too much. You make an excellent leader, and are best in a position of authority or responsibility. You have fixed opinions, and it is difficult for anyone to make you change your mind once it is made up.
>
> You are fond of large schemes, and have great organizing ability. You aim very high, almost at an impossible state of perfection. You are proud and contemptous when hurt or offended, haughty and arrogant when angry; yet you have a very forgiving nature. You have a great power of good in you, and can inspire others to accomplish much. You are inclined to be altruistic and will act in the interests of others and against yourself, if your sympathy is aroused. You are magnetic and very powerful in exerting your influence.

Your strongest point is your organizing power. You have great ideals, which lead you to undertake gigantic concerns. A generous nature, which prompts you to do much for others. Faith and trust in your fellowmen, which will often bring the best out of other people.

The weakness of your character lies in a liability to be abnormally proud and vain, and in some cases egotistical and self-applauding. Passionate and sweeping in your anger, and at times a little too presumptuous.

You must have charge of others, whether few or many, to be at your best. A subordinate position never contents you; you are too proud to be menial, and will therefore work your way up, because of your ambition to be in a superior position.

Heredity, environmental pressures—both kindly and cruel—perhaps Destiny, too, had a hand in making Garvey what he was, because of what he did.

CHAPTER FORTY-SIX

One should be judged by one's deeds and words, but no preconceived analyses of paragraphs taken out of their context can do justice to a character whose ideals were considered revolting to the ruling systems of his time. The following article "Truth our Weapon," from the July 1935 *Blackman* should counteract the tendency to perform a postmortem examination of fragments of a man's work. It presents his poetic reflections on the church on earth, inspired by the Italo-Abyssinian war:

It is said that in Nature "nothing happens before its time." This suggests that Nature or Nature's God has a unique or particular way of dealing with phenomena; so that which looks unusual to the human mind, and sometimes out of sorts, even unkind, can well be understood by properly considering the peculiarity of the great Source of Life. The Negro presents an unfortunate picture in the world from the social, economic, political and general point of view; so much so that everywhere he has been regarded with derision, contempt, and even hate and disgust. The Negro himself has often felt the lash of his own condition, but to the thoughtful student, the very conditions that our civilizations have forced upon him, are beacons showing him the way toward the harbour of human refuge through Nature's peculiarities.

Nature has a way of teaching her lessons. The Negro is being taught his, so we must not become entirely broken in spirit, and discouraged by the lash of circumstances. Handicaps placed upon him by his contemporaries of other races are but stimuli toward his reaching out after the highest and noblest in the accomplishment of the human genius of the mind. The man who does not profit from his environment is a hopeless fool. Surely the Negroes of America, the West Indies and Africa are not such fools as not to profit by their present environments. They are being forced on toward something that is bound to come. It is Nature's way of spurring them; it is Nature's way of achieving the end.

For centuries the Negro has been merely an unfortunate incident in the life of the civilizations that have surrounded him. Surely he must have learned a lot? He has not been an aggressor, but an observer. It is hoped that his sane and sober observations will supply him with the necessary human material to build a better civilization, when the white man has destroyed that of the twentieth century. There is no doubt that the Negro's chance will come when the smoke from the fire and ashes of twentieth century civilization has blown off. There are some who limit the Negro permanently to a place of inferiority, socially, politically and economically; but there may be a law which is beyond the reach of all men, which settles the affairs of humanity, and it is apparent that in the settlement the Negro has much to expect in the future, having suffered so much in the past.

Some look upon prophesy as fairy tales, but if men are really to worship under "their own vine and fig tree," then Nature must have had her plans laid down toward this accomplishment. Slowly, though it seems, the Negro is travelling toward such a destination. He must be encouraged toward this end; this is the purpose of our Organization—to stir Negro minds all over the world toward the glorious objective of the fulfilment of Nature's design. "Princes shall come out of Egypt, and Ethiopia shall stretch forth her hand unto God," was an inspired pronouncement of the Psalmist. The children of Ethiopia can be identified as being of the black race, scattered all over the world, and so with the banner of hope they look forward to a glorious future. There must be a stimulation of mind. There must be a focusing of ambition, there must be a grasping after truth, and with all a mighty determination to go through to the accomplishment of that which is right.

Righteousness shall be our breastplate, the word of Truth shall be our weapons, the Cross of Christ shall be our implement, so that those mighty races and nations shall not break through, in the mighty rush of Negro hope and aspirations. Be not downcast, black men, wherever you are. Look up, think nobly, act honestly, and as sure as the sun shines, and God reigns in Heaven, Nature shall, even through adversity, forge a place for you that you may indeed worship under your own vine and fig tree.

The Church of God on Earth today
Is scandal of the King;
It teaches men to sing and pray,
For golden wealth to bring.
It sanctifies the cause of war,
And winks at evil deeds;
It sends its 'saints' and men afar
To preach the Victor's creeds.
The Blacks and weaker sets of Men
Are robbed and killed galore;
The Church looks o'er Commandments ten,
As tyrants kill some more.
The lands that God gave men to dwell
Are taken by the sword
As preachers go, their creeds to sell
To those who heed their word.
Almighty God looks down on Earth
To see the Church in sin,
And so we pray for Cleansing Birth

To let the Master in.
And when the Gentle Jesus leads,
The Priests and Pastors too,
Shall see the growth of harvest seeds
That blend with every hue.

If Garvey had been born and grown up in America, he would not have been an international leader.

If he had not left Jamaica and traveled so extensively, he would not have had the sympathetic urge to change the conditions of the entire race.

If he had been born in Africa, he could not have had any greater love for his this Land of Sorrow; probably a born African would have limited his Messianic program to the continent. It seems destined that one of the Dispersed Sons should spearhead the struggle for its redemption and unity with those abroad.

If he were not the son of his father, he would not have had the courage to defy the powers of man with the recklessness that disregards personal safety. How else could he have been able to submerge the roles of husband and father, and make sacrifices of his family on the altar of African redemption, with the zeal and solemnity of a devotee?

If he was not inspired as a messenger of his race, he could not, and would not have suffered all he did daily. With his ability and personality he could have earned enough to live comfortably, instead of living like a hunted animal, teased, jeered, abused, his life threatened. Self-preservation is instinctive in the average man; but to Garvey, what happened to him—one man—was nothing compared to what was happening to millions of his people everywhere.

The Voice of Africa can never be silenced again, or lulled into apathy and inertia. It betokens the Spirit of New Life —the life of a redeemed people, striving toward nationhood.

Toward the end of May 1940, a black man, a news correspondent in England, in a final effort to hasten Garvey's end, sent out a news report that he had died in poverty. His secretary tried to keep the newspapers with the report from him, but overseas cables came often; he became suspicious and on the fifth of June, demanded that all his mail be brought to him. When she broke the news to him, he was sad; but when he saw the colored American press clippings—contained in letters—in which the editors, in vicious glee had drawn on their own evil imaginations, he uttered a loud groan, held his head, and slumped in his chair.

When he was revived and attended to by the doctor, he made signs that he wanted to dictate a message to the Press, but his speech was almost gone, and he shook with anguish at his inability to answer back his gloating enemies.

During the few remaining days of his life, he was conscious of happenings, not only around him, but of the major events of the world war: Belgium and Holland surrendered; British troops got their baptism by fire at Dunkirk; Italy declared war on Britain and France; the Germans occupied Paris. To all these series of events he indicated his interest by nodding his head, or turning it from side to side slowly and sadly. This Captain of the Negro Race, although no longer in command, had the satisfaction of knowing that he had weathered the storms; his logbook showed his day to day encounter with Nature's most unpredictable and unstable force—MAN. His gratification is expressed in these verses:

> Our Fathers sowed with blood and tears
> The seed that ripens with the years;—
> The glorious hour of harvest nears—
> Africa for Africans.

> We shall forgive, but not forget—
> The shackle bruises rankle yet,
> And still with blood the ground is wet—
> Africa for Africans.

The darkness thins, the dawn is nigh,
Its promise swells the pregnant sky,
And soon shall burst the thunderous cry—
Africa for Africans.

The first international leader to unite in thought and action the scattered members of his race—not as allies in a war, but as blood brothers in the pursuit of freedom, peace and security—lay in the gathering darkness of his room, on the tenth of June, 1940; his thoughts traveled from those whom he was leaving behind, and spiritually he pleaded with his Maker, in the words of his "Guiding Hymn":

Forgive, O Lord, my errors,
Help me to all forgive
And save us from life's terrors
And peaceful let us live.

Let good-will ever guide me
Till life's brief span be done,
Then with my fathers hide me
That we may still be One.

CHAPTER FORTY-SEVEN

It is said that people who live in the Tropics, live nearest to nature. When nature gets angry they feel her punishment through hurricanes, earthquakes and drought, and when nature smiles her children rejoice. The afternoon of November 4th, 1956, Dame Nature was at her best. Previous showers had made the grass green, the trees looked refreshed, fog hung over Blue Mountain Peak, and the lower ridges of Red Hills and Stony Hill showed shades of purple, deep blue, and leafy green, softened by mist. These hills formed the background of George VI Park—formerly

Kingston Race Course. This was the setting for the unveiling of a bust to the memory of Marcus Mosiah Garvey.

Nearly seventeen years after his death when many of his prophecies were being fulfilled, and his progressive plans adopted and carried out in the House of Representatives, the Kingston and St. Andrew Corporation, and the Parochial Councils, they were making amends to him. Twenty-seven years ago, through the Peoples' Political Party, he had appealed to them to help him ring in the changes in the life of Jamaica. That day, changes were evident everywhere; for the first time in its history a black man's bust would grace the main park.

All classes of the island and foreign invitees were there to take part in the ceremony, which had its inception years before when Kenneth Hill, then mayor, proposed it, and the present mayor and councillors brought it to its climax. Sculptor Alvin Marriott, a Jamaican, had done, not only a good bust, but for years had pressed to have it bronzed and erected. The arrangements for the occasion were carefully and well planned by the Corporation and representatives from government, military and social services—all willing to help, so that the ceremony would be truly representative of all Jamaica. Invitations had been sent out to persons representative of all walks of life. Thousands assembled.

On parade were the Military Band in the colorful zouave dress uniform of the Old West Indian Regiment—dark blue pants with cream leggings, scarlet tunics, cream shirts, topped with tasseled, cream, round caps, their buttons and instruments gleaming in the sun. A Police Guard of Honor, also in full dress—navy pants with red stripes, white coats, with leather belts, white spiked helmets, and rifles; they stood motionless waiting for orders. The Girl Guides and Boy Scout troops, also hundreds of school children, representing different schools, completed the uniformed ranks.

On the platform built for the occasion were seated: Mrs. A. Jacques Garvey, widow, Rt. Rev. and Hon. P. W. Gibson, Bishop of Jamaica, His Lordship, the Roman Catholic

Bishop, J. McEleney, S.J., Members of the Executive Council, House of Representatives and their wives. Among these were: ministers F. A. Glasspole, William Seivright, Sir Alexander Bustamante, Leader of the Opposition, Hon. Douglas Fletcher, Lady Allan. Members of the Chamber of Commerce included Mr. Abe Issa and Mr. C. B. Facey. Representatives of the Consular Corps; Members of the Corporation Council and their wives; Mr. Clare McFarlane, Poet Laureate, and his wife; Mr. and Mrs. Ken Hill; Rev. Jack Peel of the Anglican Parish Church; Assistant Commissioner of Police Noel Crosswell; Mr. J. Downes, Director of Public Gardens; Dr. Varma of the Indian Progressive League; Dr. Douglas of the Afro-West Indian League. Rev. Cowell Lloyd of the Baptist Denomination; Mr. Bernard Lewis, Director of the Institute; Mr. J. J. Mills, former Inspector of Schools; Solicitor and Mrs. Neville Ashenheim; other Solicitors were Messrs. Dayes, Calame and Evans. A delegation of five persons from the U.N.I.A. in America, headed by William Sherrill, President-General; Messrs. Arnold Crawford; Levi-Lord; Thomas Benjamin; and Mrs. Walters of the Garvey Club; other prominent persons too numerous to mention.

At 4.30 p.m. Sir Hugh Foot, the Governor, attended by his A.D.C. arrived, and was received by Councillor Walker, Deputy Mayor, and Mr. Russell Lewars, Town Clerk; on his way to the platform the Band played the National Anthem. Hon. Norman Manley, Q.C., Chief Minister, arrived. Two outriders of the Police Motorcycle Squad signified the arrival of the Mayor, Councillor Balfour Barnswell, in his robes of office. He was escorted by Acting Police Commissioner L. P. Browning, while the Police Guard of Honor under Assistant Superintendent Neville Ernandez gave the salute. The Mayor inspected the Guards, to the accompaniment of drums and bugles. After which he proceeded to the stage.

The Town Clerk announced the singing of the hymn (one of Garvey's favorites) "Shine on, Eternal Light." He next presented the Mayor, who presided over the function. In his address he said, "Garvey, single-handed, lit the torch and illuminated the dark corners of Jamaica, leading the people and lifting them to a higher appreciation of themselves." Dr. Leslie, Mayor of Spanish Town, then read a paper on Negro history; before doing so, he said that when he first went to New York City, he took advantage of the many meetings held at Liberty Hall—and realized how little he knew of ancient Negro history; it was from Garvey he got the inspiration and stimulus to do so much research.

A song was rendered by a large group of school children conducted by Mrs. W. Sutherland, and accompanied by the Band; followed by little Hugh Francis, singing unaccompanied, "The Lord's Prayer," which was appealingly rendered. Mr. Wycliffe Bennett, pioneer worker to establish speech festivals, read a review of the life of Garvey, which was written by Len Nembhard of the *Jamaica Times*. After an Overture from the Band, the Hon. Norman Manley gave an address, in which he said:

> I am particularly glad that Mr. Marcus Garvey's widow—Mrs. Amy Jacques Garvey, is with us on this platform. I am sure that if her husband were alive, he would have noted with pride the great strides that the Negro peoples of the world have made in the last twenty five years, and moreso in the fields where he laboured.
>
> Since Garvey dreamed his great dream in America considerable progress has been made by the people whom he sought to serve, and at this moment they are witnessing in the U.S.A. what is verily believed to be the end, the last stage of the struggle of millions of Negro people there to achieve complete equality in that land.

Continuing, he observed that if they looked across the water at the great continent of Africa they saw—in spite of difficulties that beset many countries—many groups of Negroes marching forward to nationhood and freedom. The Gold Coast—Ghana, as they call it—under the inspired leadership of that outstanding Negro Statesman Kwame Nkrumah had made great

strides. That country would outstrip all those in the Caribbean, and would become the first Negro Dominion in the
world. Here at home in Jamaica, they stood on the threshold
of self-government, and he was confident that after the
Federation was launched—after the first Federal Parliament
was elected in 1958—it would be but a few short years within
which self-government for Jamaica and Dominion status for
the British West Indies would be a reality.

It was right that those of them who had the honour and
privilege of leading the National Movement in these territories
should remember that they did not start from nowhere. They
started on the foundation of great pioneers that went before
them. In Marcus Garvey's time in Jamaica, the determination
was the great task of breaking through the spirit of Colonialism, and winning for our people the sense of self-confidence
and self-respect—an acceptance of their own history, without
which the national spirit would not have been possible.

That afternoon they would unveil the memorial in bronze
which would stand for all times, as a testimony of his love for
his people, and which would bear historic witness to the great
part he played in liberating the spirit and minds of his people.
That was a monument in bronze, but there was a greater and
deeper living monument that would go down through all
ages—because if they today had confidence in themselves, if
they today were able to look back on their own past with
pride, then, they would be worthy to be members of a great
people, to meet as equals among equals, and they owed that
in a great measure to the spirit of freedom, which Marcus
Garvey liberated in his own people.

There could be no equality among men, there could be no
one society, until all races and all admixtures met in friendship
and harmony as equals; and only free men could meet as
equals with free men. Garvey stood to liberate the mind of his
people. That was his great contribution to history, and it was
their hope that that memorial would last longer than all the

bronze statues they could unveil for history and posterity to see.

His concluding words were:

> May that great spirit abide with us always, inspire us to take up the challenge and be worthy of those who have blazed the trail and gone before.

The Mayor mentioned that the two young Garveys, Marcus and Julius, were abroad and could not attend on account of their studies. He then asked Mrs. Garvey to stand, amidst applause. Mrs. Manley, the sculptress who devoted years of her time teaching and encouraging art in Jamaica, motioned to Mrs. Garvey to accompany her, while she graciously unveiled the bust, which had been placed on a temporary stand for the convenient view of the immense crowd, who clapped and cheered.

Then followed the laying on of wreaths, by Councillor Vickie Grant on behalf of the Mayor and Council, and by the President-General of the U.N.I.A. on behalf of the American organization, who gave a eulogy. Other local fraternities also laid wreaths. The bust was later put on its base near the east gate of the park, facing north, looking up to the hills, "I will lift up mine eyes unto the hills from whence cometh my strength."

CHAPTER FORTY-EIGHT

Marcus and Julius were able to obtain secondary education only through scholarships, and to attend universities because of my continued sacrifices—having no support from the organization, although persons have used the names of "Garvey's sons," to collect funds only to pocket them. It was difficult after his death to teach them to be proud of a race which had "let them down," and a father who had left them on its charity, believing: "I have devoted my life to my people; surely if anything happens to me, they will look after my boys."

Marcus obtained his B.A. degree (majoring in economics and law) as an External Student, London University, while working in the Government Service. Later he went to England and received his LL.B. degree from the same university. He did not take the Bar Finals, as he changed over to civil engineering, for in this capacity he believed he could better serve the needs of his people in a scientific age.

Julius, after leaving high school, worked at a government laboratory. He went to McGill University, Montreal, where he graduated in 1957 with his B.Sc. degree, and gained his M.D. in 1961.

The following are their replies to invitations sent them by the Mayor and Council:

> 35 Roland Gardens,
> London, S.W.7,
> 29/10/56

Sir:

I thank you for your gracious invitation contained in— A/7/93, of the 23rd October. Owing to my preoccupation with my present course of studies I am unfortunately unable to accept your invitation to attend. But I can assure you that although I may not be physically present, all my thoughts will be with those attending this signal and unique occasion.

May I take this opportunity of conveying to His Worship the Mayor, the Council of the Kingston and St. Andrew Corporation, and all the other well-wishers who were instrumental in conferring this mark of recognition upon my father, the deep sense of appreciation which I feel at this time.

> I am, Sir,
> Yours faithfully,
> Marcus J. Garvey.

> 3509 Hutchinson Street,
> Montreal, P.Q.,
> Canada.
> 28/10/56.

Dear Sir,

In reply to your letter dated 23rd October, nos: A/7/93, I regret to say that I am unable to accept your most gracious invitation. Although I cannot attend the ceremony because of my studies here in Montreal, I shall be there in spirit, along with the spirit of every true Jamaican.

My father was dedicated to the betterment of Coloured people the world over, and I am proud and happy that his services are being recognized in such a signal manner by fellow Jamaicans.

May the Sun never set on the glory of man, for he is truly God's finest creation.

I am, Sir,

Yours respectfully,

J. W. Garvey.

EULOGY OF WILLIAM SHERRILL.

CITIZENS OF JAMAICA:

GREETINGS:

I am happy that it is my good fortune to visit this Island of Jamaica, and the great City of Kingston. We have been deeply impressed with your kindness and hospitality, and the courtesies shown our Delegation. We congratulate you on the progress you are making in commerce, industry, and the great strides toward self-government. We bring with us the best wishes of Negro America for success in your advance toward the goal of Statehood.

We have come to Jamaica at the invitation of His Worship the Mayor to share with you the commemoration of a great Jamaican—Marcus Garvey. One whose greatness and achievements extend far beyond the boundaries of this Island. Though he is a son of Jamaica's soil, he belongs, not alone to the people of Jamaica, but to those millions of the world's population that struggle for freedom and independence in the United States of America and Africa. He belongs not only to our times, but to the ages. His memory is written, not alone in bronze and stone standing in your Public Park, but in the hearts of the world's millions, who fight to emancipate themselves from economic and political bondage.

We commend you for the honour you give him today, yet

our hearts are grieved when we realize how little we appreciated him in life. It appears however to be a weakness of mankind that he never appreciates his great benefactors at the time they serve, and make their great contributions. It is only after they have passed, and time gives us greater perspective, that we are able to evaluate their work and greatness.

Garvey was indeed a great man, and when we say great, we are not simply making a play on words. His greatness is proven by the standard which measures greatness. Greatness is determined by the impact a man's work and teaching has on his times. When viewing the individual and his work, we ask ourselves—was the world different because he lived? The answer to this question as it relates to Marcus Garvey places him in the company of the Great.

Because Garvey lived, Jamaica is different; Because Garvey lived, Negro America is different; Because Garvey lived, Africa is different. His work and teaching gave birth to a New Negro, a New Africa, and this impact went a long way in shaping a New World. For his cry was not alone "Africa for the Africans," but "Asia for the Asiatics" and "Palestine for the Jews." He did more to crystallize National sentiment in so-called backward countries than any single individual of our times. Measured by the standard of change Garvey and his teachings have wrought in the world, Garvey rises to the heights of greatness.

So great were the goals he set for his Race that small minds criticized, and little men laughed. Laughed as they always have at every new idea or venture. Some called him a fool. Others branded him a charlatan and buffoon; while the more charitable called him a Dreamer. Too blind and shortsighted to realize the possibility of black men building for themselves, they sought to belittle his work by terming it a dream. Little did they realize that in calling Garvey a Dreamer they instantly placed him in the ranks of the Great.

Dreamer! Do you know who Dreamers are? They are the Architects of Greatness. Their vision lies within their souls. They peer through the clouds of doubt and darkness, and pierce the walls of unknown time.

Dreamers! They sail seas that have never been charted, because they are the makers of the charts. They scale mountains that have never been scaled, because they are the blazers of the way. They travel paths that have never been beaten, because Dreamers are the beaters of the paths.

Dreamers! The great British Empire was first conceived and given birth to by the mind of a Dreamer. The great American Commonwealth was founded by Dreamers; the world reforms that now benefit mankind were born in the hearts and minds of Dreamers. Yes, Garvey was a Dreamer, and because he dared dream of an emancipated Negro Race, and Nationhood, Negroes of Jamaica are marching, Negroes of America are marching, and Negroes of Africa are marching. The torch of freedom has been lighted in their breasts, and all the forces of hell cannot blow it out.

We from America consider it a privilege and great honour to participate with the people of Jamaica in paying tribute to Marcus Garvey. His contribution to Negro America was no less than he made to his Native land. I wish it were possible for me to do justice to the greatness of this son of Africa, but we cannot—words are inadequate; bronze and stone too frail to convey a true picture of the man. For Marcus Garvey was one of history's providential Geniuses. He came to his Race endowed with an extraordinary ability for organization and leadership, as Shakespeare had for poetry, Mozart for music, or Angelo for Art. His undaunted faith in the possibilities of his people; his courage to come forward and plead their cause, under any condition and circumstances, uniquely fitted him for leadership of the Universal Negro Improvement Association—an Organization which has been an eternal blessing to his Race and given immortal fame to his name.

You, the people of Jamaica knew him; you worked with him; some of you fought with him; you knew his strength and his weaknesses. But no man is perfect; whatever Garvey's faults, whatever Garvey's mistakes, let us now cover them with the pure mantle of love and tolerance for an otherwise great and noble character.

Nothing we say can add or take away from the stature of Marcus Garvey; the world will soon forget what we say today, but it will long remember what he did. His name has a fixed place in history. As long as black men cherish the ideals of freedom and independence, Marcus Garvey's name will live in the hearts of his people everywhere.

CHAPTER FORTY-NINE

"Africa for the Africans, at home and abroad," is the slogan of Garveyism, proclaimed by him in 1916 when there were only two independent nations in Africa; but the year 1960 was truly a year of destiny, when most of the twenty-eight nations emerged from colonial rule to use their freedom to fight ignorance, poverty and disease, by developing the resources of their territories for the uplift and well-being of all their peoples. Truly, "Nationhood is the highest ideal of all peoples."

Ghana, the first of the new nations to demonstrate to the world the fitness of Africans to control their own affairs, is relentless in her efforts that "All Africa must be free." Osagyefo Dr. Kwame Nkrumah, President of Ghana, in his address to the 15th session of the General Assembly of the United Nations, the twenty-third of September, 1960, in part stated:

> For years and years Africa has been the foot-stool of colonialism and imperialism, exploitation and degradation. From the north to the south, from the east to the west, her sons languished in the chains of slavery and humiliation, and Africa's exploiters and self-appointed controllers of her destiny strode across our land with incredible inhumanity, without mercy, without shame, and without honour. Those days are gone and gone forever, and now I, an African, stand before this august Assembly of the United Nations and speak with a voice of peace and freedom, proclaiming to the world the dawn of a new era.

In the United States of America the impact of the Representatives of the independent African states to the United Nations, their Embassies and Consulates pressured the pass-

ing of the Integration Act, the result of embarrassment to
the State Department whenever they were mistaken for
American Negroes and discriminated against or mistreated.

In commemorating Garvey's birthday, a Jamaican journalist and news analyst, Frank Hill, writing in the *Daily
Gleaner*, August 17, 1960, under the heading "The Prophet
of Black Zionism," states in part:

> What makes a man great? It is, I think, the universal
> quality of the contribution he makes to the civilization of his
> times. The accent is on the word universal, for the quality of
> his vision must be of such as to be able to hold the attention
> of mankind, rather than mere isolated pockets of men grouped
> in special circumstances. . . .
>
> Garvey's message lighted new hope as much among the
> wandering Negroes, as among the cringing tribesmen of the
> African plains. A carefully cultivated sense of inferiority in
> black men started its slow death. The emotive word, black,
> symbolic of evil, lost its meaning. Fundamental concepts of
> religion and beauty were given a new garb; the Creator be-
> came personal and intimate as vast masses of men clothed
> Him with a black skin—rich, satiny ebony; and extended the
> frontiers of aesthetic experience by adding an authentic colour
> to the range of exciting beauty.
>
> What was the significance of Garvey? The Prophet of Black
> Zionism beat the drums for the ingathering to Africa. He may
> have meant it as a summons for a physical recall. But the
> message went more deeply, more enduringly than that. Eyes
> and hearts and minds turned to Africa—to the new values and
> standards and principles that earned their validity from the
> culture that grew out of the African community.

Black nationalism has awakened in the hearts of all
peoples of African descent a consciousness of "being somebody," of belonging to a race and people striving to impress
their image and personality on a world in terms of freedom,
justice and peace for all.

Marcus Garvey was never privileged to set foot on African soil; he was always denied entry to any territory, and
warned that he was an agitator and would suffer grave

consequences if he were discovered there in disguise; so the dearest wish of his heart was not accomplished. But his contacts had kept him informed of the happenings, yearnings and desires of those on the great continent, and he used every means available to enlighten world opinion of these facts and truths which were suppressed by white news agencies. So it was with gratification and joy that I received a cabled invitation from the Nigerian government to attend the inaugural ceremonies of the installation of Dr. Nnamdi Azikiwe as Governor-General, in November 1960. After leaving Nigeria I was the guest of the government of Ghana, traveling to and from West Africa via England and the United States.

As one closely connected with Africa for years I expected to see the modern developments; but to get the feel of what's going on one has to be in the atmosphere of Old and New Africa to capture the spell of the African tropics—the trees, flowers, animals, the mysteries surrounding them; the people of so many tribal backgrounds, all giving one a sense of purposeful active living; belonging to the whole, yet sharing it, with the joy of knowing that they are now masters of their destiny in their own country.

Ghana, Nigeria and Ethiopian Airways have modern, comfortable planes, wholly or partially manned by Africans, also air hostesses, efficient and charming. On the seas Ghana has her Black Star Line fleet of ships. The railroads of Ghana and Nigeria are efficiently run, as are the buses. The roads run hundreds of miles into the interior linking villages with towns. City banks are large and modern, with African directors, managers and staff. White technical advisers are kept in the inner offices. Office buildings up to ten stories are quite common. The interiors contain modern furnishings and equipment, air-conditioning and elevators. New schools, technical colleges, universities, hospitals and clinics are a part of the rapid progress made during and after the period to preparatory independence, which both

England and France were wise enough to agree to as a period of extensive training.

There are no drunks around the streets. Moslems do not drink intoxicating liquors; Christians and others act in moderation, because of their home training. Women are not allowed to work in foreign homes and hotels, so as to preserve their chastity. Young men cook and wash, and are called houseboys. Children, no matter how politically and educationally advanced they become, respect their parents. Men do not leave illegitimate children with their mothers without support, care or training; their tribal, communal mode of life helps to weld them into responsible, easily disciplined citizens.

Foreigners who do business in these countries are not allowed to send large sums of money abroad. An African must be on each directorate, and an understudy for the manager. The economies of these countries are geared to the needs of the people; their livelihood and happiness come first. They realize that the masses form the foundation of the nation, and as such must be strengthened to carry the weight of expansion and progress. The human element must be of the finest quality in nation building.

In Ghana unemployed men and women are put in separate camps, given work and taught skills; they wear khaki uniforms and bear the dignified name of Builders Brigade. The children are organized as Young Pioneers.

During my stay in Ghana, Emperor Haile Selassie of Ethiopia paid a state visit there to cement the ties of friendship between the Old Kingdom of the East and the young Republic of the West. The Emperor conferred on Dr. Nkrumah the Exalted Order of the Queen of Sheba; Dr. Nkrumah in turn conferred on the Emperor the Exalted Order of the Star of Africa—the black star.

I was treated royally everywhere I went: To the African I represented the spirit of Marcus Garvey, the "Returned One." We reminisced about the early years of awakening

and struggles in America, England and France, and now . . .
full credit is given him for his prophetic warnings and
declarations. As a prominent Nigerian said to me: "Whatever our leaders say today, Garvey said more than forty
years ago."

Another said: "This son of Africa saw the light of day in
an Island in the West Indies, but he followed the call of
Africa to his dying day."

His dreams of a redeemed continent, of a United States
of Africa, is almost a complete realization. Jamaica, Trinidad are independent, and the "Little Eight" islands of the
Eastern Caribbean are following this lead.

Africa and Asia will play leading roles in this civilization,
and Africa gave the cue when Dr. Azikiwe in his inaugural
address stated:

> The challenge of Nigeria as a free State in twentieth cen-
> tury Africa is the need to revive the stature of man in Africa,
> and restore the dignity of man in the world. Nigerians believe
> passionately in the fundamental human rights. We regard all
> races of the human family as equal. Under no circumstances
> shall we accept the idea that the black race is inferior to any
> other race. No matter where this spurious doctrine may pre-
> vail; it may be in Lodwar, or Sharpeville or Decatur, we shall
> never admit that we are an inferior race, because if we accept
> the Christian or Muslim doctrine that God is perfect, and that
> man was made in the image of God, then it would be sacri-
> legious, if not heretical, to believe that we are an inferior race.
> . . . Respect for human dignity is the challenge which Africa
> offers to the World.

EPILOGUE

The Source and Course
of Black Power in America

What depths of emotion a small word can evoke! Hate and love seem to take the highest rating of all. While words by themselves seem harmless one combined with another can have explosive reaction. The word "Africa," and the words "the Africans"—that seems like a logical combination; but substitute the word "for" in place of "and," then we have: "Africa for the Africans," the slogan of Marcus Garvey 40-odd years ago—a challenge to European Imperialists in Africa, and a hope and goal to Africa's sons and daughters all over the world.

Black Power now confronts the United States of America. This slogan, in the minds of whites, seems to conjure up black magic, for it strikes fear in their hearts, and even causes the government to become concerned as to what actions these two magic words may cause black citizens to commit.

"White Supremacy" has been the slogan of White Power for centuries, but the last two world wars proved that blacks were physically as good soldiers as whites, and white colonial empires disintegrated politically.

Let us trace the source and course of Black Power to determine its effectiveness as a weapon of defence of a black minority. I propose to do so by submitting questions sent me by a student of research on the work of Marcus Garvey. I have added other questions and their answers, so as to round out my subject. Here they are:

Is there any connection between Marcus Garvey's teachings and the philosophy of Elijah Mohammed and Malcolm X? Have Garvey's teachings been corrupted?

This question can be partially answered by my quoting from a letter written by Mr. Thomas Harvey, President-General of the Universal Negro Improvement Association, to the *Jamaica Gleaner*, November 17, 1964, in which he states:

> Please allow me space to express my thanks to your Government for inviting us down from America to attend the ceremonies in connection with the re-interment of Marcus Garvey in George VI Park.
>
> I think I am in a position to speak on behalf of Negroes in America and Canada, and to affirm our belief in the sincerity and courage of Marcus Garvey as the only international Negro leader at the close of this century.
>
> He paved the way for all local leaders who have emerged since his death. Most of them were his understudies or followers who were inspired by his dynamic leadership, and the universality of his appeal for justice, equality and independence for the Negro peoples throughout the world.
>
> For instance Elijah Mohammed was formerly a Corporal in the uniformed ranks of the Chicago division. Malcolm X's father was a Vice-President of the Detroit division; so Malcolm X grew up under the influence of Garveyism. Mrs. M. L. Gordon of the Peace Movement of Ethiopia was formerly an active member of the organization in Chicago. The Ethiopian Federation is also an off-shoot of Garveyism.
>
> The awakening of the Negro in the deep South, and in the industrial North made him militant and courageous for his rights as a citizen; and from early 1920 he was called a NEW NEGRO. So Martin Luther King and others before him, rallied their forces from people who were prepared and ready to fight for their rights.
>
> But the Negro is suspicious of local leaders who are backed by white people, and time will tell if they can stand the test.

Less than eight months before his assassination in New York on February 21, 1964, Malcolm X, in an interview with

Yael Lotan, journalist, in the *Daily Gleaner*, Jamaica, W.I., under date July 12, 1964, states his policy thus:

> Our religion is still Islam. But we don't involve our religion in the social, political and economic problems that confront our people in this country. We confine our religious practices and preachings to our Mosque; after we leave the Mosque, then we tell all other Afro-Americans, whether they are Christians or atheists, that we all have the same political, social and economic problems, and the only way we are going to solve these problems is to leave religion out of it, and form a united front against the common enemy, who is responsible for those evils that exist in the community.
>
> The racial deadlock in this country can never be resolved peacefully by any passive resistance methods; it is a question of power, and no one who has power—illegal power and immoral power, unethical power—ever gives it up legally, morally and ethically. You have to fight to get it back.

Asked if he felt that his thinking as a black man in America had been affected by the fact that his mother was a West Indian, he replied:

> Well, it probably did. . . . Historians have written the fact that slaves were never brought directly from Africa to America, but rather they were first taken to the West Indies or Caribbean area, where there were special persons whose job it was to break the will of the slave. Once his will was broken, his language and cultural characteristics were destroyed, then he was brought to America. So that the black people or the Africans, who remained in the Caribbean Area, their will was never broken as thoroughly as the will of those Africans who ultimately ended up on these shores.
>
> For that reason you will find that most West Indians, most people in the Caribbean area, are still proud that they are black, proud of the African blood, and their heritage; and I think this type of pride was instilled in my mother, and she instilled it in us, too, to the best degree she could. She had—despite the fact that her father was white—more African leanings, and African pride, and a desire to be identified with

Africa. In fact she was an active member of the Marcus Garvey movement.

My father, besides being an active worker in the Marcus Garvey movement, was a Christian clergyman—a Baptist Minister. He was lynched in Lansing, Michigan, in 1954, by being thrown under a street car. I grew up, after leaving home and Michigan, and moving through the streets of Harlem I turned into a complete atheist—I disregarded religion completely. While serving a sentence in prison in the state of Massachusetts, I was first exposed to the religion of Islam, and I studied it, and could see that it did for me what Christianity failed to do . . . also because of the historic part it played in the culture of the African continent.

In any movement of liberation—religious or political, one finds conservatives, pacifists and extremists. The younger people chafe under restraint and break away "to do things their own way." Their wanton assault usually brings pressure to bear on the power structure, who palliate the pacifists and exterminate the extremists. While one may be compelled at times to deplore the actions of some extremists, yet they are the battering rams in the forefront of the fight.

The strategies of freedom fighters should make them mobile, able to cover unexpected distances, and flexible in expression and pronouncements so as to cope with the exigencies of the moment, keeping the goal always in mind— to change an existing system that holds him down. It takes courage and determination to go through to the bitter end.

Regarding Marcus Garvey's influence on Malcolm X, in the same interview he volunteered this opinion:

Every time you see another nation on the African continent become independent, you know that Marcus Garvey is alive. It was Marcus Garvey's philosophy of Pan Africanism that initiated the entire freedom movement, which brought about the independence of African nations. And had it not been for

Marcus Garvey, and the foundations laid by him, you would find no independent nations in the Caribbean today. . . .

All the freedom movements that are taking place right here in America today were initiated by the work and teachings of Marcus Garvey. The entire Black Muslim philosophy here in America is feeding upon the seeds that were planted by Marcus Garvey.

Another question asked is: "What do you think of Martin Luther King as a Civil Rights leader? The Rev. Martin Luther King came to Jamaica, West Indies, in June 1965, at the invitation of the University of the West Indies, and spoke at a reception at the National Stadium. He declared that, "in the light of the many unpleasant and humiliating experiences with which I have to live, I am glad to feel like somebody in Jamaica. I really feel like a human being."

He laid a wreath at Marcus Garvey's shrine, and said, in part:

Marcus Garvey was the first man of color in the history of the United States to lead and develop a mass movement. He was the first man, on a mass scale, and level, to give millions of Negroes a sense of dignity and destiny, and make the Negro feel that he was somebody.

You gave Marcus Garvey to the United States of America, and he gave to the millions of Negroes in the United States a sense of personhood, a sense of manhood, and a sense of somebodiness.

As we stand here let us pledge ourselves to continue the struggle in this same spirit of somebodiness . . . in the conviction that all God's children are significant . . . that God's black children are just as significant as His white children. And we will not stop until we have freedom in all its dimensions.

The Rev. King had the financial support and sympathy of influential white Americans, and he was doing what he was guided to do in the interest of Civil Rights for Negro Americans. On April 4, 1968, in Memphis, Tennessee he was stopped forever, in the midst of his work, by an assassin's bullet.

Next question: How did Garvey view the Negro problem in America?

The Negro only became a problem because white America refused to treat the descendants of African slaves as MEN and relegated them to ghettos in the industrial northern cities and peonage farms in the South; used them as strikebreakers to suit their whims; made them economic serfs, political pawns in the North; disenfranchised them in most parts of the Southland; jim-crowed and lynched them, treated them with contempt as sub-human, or with apathy —not caring sometimes whether he the black man was dead or alive. The Negro was used and abused at will, but two world wars jolted isolationist America, and she was forced to call on black Americans "to make the world safe for democracy." They fought valiantly only to realize when they came home that America was still not safe for Negroes born and bred there.

The contacts that the American Negro made abroad opened his eyes to the fact that his group was only a minority in a white population of ten to one. This majority increases rapidly by opening its gates to millions of Europeans and by the healthy rate of increase of a well-fed population; while foreign Negroes are restricted from general entry, and bad conditions hold the minority population in check.

But the great awakening came, and with it strength through UNITY with people who look like him on the continent of Africa and in the West Indies. The bond of fellowship developed through Marcus Garvey's leadership of "One God! One Aim! One Destiny!"

The New Negro was aroused not only to fight as a minority group for Civil Rights, but to take a lively interest and help African nationalism all over the world, which gives him—the minority—prestige and international backing.

The presence of the United Nations' headquarters on American soil, and with African and Asian Delegates and representatives in the majority, pressurized the passing of the federal Civil Rights laws. As the late South African Prime Minister Verwoerd once said: "The complexion of the United Nations has changed from white to black."

The United States of America has taken on the burden of being leader of the West; in fact, it was thrust on her. She has spent millions of dollars and lost thousands of lives in Korea and Vietnam to "teach Asians the democratic way of life." But until white Americans allow their fellow citizens of a darker complexion to live, work and enjoy their lives to the fullest, the image she presents to the world is that of a shameless hypocrite fighting to give Asia that which she denies to her own brethren within her borders.

It was Marcus Garvey's contention (and justifiably so) that no white man can adequately speak for and represent the sufferings, persecutions, frustrations, ambitions and longings of the Negroes.

True, there are sympathetic white people who hate the injustices meted out to Negroes, but the Negro must have an all-Negro organization, and evolve his own self-sacrificing leaders—who will refuse white handouts; preaching always self-denial, self-help and self-determination. Black men must unitedly guide their own destinies. The New Negro is a man. Let him stand on his own two feet, unaided, and think for himself, and of himself, then ACT as wisdom directs.

Another pertinent question is: Can Negroes and whites ever live together in the United States of America in peace and harmony?

White Americans are merely human beings, with all the weaknesses and prejudices common to man, demonstrated through class, religion, and race. So federal legislation is but the first step toward Negro freedom. The greatest handicap is its implementation. In this endeavor we are dealing with the mind of man. Men with ideas fixed for generations cannot be made to think differently by legislation. Laws are intended to govern the conduct of citizens. The Police—the officers of the law—are employed to enforce them, but when new laws are against old traditions and social and economic barriers made and ingrained in people from birth, and practiced by their forbears, what kind of enforcement can one expect? The policeman's heart is with the white lawbreakers, while his uniform represents "law and order"; for whom?

There should be a national campaign on the part of white legislators, preachers and businessmen to accord justice and fair play to Negroes in all walks of life; not because they love them, but because America—leader of the West—cannot afford to continue to spend millions of dollars abroad without achieving her aim, as her image is tarnished with black unrest against injustice at home. Peoples in a nation cannot live in peace until each respects the rights of the other. "When the strong oppresses the weak, wars and discontent will ever mar the path of man."

If a nuclear war is hurled against the United States of America from Asia, without warning, then those who survive in good health (black and white) will have to journey to areas that are not polluted and contaminated by fallouts and rebuild the nation.

Methinks the ego of the white will be so blasted by the yellow man's scientific onslaught that he will be reduced to a reasonable state of mind and stretch out the hand of fellowship to his black countrymen. War is a leveler, and arrogant men must be humbled in order to see and feel man's injustices to man—injustices generated by color difference alone or compounded by economic differences.

Despite the geographic alignments going on, the call of RACE by whites, which is always a rallying appeal to "close ranks," will be countered by a similar appeal of the colored races, who are being scientifically trained so that in the long run they—black, yellow and brown—will dominate the world. Civilization moves in cycles. While it takes centuries to complete one, a new one is coming. It looms in sight.

Russia unwittingly trained 700 million Chinese along scientific lines, while regimenting their lives to communistic living. But an ideology in the yellow man's mind is practiced differently from the white man's interpretation. Today China is back-talking Russia, and has assumed the leadership of Asia as a red firebrand. She has got the population, and can afford to lose a few millions; she has got the scientific knowhow and the land area, enough to abandon a portion and still have enough to rebuild a strong nation. Besides, her people are accustomed to tighten their belts and fight and work like stoics. Who can stop them?

The younger group of freedom fighters have split with the conservative interracial groups, such as the N.A.A.C.P. and the Urban League, and demand black power, which they describe as a "drive to mobilize the black communities, as the only way to achieve meaningful change." What's wrong with that?

On the other hand the N.A.A.C.P., leader of the moderates and interracial in membership, has condemned the call for Black Power as "a separation and a ranging of race against race."

Who separated the races, and has consistently kept black people down? Are not the slogan "white supremacy" and the violence and murders by white supremacists "ranging race against race"?

If regardless of religion and political affiliations, the UNITY of Negroes to combat these evils were achieved, it would be a voting weapon, voting solidly for black freedom. Is this wrong?

Black unity is black power, the only power a despised, oppressed minority is capable of attaining. The use to which it is applied is best achieved in its organized voting strength. The abuse of this power by individuals—frustrated, despised and under financial pressure by the white majority—is to be expected, as is also the misuse of this power by splinter groups to wreak vengeance on others.

Human nature under pressure is unreasonable and unpredictable. The surest way to stop community violence is to remove the causes that make black men and women, even children, violent, forgetting God, whom they feel has forgotten them in their misery, and striving momentarily to create havoc with their bare hands or any sort of weapon handy.

The cost of their wild actions, and the fact that they suffer financially and physically does not occur to them in their emotional despair. All they feel is that they are fighting back—even in the face of policemen's bullets, dogs, teargas and night sticks. As these incidents occur all over the United States, the black minority get world sympathy, and Uncle Sam is seen as Simon Legree. The international role of leader of the West suffers from bad characterization; it is time to see yourself as others see you. For bullets cannot destroy an ideology (whether it is red or black), in the minds of people. Nor can dollars buy or bribe the acceptance of another ideology, when its demonstration shows that it is against the best interests of the colored races.

Blind prejudice must give way to scientific deductions, which will reasonably defeat hate and fury.

The Impact of Marcus Garvey on Africa as Told by Africans:

J. I. G. Onyia, writing in the *West African Pilot*, November 4, 1960, on the fighters against imperialism and oppression, states:

> The second stage of the struggle against imperialism started among the readers of the *Negro World*—a paper published by Marcus Garvey in America. It was an eye-opener to the few educated elements, and others who rebelled against the imperialistic haphazard division of their continent into colonial territories for exploitation by Europeans. Discussion groups were formed.
>
> Negroes of America were expected to land in Africa under the leadership of Marcus's Group to save the African from bondage.
>
> It was at this time that the West African Congress under

BIG MASS MEETING

A CALL TO THE
COLORED CITIZENS
OF
ATLANTA, GEORGIA

To Hear the Great West Indian Negro Leader
HON. MARCUS GARVEY
**President of the Universal Negro Improvement Association
of Jamaica, West Indies.**

Big Bethel A. M. E. Church
Corner Auburn Avenue and Butler Street

SUNDAY AFTERNOON, AT 3 O'CLOCK
MARCH 25, 1917

He brings a message of inspiration to the
12,000,000 of our people in this country.

SUBJECT:

**"The Negroes of the West Indies, after
78 years of Emancipation." With a
general talk on the world position of
the race.**

An orator of exceptional force, Professor Garvey has spoken
to packed audiences in England, New York, Boston, Washington,
Philadelphia, Chicago, Milwaukee, St. Louis, Detroit, Cleveland,
Cincinatti, Indianapolis, Louisville, Nashville and other cities. He
has travelled to the principal countries of Europe, and was the
first Negro to speak to the Veterans' Club of London, England.

This is the only chance to hear a great man who has taken
his message before the world. **COME OUT EARLY TO
SECURE SEATS.** It is worth travelling 1,000 miles to hear.

All Invited. Rev. R. H. Singleton, D.D., Pastor.

the leadership of Sir Casely Hayford of the Gold Coast (now Ghana) was founded. The late Governor, Sir Hugh Clifford, described the members as "Europeanized Africans in the coastal region, who did not represent their people!"

The *Negro World* was banned; but some courageous Africans in various walks of life started individually to revolt against the slavish and tyrannical treatment of them by Europeans, who hitherto were regarded as "tin gods." A civil servant in the northern region shot a European dead in resentment of the treatment meted out to him and shot himself afterwards.

Henceforth any African employee who was bold enough to protest against ill-treatment by Europeans was marked, shadowed and victimized. Acquisition of higher education was discouraged.

Peter Abrahams, South African author, writing in *Public Opinion*, November 3, 1956, states:

Marcus Garvey gave to the Negroes of the twentieth century a sense of self-awareness, a sense of pride and dignity that largely overcame the inferiority complex bred by centuries of racial and colour oppression.

And since the first state in any kind of liberation is the liberation of the mind, Marcus Garvey can justly be regarded as a primary source of the great freedom movements in the colonial world today. And that Jamaica honours him shows the extent to which Jamaica has changed.

Chief Nana Kobina Nketsia, Director of the Institute of Art and Culture in Ghana visited Jamaica, July 1965. In placing a wreath at the shrine of Marcus Garvey, he unloosed his sandals, and with bare feet, he bowed before the tomb, and performed absolution with water and devotion according to his spiritual ritual. Then he said:

I am pleased to be present at this sacred spot where Marcus Garvey my international leader is enshrined. Seeing you, my brothers and sisters, gathered here in your hundreds to pay homage, inspires me to higher endeavour as a noble descendant of a proud African race.

It urges me not only to play a decisive role and fulfil a destined mission in a modern world, but also to strengthen and build on the ruins of the past a better future for posterity.

I sincerely believe our mission for freedom is not an accident of history, but the work of Divine Providence, being manifested through the ages. Through UNITY among Africans, the black man's place in the world is secured for all times, despite misfortunes brought by opposition forces. Thanks be to God and Marcus Garvey's teachings for the light that is shining over Africa today, and will always shine.

The *Panama Tribune*, April 30, 1944, under the headline "Eboué, French Governor-General joins demand of 'Africa for Africans,' stated:

> *Adolphe Félix Sylvestre Eboué*, Governor-General of French Equatorial Africa and France's most distinguished Negro, talked proudly in Cairo last week about the future of the black man in his native continent.
>
> At last February's trail-blazing French Empire Conference in Brazzaville, he had served as honorary chairman, helped promote a policy of "Africa for the Africans." Now within the French Empire, the Governor-General said optimistically, his people stood on the threshold of full citizenship, even of social and economic equality with whites.

Governor-General Eboué attended a conference in Cairo, and it is alleged that he died from food poisoning. The *Pittsburgh Courier*, commenting on his death, said:

> By the terms of the armistice, the French politicians in France and North Africa were impotent, and General de Gaulle was merely a refugee in a London which was being shaken to its foundations by savage air raids by Goering's Luftwaffe. Only Félix Eboué had troops and territory to provide a rallying point for Free Frenchmen. . . . In the white press one heard everything about de Gaulle, but nothing about Eboué. . . . Eboué was black, and in the Anglo-American world no black man must become too powerful. Even

worse, Eboué had ideas about "Africa for the Africans."
which is a treasonable thought in the minds of the Wall St.
and Bank of England crowd that owns Africa and controls the
administrators who run the continent.

The *Chicago Defender* stated: "Eboué was modern Africa's brightest hope in the welter of intrigue, confusion and
misrepresentation that became accentuated with the fall of
the French Republic. To Africans, he was more than a
bright, competent administrator. He was *a symbol* of eventual redemption and autonomy."

Mr. Godfrey Binaisa, leader of the Uganda Delegation to
the Commonwealth Parliamentary Conference, held in
Jamaica (November 1964), speaking at a symposium audience of the Extra-mural Department of the University of
the West Indies, was reported in the *Daily Gleaner* of the
seventeenth as follows:

> Mr. Binaisa was speaking along with other Delegates from
> Canada, Nigeria, Malaysia and Tanzania in the symposium
> on, "New developments in Commonwealth countries." The
> Speaker said that in his youth he was familiar with the Gar-
> vey pamphlet *Blackman,* which though banned, was still cir-
> culated. Garvey's contribution, he said, was to show that the
> black man could stand up and demand his rights. This was
> the beginning of the movement of Black Nationalism.

Hon. Tom Mboya in 1963 Minister for Justice, Kenya,
East Africa, in a letter to Mrs. Garvey, said: "I am delighted to know that you have mailed me your latest book
which I will wait to read with interest and excitement. I
have followed very closely the writings and speeches of
Marcus Garvey, and believe he made a tremendous contribution at a time when the people were not aware of the
Negro heritage."

Mr. Dennis Ejindu, reviewing the book, "Garvey and
Garveyism" in the *Morning Post*, Ghana, February 18,
1966, wrote:

Garvey's aim was to destroy the conventional inferiority complex of the Negro and prove that the Negro is more than capable of designing his own future and fortune.

He was infuriated by the exploitation everywhere of the black man, and therefore decided that the black man should grab a chance to improve his lot, and ultimately to fashion a civilization worthy of human dignity.

For this Garvey was feared and hated by the Governments of Europe and America, who hounded and destroyed him.

But not before Garveyism had intoxicated more than two million followers all over the world, who henceforth re-echoed his theme of Africa for the Africans.

He was dubbed a racist, or at best a dreamer. The honesty of the man, the strength of his message, and the popularity of his Cause so overwhelmed the society-climbing Negro intellectuals of America and the West Indies that they joined hands with the negrophobists to ruin him, instead of interpreting him. It is, for instance, lamentable that a man like Dr. W. E. B. DuBois would condemn and subvert Garvey's Back to Africa programme in 1924, only to come back to it in 1960 when he himself returned. What a progress both men would have made if only they had worked together.

Garvey, however, is dead. But our hope is that we, at least, will remember that he died for the black man. Yet the lessons of Garvey's tragic death remain to be learnt by those so-called pragmatists in African politics. They should, for goodness sake, see themselves now, the way we today see the Negro intellectuals in their opposition to Garvey's idea of African unity forty years ago.

Dr. Kwame Nkrumah of Ghana, speaking at the closing session of the All-African Peoples' Conference in Accra, December 13, 1958, stated in part:

It has warned us that so many of our brothers from across the seas are with us. We take their presence here as a manifestation of the keen interest in our struggle for a free Africa. We must never forget that they are a part of us.

These sons and daughters of Africa were taken away from our shores, and despite all the centuries which have separated us, they have not forgotten their ancestral links.

Many of them made no small contribution to the cause of African freedom. A name that springs immediately to mind in this connection is Marcus Garvey. Long before many of us were even conscious of our own degradation, Marcus Garvey fought for African national and racial equality.

George Padmore writing in the *Jamaica Gleaner*, October 23, 1952, on Jomo Kenyatta, "the man with the burning spear," stated:

Kenyatta was repeatedly spurned by the Colonial Office, and the Communists invited him to visit Moscow in 1939, but he returned to England when he refused to let African nationalism be exploited for Russian foreign policies.

Kenyatta met Marcus Garvey and became converted to the philosophy—"Africa for Africans," and after Garvey's death Kenyatta and other Africans and West Indians formed the Pan-African Federation, and called a Congress at Manchester, England in 1945 to plan a broad strategy of African liberation.

Kenyatta returned to Kenya in 1946 to assume leadership of the African Union. Within one year over 100,000 members were enrolled. In the following year Nkrumah returned to the Gold Coast to lead West African Nationalists. Other Pan-African leaders returned to South and Central Africa to organize poltiical parties, trade unions and co-operatives.

Rev. Clarence Harding, Commissioner to Africa for the U.N.I.A., wrote the following to Mr. Harvey, President-General, in a report dated October 30, 1967: "I arrived at Nairobi, capital of Kenya, on the 18th and was greeted by a Protocol Officer, and driven to the Hotel Clive; the following afternoon I was presented to President Jomo Kenyatta—a dynamic man, a sincere Nationalist. He informed me that when he was a young man he met Mr. Garvey in London, heard him speak several times, and considered himself a member of the U.N.I.A.

In the same report Rev. Harding stated as follows regarding Joseph Mobutu, President of the Republic of Congo:

I arrived in the capital city of Kinshasa. I was met by the Deputy Minister of Foreign Affairs—Mr. Bokondo. I was

taken to the Patrice Lumumba Hotel. The following morning
I was escorted to the Presidential Palace, where I was received by President Mobutu. He is a staunch admirer of Marcus Garvey, and was surprised to know that the U.N.I.A. was
still in operation. I spoke to him about our problems, and the
opposition by groups and Governments. He said that he fully
understood our position, and that our survival was a miracle,
but a blessing to Africa.

The *Jamaica Star*, November 23, 1966, reported as follows:

A delegation from the Universal Negro Improvement Association consisting of Messrs. E. E. Whyte, Vin Bennett, J.P.,
Rev. K. A. Bailey, met President Kenneth Kaunda at King's
House yesterday morning, and presented him with an address
on behalf of the Association.
Dr. Kaunda thanked the delegation, and said how much the
teaching of Marcus Garvey, the founder of the U.N.I.A. had
helped him to build his NEW NATION. He expressed the
hope that the U.N.I.A. would continue in the work to inspire
Africans at home to obtain their freedom.

The slogan of Dr. Kaunda (President of Zambia) is: One
Africa! One Nation!

The Power of the Human Spirit

Normally, a man's mind is the activating force that directs him. He does as he thinks.

If he is stimulated into action by impulses that override
thought, quite often he has to stop and think over the consequences. In this age of technology one may well liken
man's mind to a computer machine, because the output
depends on the intake.

From early history we learn of tribe subduing tribe;

nation conquering nation; where the warriors leave off, the administrators take over the task of subduing the conquered —physically and mentally.

The methods employed have become more advanced scientifically, but the intent remains the same—break the spirit of a man, and he easily becomes a serf, a peon, a good-for-nothing person, a frustrated human being, without hope, engulfed finally in futility and despair.

"Peace in our time" has been the wish of many generations, witnessing the holocaust of war and the poverty and misery consequent thereon; but man has predatory instincts, and particularly the white race in modern times has acquisitive traits; thus they build up material wealth, and this ensures them power.

Within the last twenty-five years the empire-holding nations of Europe have had to give up their rich possessions in Asia and nearly all of Africa and the West Indies. This was brought about finally after two bloody global wars in which Germany, aided by her satellites, sought control of more of the mineral-laden territories of Africa.

The result is that the United Nations General Assembly has more Representatives from Asia, Africa and the Caribbean areas than Europe, the United States of America, Australia and New Zealand. This means that the opinions and decisions of the colored races of the world dominate the International Forum, which in the closing years of this century augurs hopefully for justice and fraternity.

Now that this planet earth offers no more exploitable areas with the possibility of rich material resources (ruling out the North and South poles, which would not justify the efforts), the white race has encouraged and supported their national scientists to explore the possibilities of other planets having mineral wealth, and other means of sustenance for man's comfort and livelihood.

The moon is the first experiment, and landing on the moon is the first step towards exploration and exploitation.

The science fictions of yesteryear are the scientific achievements of the years ahead.

The replacement of diseased organs in human beings is an effort to prolong useful, skilled lives; but can that offset the decimation caused by a nuclear war, or germ-laden war maneuvers? Scientific minds trained politically to work for national power are more often debased by selfishness, greed and hate.

The spirit of man—the mind—is the link between God and man. He breathed into man the breath of life, and man became a living thing. Quench the spirit, and you slow him down—he marks time, he does not move with the tempo of his contemporaries.

Debase his image and his symbols, and you remove from his view the elements of greatness, the purpose for achievements, and you stultify the urge in him to go forward progressively. Instead of looking up, he hangs his head and looks down, only to be kept down by his deceivers, who know full well that "as a man thinketh, so is he."

This axiom—this truth, so self-evident, assails the conscience of people of color to be aroused as they see beneath the layers of brainwashing, and behind the façade of mawkish propaganda imposed on their race, designed to keep them fooled, as this conditions their thinking to the low levels set them, so as to prop the "master race."

For centuries whites have studiously and physically debased the spirit of black peoples everywhere, and used and abused their bodies to a state of trauma and inertia; but the spirit of God in black bodies cannot be extinguished as long as they live and have their being among others.

The awakening came when Marcus Garvey in ecstasy of spirit shouted to his people—"Up, mighty race! Your homeland must be redeemed, and our people everywhere rehabilitated and working unitedly toward the goal of full freedom —which alone can bring unlimited achievements and happiness." This was the almost superhuman task he set for himself, and those who looked like him—the revival of the power of the human spirit in black people everywhere.

This was achieved by changing their thinking. Garvey instilled in them new concepts of their rightful place on earth as God's creation; of their economic potentialities for their security and happiness, in which he pioneered industrial and commercial undertakings, and paid the price for his daring.

He not only created an ideology—Garveyism—but cultivated and nurtured it with the full capacity of his being to endure ridicule, abuse, imprisonment, persecution and anguish.

He made all peoples of African descent political aspirants for the continent of Africa and the West Indies, when he shouted his challenge to the colonial powers in those parts: "Africa for the Africans, those at home, and those abroad."

He gave to them a stimulus to the "old-time religion," by teaching them to visualize Christ—the Redeemer of all Mankind, as a man of color; for who can best portray "the man of sorrow, and acquainted with grief," but the downtrodden Negro in modern times? The wandering Jew did many years ago, when he was the persecuted, the spurned, the wanderer on the face of the earth, seeking a return to his homeland. Today, in this new era, the New Negro's icon is of dusky hue.

The Virgin Mary, the Mother of our Lord and Savior, Jesus Christ, is of dark complexion; she is depicted as bearing the burden of motherhood and loving care for her own and for whites as well. Psychologically, he lifted his race's fervor to a picturesque representation, in which he is symbolized as a part of God his Maker, and thus he takes pride in his black skin.

In the past the paradox of Christian teaching to "the poor benighted heathen," (people of other beliefs) of love and unity, in contrast to the practice of it—especially by Christian administrators and traders in Asia and Africa—has been challenged by the peoples of these continents, as being meaningless to them who suffer oppression because of the selfishness and greed of those who profess Christianity as a religion, but not as a way of life.

Moslems are attempting to fill the vacuum thus created in these countries, and this crusade has speeded up the unity of many Christian denominations, who are forced to present a united front to counter Mohammedism, Buddhism and Confucianism, etc., among three-quarters of the world's population—who not only want to hear about a religion but to feel it deep down in their hearts so as to express it in their daily lives.

Ecumenical unity calls to them in 1968, stressing the belief in "the Fatherhood of God," which is inconceivable without "the brotherhood of man":

> Join hands, then, brothers of the faith,
> What'er your race may be:
> Who serves my Father as a son
> Is surely kin to me.

He gave them goals at which to aim for generations to come. His was a shout to awaken, a command to his race: "Acquit yourselves like men, worthy of your Creator—the All-Wise, the Omnipotent."

He appealed for UNITY, to exercise love and drive out hate which warps the mind. Prayerfully he exhorted his people in his ritual, used at all meetings of the Universal Negro Improvement Association:

> "Take from us envy, hate, malice, and whatsoever may hinder us in Unity and Concord; as there is One Body, One Soul, and one hope of our calling, One God! One Aim! One Destiny! we may all with one mind, one heart, and one soul glorify Thee."

For, observed he: "As long as the strong oppresses the weak, wars and discontent will ever mar the path of man; but with love and charity towards all, the era of peace and plenty will be ushered in, and generations to come shall call us blessed."

These are the indestructible values of Garveyism.

If one can count those millions who were inspired by Garveyism, and thus changed their attitude towards life, and their way of life, then, you can count Garveyites all over the world.

> Outsiders will never understand the psychology of those they call *Garveyites*. We doubt if we who are thus nicknamed understand it ourselves. The binding spell, the indefinable charm which Mr. Garvey exercises over us beggars description. But we find reason for it in our conviction that no man has spoken to us like this man, inculcating pride and nobility of race, and clearly pointing out the Star of Hope to a discouraged and downtrodden people.

Thus wrote Archbishop George Alexander McGuire, in *The Negro Churchman*, September 1923.

LOOKING BACK ON GARVEY

We call the noble and the grand
From History's silent page
And let them gaze upon the land
Our glorious heritage.
Let's call Garvey from the lot
Who for Jamaica strove
And tell him we have not forgot
His labours and his love.
We venerate the feeble dust
And search for deeds untold,
We raise him stone and bronzed bust
And write his name in gold.
But these can never take the place
For what he fought and won
That however dull or black the face
He is an equal son.
That black men must themselves equip
To rule their native lands

And freedom gained must never slip
From out their sinewy hands.
He scanned the final page to look
On things he spoke about—
One God! One Aim! He closed the book,
And triumphantly passed out.

—REV. A. F. BULLOCK

INDEX